THE LAST DAYS

VOLUME TWO

Zion's Trail

by

Kenneth R. Tarr

ISBN: 1-55517-530-9
v.1

Published by Bonneville Books

Distributed by:

925 North Main, Springville, UT 84663 • 801/489-4084

CFI | Publishing and Distribution Since 1986

Cedar Fort, Incorporated

CFI Distribution • CFI Books • Council Press • Bonneville Books

Typeset by Virginia Reeder
Cover design by Adam Ford
Cover design © 2000 by Lyle Mortimer

Printed in the United States of America

THE LAST DAYS

VOLUME TWO

Zion's Trail

PROLOGUE

After the year 2000, Babylon and its wickedness reigned supreme on the earth. Man worshiped wealth, power, and pleasure rather than God. A great secret combination sought to destroy the freedom of all nations. Then, because of man's terrible sins, God's wrath was poured out almost without measure upon the inhabitants of the world.

The structure of world society was shaken to its foundation, but still managed to maintain a semblance of order. The greatest disintegration occurred in North America, where the land was filled with scenes of brutality, devastation, and anarchy. This was the home of those who had been most favored of the Lord, but who had rejected Him in favor of the excesses of Babylon.

The only place in North America where decent people could find refuge from the storm was in the Rocky Mountains. Here society was held together by the influence of God's church and the faith of the Saints. Yet even in this place civilization was hurled into primitive conditions. The region had been so profoundly linked to the economy of the rest of the nation that its supply of power, fuel, and consumer goods quickly dried up. Mobs stormed stores and fought violently over anything they could find. Within days markets were empty. Since most of the Saints had not stored food as their leaders had taught, there was widespread starvation and misery.

The people with health problems agonized the most. Because medical equipment became useless, and the supply of medicines quickly disappeared, the doctors were relatively helpless. As a result, those who were seriously ill found themselves in peril. Some perished swiftly. The others had two options: adjust or suffer helplessly. Most adapted by finding natural remedies, but many settled for suffering.

But eventually the people learned to work together to solve their prob lems. Within six months after the great collapse, they had established thousands of home-based businesses, which supplied the basic needs of the people. Since the banking system had also fallen, they used barter instead.

Then the Prophet, a seer like Moses of old, announced that now was the time for the Saints to begin the great work of establishing the New Jerusalem. Their great task was to create a Zion society, which must be the opposite of Babylon. The leader of the first wagon train to leave for Missouri was a young man named Steven Christopher, who had been selected by the Lord Himself. The saints who were chosen to go, the new pioneers, were eager to start the journey and hoped they were equal to the task. It wouldn't be easy, for the Lord had declared that Zion, which was destined to fill the American continent, could only be built upon the principles of righteousness, those of the celestial kingdom. No one but the pure in heart could live there, and the people had to be of one mind and one heart. Because of their genuine Christ-like love, there would be no poor among them.

However, the saints who started the difficult trek did not fully realize that before they reached their destination, they must face the chastening hand of the Lord until they were a people truly sanctified.

Chapter 1

When Pioneer One left Provo on Friday, April 14, heading for Zion, the modern pioneers were full of energy and enthusiasm. As they rushed along Interstate 15 toward Salt Lake City, they chattered, laughed, danced, and sang, enjoying themselves thoroughly. What a shocking sight it was to see the strange assortment of vehicles they used. There were old-fashioned wagons and handcarts, modern cars, vans, pickups, trailers, and a swarm of two- and three-wheeled bicycles. Those who rode bicycles pulled children or provisions in bike trailers. One brother had even converted a small bus.

Since there was no oil or fuel, they couldn't simply drive to Missouri. But when some Saints saw how difficult it would be to build new covered wagons, they decided to use the modern vehicles rusting away in their drive-ways, or they accepted more functional ones from friends. They stripped the metal carriages of every unnecessary part and packed the empty engine compartments with supplies. Their greatest challenge was to figure out how to attach tongues and hitches between the frames of the vehicles and the animals which would pull them.

As for those who had built covered wagons, or "prairie schooners," they gazed at the converted vehicles with amusement or disdain, depending on the bent of their minds. Most were proud of their creations, which they had furnished with every kind of "modern" convenience. There were spring seats, shaded seats, fancy braking systems, exterior tool boxes, double board boxes, full suspension, rubber wheels, and many other amenities. The builders and the converters made bets as to which type of vehicle would best survive the arduous journey. As time passed, the two groups adopted names to describe themselves and their rivals. The wagon builders used the terms "Creators" and "Converters," while those who drove altered vehicles preferred "Ancients" and "Moderns." If you knew who was doing the talking, it was never hard to figure out what they were referring to.

All of these conveyances, except the bicycles, were pulled by mules, work horses, or oxen. And in order to spare the draft animals, which had to pull wagons heavy with supplies, most of the travelers found it necessary to walk. Of course, drivers were always needed for the converted vehicles and the wagons which were drawn by mules or horses. As for conveyances pulled by oxen, someone needed to walk beside the leading team and control the animals with whip or goad.

Steven Christopher, the leader of Pioneer One, rode up and down the caravan on his sturdy mustang to check the progress of the company, amazed at the surprisingly brisk pace of the people. He decided to let them go, figuring there was no way to hold them back. After all, they were the courageous ones who would make history by being the first to reach Missouri and begin building the eternal city of the New Jerusalem! And yet he felt a certain trepidation, seeing all that exuberance and overwhelming self-confidence. He noticed that many were not wearing proper clothing, in spite of the instructions and guidelines he and his counselors had given them. Most had bare heads and arms, and wore shoes that would be more appropriate at a dance than on an eleven-hundred-mile trek under the most trying circumstances.

Steven was especially surprised to see many teenagers—and even adults!—wearing T-shirts and shorts. Some of the beautiful daughters of Zion pranced along merrily, although awkwardly, on platform shoes. It was as if they were going to some delightful outing at a nearby shaded campground! Steven wondered if they had remembered to bring their homemade sunblock and mosquito repellent.

"They don't look too prepared, do they?" Steven's brother, John, called as he rode up on his rugged horse. "You know, the way some are dressed."

"I'm afraid not. I guess a lot of them didn't take our guidelines seriously."

"Well, it won't be long before reality hits them," John declared with a grin. "They'll get more blisters and sunburns and whatnot than they ever dreamed possible...but there are other things which worry me more than their clothes."

"Like what?"

John struggled to control his frisky horse. "Some of these people don't look too fit. We warned them to take long hikes and trim up as much as possible, but it doesn't seem they paid much attention."

"Don't worry. The trail and the sparse diet will shape them up in no time." Steven guiltily touched his own stomach. It certainly wasn't as trim as it could be.

"I guess you're right. I only hope they don't suffer too much before that happens. And I suppose it's only a matter of a few miles before they get the idea to maintain a slow, steady pace."

"Yes, I know what you mean," Steven replied as he watched one brother chugging along as fast as he could go.

"Well, I'd better get to my post at the rear," John declared. He turned his horse and trotted down the caravan.

A mile further along the freeway, Steven noticed many of the pioneers eyeing their wagons with longing. Soon, along the entire length of the caravan, they began to hop onto wagons, desperately needing to rest. A rest which would last a long, long time. The draft animals slowed their pace. After another mile, nearly every pioneer was hitching a ride, and the wagons slowed even more. At first Steven was irritated to see such laziness, but then a pang of guilt hit him. He had to admit that he was no paragon of physical fitness, and he started to worry about whether or not he'd make it through the day without embarrassment. After all, he was supposed to be a good example. Thank heavens he had to ride around on his horse for a while—to check on the welfare of his people, of course! He wondered how long he would get away with that excuse.

On that first day of the journey, Steven wondered if he'd already made a mistake. He had planned to increase travel time by one hour a day every two weeks: first ten hours, then eleven, and finally twelve. In that way, he had hoped to break the pioneers in gradually, to make the transition from unfitness to fitness less painful. But from the looks of the Saints, maybe he should have asked them to walk no more than three or four hours a day at the beginning, and increase the time gradually. He asked himself if he should make a quick change of plans.

Four days later, on Tuesday, April 18, as Pioneer One struggled up the six-percent grade on I-80, a mile from Parley's Summit, Steven knew for sure he had made a mistake. He walked beside his wagon slowly, and his legs and feet hurt terribly. Mary, Steven's bride of eight days, drove their wagon and glanced at him often with sympathy on her face. Steven couldn't imagine a worse way to spend a honeymoon. It was only 11:30 a.m., and already the temperature was ninety degrees. And since there was no breeze and the skies were cloudless, the heat was sizzling on the hot freeway surface. John had informed him that the temperatures of the last few days were twelve degrees higher than normal for this time of year. Steven wasn't surprised, because the weather had been erratic and extreme around the world for a long time. The peaks to the south were covered with snow, but that seemed to have no effect in moderating the temperature.

"Do you want to take the reins for a while, sweetheart?" Mary said tenderly, looking down at him. "You need rest."

"No, I'm okay. Maybe later." Steven agonized over what the other pioneers must be going through. At least he was wearing sneakers which gave his feet good support. They were two sizes too large so he could fill the bottom with foam pads to absorb as much shock as possible. He had wrapped his lower legs with Ace bandages just tight enough to give his muscles a measure of support. He wore a long-sleeved shirt and a wide-brimmed hat. Yet, in spite of this preparation, he had shin splints, aching muscles, blisters, dry skin, red eyes, and chapped lips.

He knew that others must be suffering even more than he, because they were older and less fit. They had not made careful preparations and had not worn the right clothes. Already most of the company was smitten by sunburn, blisters, pulled muscles, fatigue, dry skin, and a multitude of other ailments. Steven and his brothers had instructed the pioneers from the beginning to take regular doses of water, but many had not done so and were suffering from heat exhaustion and dehydration.

Steven knew that even the early Mormon pioneers, who were used to hard labor and physical exertion, had endured great physical exhaustion and pain as they made the journey to the promised land. But the new pioneers had lived lives of relative ease and inactivity. After only four days, several families had already given up and returned to the city, protesting that nothing was worth the agony they were going through. A number had no choice: they had developed such severe symptoms that the camp doctor, Quentin Price, had warned they might die if they didn't return to civilization.

Steven was proud of those who persisted despite great distress. He felt especially sorry for those who were overweight. Their initial brisk pace had soon turned into painful trudging. Their agony was so great that they moaned from pain during the night instead of getting the sleep they needed so badly. Many Saints still found it necessary to hop into wagons or mount horses to continue the journey. This added to the burden of the animals which had to pull overloaded wagons. Steven wondered how many more Saints would have to go back to Salt Lake City, and how many draft animals would perish from exhaustion.

He was surprised to see that the people using converted vehicles did not seem to have more difficulties than those employing wagons. But the bicyclers had given up trying to climb the steep road, and had fastened the bikes to hooks on their wagons. The people pulling handcarts had the most trouble, and it took every member of the family to keep the carts moving. Steven knew their struggle would ease as soon as the highway leveled out.

The Prophet Josiah Smith had warned Steven that not all the pioneers would have the strength of character to endure the trials the Lord would send them on the road to Missouri. Some would abandon the wagon train, and others would become traitors before the trip was over. One of the purposes of the difficult journey was to prepare a sanctified people who would be worthy to establish the New Jerusalem. He told Steven that he must use his own judgment in solving problems, after seeking the counsel of his assistants and the wisdom of the Lord, but he advised him to maintain strict company rules and to travel as fast as the Saints could bear.

The previous evening, on Monday, Steven had called a meeting with the caravan leaders, John and Paul, his brothers, and four colonels. They had decided to allow the company to stop shortly after reaching the summit and rest a day and a half. Tonight, on Tuesday, the usual strict schedule would be relaxed, and the pioneers, instead of retiring or quieting down by 8:00 p.m., would be allowed to enjoy one another's company until midnight. Then on Thursday morning, April 20, the company would start again and travel only five hours a day for at least a week. They had made this announcement immediately, and those who heard it smiled gratefully and hurried off to spread the good news.

"Steven, please take these reins," Mary called down. "You've been walking almost three hours now. I can see that your legs are hurting you."

"Don't worry. I'll be fine. It isn't far to the resting place." Steven saw a sign on the right which indicated that Parley's Summit was only a mile ahead. He knew the going would be easier after they reached that point. He looked at his three children and felt a wave of pride as he saw them maintaining the pace without complaint. Only Andrew, who was nine, found it necessary to jump into the wagon at times. Jennifer, his eleven-year-old daughter, doggedly kept up with William, who at thirteen, was proud of being a teenager. Steven looked back and saw his non-Mormon friend, Douglas Cartwright, plodding wearily beside his wagon, his eyes staring at the road in front of him. Apparently, this march was taking its toll, even from a man as strong as Douglas. Steven gritted his teeth and made up his mind that he was going to set a good example for his children and the other members of the wagon train, no matter what the cost. His legs had always been a weak spot, his Achilles tendon. In past years they had prevented him, during workouts, from running too fast or jogging more than three or four miles.

He looked at Mary again and shouted, "We can stop in about two hours. In three miles we come to a wide valley, where there will be plenty of room to place the wagons into circles. It's near Jeremy Ranch." Mary nodded and threw him a kiss.

The next few miles seemed endless, but finally the road began to level out, then turn downward. Steven felt immense relief. He looked to the right and saw what used to be a community of cabins and other buildings on the side of the mountain, not far from the freeway. He was astonished to see that all of them were demolished, and there was no sign of life. It reminded him of the developments he had seen on the bench east of I-215 on the third day of their journey just before the wagon train turned northeast into the canyon. They too had been flattened by some gigantic force. At the time Steven had wondered if the devastation had been caused by the great earthquake that had struck the Cottonwood Fault nearly a year ago in May. Or was it the result of the massive mud slides which had occurred this year after three weeks of ceaseless rain? He had concluded that both disasters might have taken their toll.

But in the case of this mountain community, marauders may have been involved also because many of the cabins looked as if they had been burned out. A sudden chill went up his spine. He remembered the words of the Prophet, who had warned him several weeks ago that Pioneer One would face dangers from wicked men which would be almost insurmountable.

After the wagon train had traveled another mile, Steven's thoughts were abruptly interrupted. "We can camp over there," a voice said. It was Paul, who appeared beside him as if from nowhere. Steven looked in the direction indicated by his brother and saw a wide-open space on the left, large enough for hundreds of wagons. It was about a mile south of Jeremy Ranch. Since the ditch on the side of the freeway was shallow, Steven knew they would have no trouble crossing it to reach the site.

"Looks good, Paul," Steven said, climbing into his wagon.

Paul waved and disappeared. As Mary slid to the right on the seat to make room for her husband, she handed him the reins. He drove the mules toward the field, and then turned his wagon into a vast circle. If the other drivers followed him, as they had been instructed weeks ago, they could form a ring of about a hundred wagons. As soon as he finished the first circle, he jumped from the wagon and, with the help of Paul and Douglas, guided the second line of wagons into another circuit.

They repeated the procedure until the final section of wagons formed the last circle. The result was three complete rings of about a hundred wagons each, with openings at opposite sides. The handcart pioneers parked their carts in the center of the circles. Most of the cattle and horses were herded to forage on the north side of the camp, where Paul posted several bachelors as guards. John put sentries around the entire encampment.

It was the first time Steven had tried to form the wagons into such large circles. On the freeway there was only enough room to place the wagons into many small circles of six to ten wagons. On the three days when they had made camp for the night, it had taken no more than five minutes to make the rings. But today the pioneers spent almost an hour to complete the three large camps. Steven figured that this was natural since it took time for the vehicles to move up the freeway to the camp site. And yet he began to see how vulnerable the wagon train might be in case of attack. It was a problem he would have to present to his assistants and the colonels as soon as possible.

It was 2:30 p.m. when the Saints finished the work of organizing the encampment. Most of the travelers found a shady spot and fell asleep immediately. But many found it necessary to nurse their aching bodies before they were comfortable enough to rest. None showed the slightest interest in visiting neighbors, telling stories, or playing games, as they had that first night on Interstate 15.

Paul, John, and Douglas Cartwright gathered at Steven's wagon as soon as their chores were completed. They hugged Mary and Steven's three children. A few minutes later, Jarrad Babcock and Leonard Reece, Paul's traveling companions, turned up. Like Paul, they were bachelors.

"I suggest we mount up and check the region east of here," John said. "There are several communities farther along the freeway. Or at least there used to be."

"I agree. We need to check it out," Paul said.

Steven detected fear in the eyes of the other five men. He guessed that they too had seen the destruction at the entrance to the valley. "All right. Let's go." He turned to Mary and said, "We won't be long."

"Please be careful, Steven," she said.

"I will," Steven replied as he kissed her.

Mary said no more. She knew it was something they had to do. What if someone was still alive and needed their help? She realized her husband was a very careful man, but still she felt nothing but dread.

"Can I go, Dad?" William said.

"Not this time, son, I'm depending on you to stay here to help protect the camp." Steven was afraid for the boy's life if they ran into trouble. William frowned, but did not protest. Steven knew his son was pleased that he depended on him.

The six men mounted their horses and trotted east on the freeway. Each carried a rifle. With great caution they spent two hours exploring the area several miles from the encampment. Desolation was everywhere. It was evident that some great natural disaster had struck the region. Nearly every building was smashed to the earth and covered with a thick layer of hardened mud. Yet the searchers found something even more sinister.

Some of the buildings had been consumed by fire, and there were numerous people, including women and children, who had been shot or stabbed to death. Whoever had committed these crimes had also poured out their rage upon pets and farm animals. The situation became even more frightening when they realized that the tragedy had taken place only a few days earlier. Having found no life and sickened by what he saw, Steven called off the search, and the men headed for camp.

Before they reached the encampment, they agreed to report the destruction in general terms, but to avoid revealing the violence committed by human hands. Steven did not want to provoke terror in the hearts of the pioneers. As they reached the outskirts of the camp, they were met by two colonels and seven captains. The colonels were in charge of fifty families, and the captains oversaw ten families. Steven told them what they had found and asked them to be cautious as to what they told the families in their charge. He also asked John to make sure he doubled the guard. The leaders left immediately to do what he requested.

After saying goodbye to Douglas and the others, Steven joined his family, who had gathered around a campfire not far from their wagon. It was nearly 6:00, and Mary was preparing supper. Steven sat beside his wife and kissed her gently on the neck. The children snickered at his display of affection. Suddenly, the feeling struck him that he wouldn't want to live another minute if anything bad happened to Mary or the kids. Even though Mary was his second wife, and not the mother of his children, Steven knew that she loved them almost as much as he did.

Mary stopped her work and insisted that Steven take off his shoes and roll up the legs of his pants. The children giggled at his white legs, but Steven didn't care, because Mary began to rub them with pain-relieving ointment.

"Why don't we invite the Cartwrights and the three bachelors for supper?" Mary asked as she worked on him, her face glowing like that of a typical newlywed.

"Of course!" Steven replied. The Cartwrights and the three bachelors sometimes ate meals with them, and Steven was especially anxious to have their company tonight.

"I'll go get them," Andrew yelled enthusiastically, not waiting for his father's approval.

Andrew had unofficially become the family courier, and Steven didn't mind as long as the boy didn't stray too far. He watched as his son ran the forty feet to where Douglas was doing some chore. Hearing Andrew's message, Douglas smiled and waved his acceptance to Steven. The boy ran to the second wagon and spoke to Paul. Paul said something to Andrew and the child quickly sped away toward the center of the camp. Steven figured he was hurrying to find Leonard and Jarrad. No doubt the two young men were hanging around the best-looking young ladies of the camp, hoping to score points. Steven was sure that Anastasia Borisovich would be one of them.

Mary had just finished working on his legs, when Paul and the Cartwrights arrived and sat around the fire. Elizabeth Cartwright, Douglas' wife, had brought a huge bowl of potato salad with her. She and Douglas had six lively children. Like her husband, Elizabeth was not a member of the church. As time passed, Steven grew concerned that Andrew had not yet returned. But he was relieved when he finally saw the boy hurrying toward them, pulling on the bachelors' arms.

"What took you so long, Andrew?" Steven asked.

"Well, to make a long story short, Dad," the ten-year-old said disgustedly, "I couldn't get these two lovers away from the chicks."

"Hey, what's the problem, Andy boy?" Jarrad said with a twinkle in his eye. "We were merely having a profound religious conversation with two serious young women."

"Yeah, right," Andrew said, smirking. "You looked pretty goggle eyed to me."

Everyone laughed at Andrew's choice of words. Steven was astonished to hear his son use terms like "lovers," "chicks," and "goggle eyed."

By that time Mary had finished preparing the fried chicken and the pork and beans, and Douglas offered a prayer of thanks. Steven looked at all the food and wondered how long they would be able to enjoy such feasts. He felt guilty that he hadn't done a good job of encouraging everyone, even his own wife, to ration food. Obviously, other people were ignoring the guidelines also. Maybe he would have to do what John said—put the food in special wagons and give every person a specific allotment each day. Another thing to bring up in the leadership council! As they ate, the group discussed the difficult trip up the mountain, the ailments of the pioneers, and especially the terrible destruction around them. At 10:00 Mary put Andrew and Jennifer to bed, but William begged to stay up until midnight. As a teenager, he felt he had the right to listen to the adults talk. In spite of the frown he saw on Mary's face, Steven agreed to this. Just as Mary returned to the campfire, John and Tania Christopher joined the group. Steven was pleased to see his brother and sister-in-law.

As soon as everyone had settled down, Paul said in a mysterious voice, "I wanted to tell you all that I think something very strange is going on."

Steven looked up at him in surprise. "What do you mean?"

Paul looked around the campfire as if to make sure he could speak freely in this group. Seeing William, he declared, "William, what I'm about to say is a secret. It's important that you don't repeat it to anyone, no matter what."

Normally, Steven would have considered Paul's attitude to be no more than one of his usual jokes. But after the terrible things they had seen that day, he sensed that Paul was serious. He noticed that no one in the group was smiling.

"Don't worry, uncle Paul," William said, "I'm an expert at keeping secrets."

"I'm sure you are... Okay, as everyone here knows, Leonard and Jarrad have spent a lot of time in the last few days visiting the available females in the caravan."

"Hey, we were only doing a little quality home teaching," Jarrad protested.

Paul smiled. "That's understood... Anyhow, Jarrad and Leonard tell me that some of these young ladies couldn't resist pouring out their tender hearts to them. But to make a long story short, these young ladies inadvertently revealed that they had heard a lot of murmuring."

Douglas Cartwright said, "Murmuring? What kind of murmuring?"

Paul leaned forward and placed another branch on the fire. "Well, it seems that someone is spreading rumors about us, the leaders of Pioneer One. According to the gossip, we are dangerously incompetent. The brunt of the attack seems to fall on Steven."

"You're joking!" Douglas said angrily.

"No, I'm serious."

Steven felt the heat of shame flow from his neck to his face. The idea of incompetence was particularly embarrassing, since he had always believed that everyone else, almost anyone else, would be better qualified than he to lead Pioneer One. "Incompetent in what way?" he asked nervously.

Jarrad answered for Paul. "In lots of ways. Not establishing rules that are strict enough. Neglecting to enforce the rules we have. Supporting the weaker Saints, who are slowing us down. Refusing to make the people ration their food more carefully. Not posting enough guards at night. Choosing a poor route... And believe me, that's only the beginning! Those sisters couldn't stop talking."

"The attitude seems to be," Leonard added, "that you are endangering the lives of everyone in the company by not doing your jobs properly."

"But it was the Prophet who chose this route for us, not Steven," Elizabeth objected.

In spite of his humiliation, Steven was pleased to hear Elizabeth, who was not a member of the church, refer to Josiah Smith as "the Prophet."

Mary was visibly upset. "Paul, do you think these criticisms represent a general opinion, or is it just gossip spread by a few individuals?"

Before Paul could respond, John piped up, "It's obviously a conspiracy. I've talked to a lot of the pioneers. Most of them like Steven and have complimented us on the way we're handling the trip. I believe someone is trying to corrupt the others and undermine our authority by circulating lies."

"But why?" Douglas said. "What do they hope to gain?"

"That's what we need to find out," Paul said. "Also, we may have another problem. Several people have told me that someone is stealing supplies."

"I've heard the same thing," John observed.

Steven was stunned. "Stealing? Are you sure?"

Paul replied, "Yes. Two wagoners told me this morning that someone stole tools and ammunition from their wagons. They've no idea when it happened, but both are fit to be tied."

"And what did you hear, John?"

"What I heard came from Byron Mills."

"Oh, yes. I remember him," Steven said.

"Well, Byron said he had a sack of wheat and a rifle stolen. He doesn't know when it happened either."

"Do you think these people simply made a mistake? Maybe they forgot to bring the items they believe were stolen."

Both Paul and John shook their heads. The group discussed the matter another half hour without coming to any firm conclusions.

Finally, Steven said, "Listen, everyone, we're not going to find the truth without more information. I want you to keep your eyes and ears open. I suggest you enlist the aid of as many people as possible, if you know you can trust them. I especially want Paul, Leonard, and Jarrad to use their special talents to uncover some solid evidence. We need to resolve these problems quickly."

After the guests left, Steven and Paul walked around the camps to check the guards, who reported that they hadn't seen or heard anything unusual.

"You sure are lucky, Steve," Paul said as they trudged back to their wagons.

"Lucky! What do you mean?"

"You get to go home to a beautiful tender wife, while I have to put up with two dirty bachelors who burp constantly and think it's funny to let smells."

"You poor boy! Look, I happen to know that your companions are pretty high up on the cleanliness chain. So don't give me a line of bull."

When they reached the wagons, Paul sighed, "What a life without a wife! How can I bear it?"

Steven laughed. "Good night, Paul."

"Good night, you lucky devil."

Later, as he snuggled close to Mary, Steven couldn't sleep. He struggled to think of something pleasant, but failed. The problems of the wagon train and the murdered people he had seen in the nearby communities tormented him.

"You can't sleep, sweetheart?" Mary said gently. "You're tossing and turning constantly."

"Sorry to keep you awake."

"Listen. There's no problem we can't solve with the Lord's help. Maybe we should ask Him."

"Yes, of course." Steven was grateful for the suggestion because he had forgotten to have prayer that evening except over the supper. Another thing to feel guilty about! They kneeled, and Steven asked God for protection and help in solving the troubles of Pioneer One.

After putting more balm on his legs, Mary said, "Now, roll onto your stomach, so I can rub your back."

The gentle touch of his wife and the warm ointment made him feel better immediately. He remembered how Selena, his ex-wife, had rubbed his back sometimes when they were first married. Strange how it was that you never seemed to forget completely a woman you once loved. And yet, because of Mary, he could think of Selena now without the terrible pain he had felt before. What would his life be like today if Selena had not abandoned him and the children three years ago to join a polygamous cult? Would it be her rubbing the pain out of his legs instead of Mary? Then the great fatigue of the day gradually overtook him and he fell into a deep, dreamless sleep.

Chapter 2

Gerald Galloway sat back in his luxurious couch at his country mansion in Hampshire, England. As he sipped a glass of 1903 Chardonnay and contentedly smoked a Gauloise, he thought about the recent renovations to his estate. They had cost a fortune, but as the Supreme Leader of the new world government, UGOT, he could afford it. Fortunately, the final changes had been completed three days ago, in plenty of time for the meeting later today with his associates. He knew his confederates would be elated because of the stunning success of their plans for world domination. Especially significant was the fact that it had taken less than a year to undermine and destroy the European Union.

Yes, it had been necessary to kill a few people and bribe others, but their most effective tool had been to accuse—through his European network of propagandists—some member nations of abusing the terms of their agreements. He had undermined political harmony in these countries by placing operatives in important positions, so they could plant false evidence against national leaders. He had hired a secret society to destroy factories and poison harvests. All of it had required a great deal of planning and money...Gerald laughed at memory of the turmoil he had caused by promoting Marcus Whitman as Prime Minister of Germany, and then leaking to the press that Marcus had a secret affiliation with neo-Nazi organizations.

And his success in gaining control of the United Nations had been equally as spectacular. After the fall of the American government, the global natural catastrophes, and the collapse of the international banking system, the UN had been in chaos. Thirty nations had declared war on one another and had begun immediate hostilities to settle old scores. Pakistan had made the mistake of attacking India with nuclear weapons, and the Indian retaliation had been dreadful. India had struck the largest Pakistani cities with four one-megaton hydrogen bombs, and then had invaded with an army of a million soldiers. The war had lasted only five weeks, with violent repercussions in surrounding nations. There was a grave shortage of grain and food stuffs throughout the Middle East and the Russian Federation. Millions of starving people had fled poor countries and illegally entered rich nations: from Africa, Afghanistan, Eastern Europe, Vietnam, Cambodia, and North Korea they had escaped to Western Europe, New Zealand, Chile, Taiwan,

South Korea, and Japan. War, civil disobedience, natural disasters, drought, and famine had been everywhere. The disintegration of world society seemed imminent.

Therefore, when Gerald Galloway came to the UN and offered the help of his wealthy megacorporation, a desperate world accepted his leadership gratefully. His plan was tough and radical, but he convinced the UN that it was essential. A council of twelve people would govern the United Nations, with Gerald Galloway as chairman. This inner circle would be called the Supreme Committee of the Twelve. Their power would be absolute. The member nations would continue to send delegates, but they could no longer vote. They would function only as representatives to inform the Committee of the needs of their homeland. Every country must show implicit trust in the wisdom and goodness of the Committee to handle their needs in the best ways possible. Their governments could stay in power if they strictly followed the will of the Twelve. Gerald promised the people of the world that the new regime would be just, effective, efficient, absolute, and righteous. The first step that the nations must take to show their good faith was to replace many of their current administrators with the new leaders whom the Committee would send.

Gerald vividly recalled his moving speech to the assembled representatives, and he had to admit that he had been brilliant. They had bought his provisions virtually without question. And what was the name of the new world government? The Universal Government of the Twelve, or UGOT.

But his joy and satisfaction were not perfect. Thirty-one nations had not sent representatives to the assembly where he had taken control. Some of these nations, such as China and Japan, were very important. Without them, he knew it would be difficult, perhaps impossible, to make his rule universal and to reach his ultimate goal of destroying Israel. That was why he had called today's meeting with his associates. Together they would have to create a master plan to capture the allegiance of the uncooperative countries. Gerald was confident that they would succeed, eventually, in making the disobedient fall into line. He also looked forward to the meetings because he knew that they would give him an excuse to spend time with Lucienne Delisle, his lover, who planned to attend.

A few minutes later, at 5:00 p.m., the inner circle began to arrive. As usual, the associates greeted one another with the secret words and gestures. The first person to appear was Dominic O'Brien, whom Gerald had appointed three months earlier as the twelfth associate. Lucienne was the last to arrive. These were the chosen ones who made up the Supreme Committee of the Twelve. Other trusted people had been selected to replace them in the areas of the world where they had functioned as Gerald's operatives.

After they had taken seats in his vast study, Gerald said, "I'm glad you all arrived in time for supper. My cook is a master chef, and I'm sure you'll be delighted with his creations."

"I know we will, Mr. Galloway," said Randolph Benson, Gerald's former associate in the Middle East. "You always do things in style."

"No, not Mr. Galloway! I want each of you to call me Gerald from now on. After all, we're trusted friends, aren't we?"

"Yes, of course, Gerald," Lucienne observed. "We can always trust you to give us the best you have."

"Thank you, Lucienne," Gerald said with a straight smile.

After a half hour of small talk, they moved into the dining hall where domestics served them a six-course meal. Later the associates returned to Gerald's study, where they enjoyed bottles of dry sherry and more light conversation.

At 8:00 p.m. Gerald asked them to pull their chairs into a circle. "I think it's time we got down to business. First, let me compliment you. As members of the Committee, you've done a remarkable job. You've given me excellent advice and handled your individual areas of responsibility with amazing competence. I called you here today because I know you get tired of meeting in our regular chambers in London or Paris. I feel the same way. Here we can be more intimate, let ourselves go, and say what we really think."

On hearing those words, the visitors stiffened. They knew that their fate depended completely on the whims of the powerful man before them. As a result, they did little without his approval. The very idea of offering alternative suggestions or objecting to Gerald's position was extremely dangerous. Most of them hated their arrogant master and secretly conspired to bring him down. Only Lucienne dared to challenge Gerald's ideas openly, and she did so often, but always with charm and skill.

"Yes, it's nice to be able to say what we really think," Lucienne said with subtle irony.

Gerald smiled and took a sip of sherry. "Let me say that as masters of the world, we have accomplished a great deal." Several associates nodded. "But we also have many important things we still need to do."

"You are referring to Israel, of course," said Francis Bonnard, the former associate to Africa.

"In part, yes. Israel is still strong and independent and refuses to acknowledge the authority of our new government. We must bring her into line." Everyone in the room knew Gerald meant that Israel must be annihilated. "However, Israel is not the only government we must reach. There remain thirty-one nations which have ignored our invitations to become part of our new world government. They neglect to send delegates to our general assemblies, and have refused—no, not refused, but declined—to participate in our economic, political, and military operations."

"Still, most of those countries are fairly small," Alexi Glinka observed. "Do we really need them?"

"You are forgetting China, Alexi," said Janet Griffin, the ex-associate to China. "It has the bomb, a skyrocketing gross national product, and a population of almost 1.7 billion people."

"Oh yes, of course," Alexi mumbled. Gerald had always despised Alexi for his naive stupidity. This was a perfect example of it.

"What about the United States?" Randy Benson asked.

Gerald replied, "The United States is a wasted land full of anarchy and pollution. There is no civil authority whatsoever. We, of course, played a role in that. At this time it is in a world apart, and we don't have to worry about it. The same is essentially true of Mexico and Canada. Central America and South America, however, are a different matter. If any of you want details concerning the United States, talk to Lucienne before you leave in the next few days." Lucienne was Gerald's former chief operative in the United States.

"I'd be happy to answer their questions," Lucienne indicated. "But what do you want to do about the rebellious countries, Gerald?"

"I'm open to suggestions."

"I think we should send delegations to them," Ernest Hopkins said. Ernest had been Gerald's associate for the Far East.

"To do what?" Gerald asked.

"Well, to encourage them to join us," Ernest replied. "We might offer them various types of incentives."

Lucienne said, "What kind of incentives?"

"Well, mostly economic. Send them money to develop their infrastructure. Things like that."

"And if that doesn't work," Randy said, "we could make it clear that we would see their refusal as a sign that they don't care about their neighbors. They don't want to participate in solving the world's predicaments, such as global warming, the wasting of earth's resources, and rampant overpopulation. We could let them know that these problems are so vital that we are ready to use military force to ensure that every nation cooperates in solving them."

Gerald was surprised because he had considered Randy to be as stupid as Alexi. "Excellent, Randy! I like the way you think. The end justifies the means. We want a peaceful, happy world, and we may have to break a few traditional rules to get it." Randy blushed with happiness. "First we appeal to their greed, and then we threaten them. Now, what else, people?"

Lucienne knew perfectly well where Gerald was leading. She had spent many hours beside him at night, listening to his biases and hatreds. "Well, we might also appeal to their altruism," she said. "We explain our concerns about Zionism. We convince them that the Jews are wealthy because they've exploited the people of the world through their multinational corporations and their international banks. We might even blame genetic engineering on the greed of the Jews. We try to persuade them that we truly need their help in ridding the world of the Zionist plague. We maintain that without them, it will take decades for us to accomplish it. At the same time, we promise them a significant portion of the wealth of Israel." The other associates were impressed by Lucienne's rhetoric.

Gerald smiled pleasantly and said, "Very good, Lucienne! I want you people to think about the ideas which have been mentioned. Remember that this group is generally responsible for converting the thirty-one recalcitrant nations. Since I believe in giving you great independence in your areas of responsibility, I leave the details up to you. I'm only concerned that you bring me results. Of course, I have assigned a number of you to visit the defiant nations in person in order to obtain their compliance. These people will have a very special emissary at their disposal. Most of you already know him— Colton Aldridge, the American prophet recruited by Lucienne. I've seen him do miracles with my own eyes, and I know you can use him to convince many gullible leaders that our cause is holy and just."

After the twelve associates discussed the goals of UGOT until midnight, they retired to comfortable beds. Gerald and Lucienne were proud of themselves. The meeting had been a great success. For an hour they planned how they would use Colton Aldridge and their other key operatives to consolidate their power.

*****

Pierre Laborde entered the foyer of the three-story building and pressed the button to his friend's apartment. The building was located in Rueil-Malmaison, a suburb of Paris.

"Yes?" a voice said through the speaker directly above the row of buttons.

"It's Pierre."

"Okay."

After waiting to hear the hum which indicated that André had released the lock on the inner door, Pierre pushed it open and hurried to the elevator, the only access to the upstairs apartments. André Renan had given him an urgent call a half hour earlier, asking him to rush over as quickly as possible, but refusing to give details on the telephone. Pierre was intrigued and a little nervous. These were dangerous times, and André wasn't the kind of person to play silly games. Pierre was glad that his friend had been able to find his excellent apartment. André and his wife Mireille were the kind of Saints who opened their home and their hearts to any members who were in need.

There were almost eighty thousand Saints in France, and when the Prophet had made his call last July, most had sought safety in the main branches of the church, located in Paris, Marseille, and Lyon. But often it was difficult for them to find work and accommodations. Most of the Saints who had gathered to the Paris area had to live in the nearby countryside with friends or church members. Others had no choice but to live in abandoned farm buildings or other structures. Pierre had been a civil engineer in Vendôme, a city seventy-five miles southwest of Paris. But now he and his wife Diane, and their two young children, lived in church facilities in Paris. Since Pierre had appeared on television a number of times in opposition to UGOT, landlords were afraid to rent to him.

Pierre was grateful when the elevator door slid open because the smell of perfume was nauseating. He knew that many French women covered themselves with the stuff instead of taking daily baths. Obviously, one of them had just used this elevator. He rushed out, turned right, and knocked on the first door he came to. Almost immediately, André unlocked the door and let him in.

"Have you heard the news yet?" André said after closing the door.

"What news?"

"Come in and sit down."

Pierre entered the living room and was surprised to see that two other families were visiting André and Mireille. Pierre recognized them as members of the church. He was surprised at the terror he saw in their eyes. As Mireille turned off the television, the others made room for him on the couch.

"What's going on?" he asked.

André said, "Pierre, an hour ago we heard a news report which said that French authorities are requiring all Mormons to register with the government within three weeks."

Pierre was shocked. "Only Mormons? But why?"

"No one knows for sure. They want us to bring our official papers: birth certificates, mortgages, a list of assets, bank accounts. We'll also have to answer personal and family questions."

Pierre was furious. "The lousy tyrants!"

One of the visitors, Carl Mauriac, said, "I got a call this morning from a friend of mine who is visiting relatives in Rome. He told me that the same thing has been going on for weeks in Italy."

"It's restricted to members of the church?" Pierre asked.

"Yes, only Mormons. My friend said he heard that UGOT is disenfranchising Mormons in many countries, confiscating their property, and forcing them to live in special camps."

"Sounds like the Nazis all over again to me!" Mireille exclaimed.

"Yes, it does, but I wonder how accurate these reports really are," André said

"We may not find out until it's too late," Pierre observed.

"We should get counsel from our local church leaders as soon as possible," Carl's wife declared.

Mireille added, "And do a lot of praying."

André said, "Yes, of course. Most of all, we need to find out for sure what UGOT is doing to the Saints in other countries. I don't intend to report to the government unless I get the facts."

"Well, I'm not putting my family into their hands—no matter what," Pierre replied.

Chapter 3

On Wednesday, April 19, the bugle which normally announced the beginning of the day for Pioneer One did not sound. Since it was a day of rest and recovery, the pioneers did not have to arise early. Steven, however, awoke at 6:00 a.m. and couldn't go back to sleep. Afraid his tossing and turning would awaken his family, he decided to get up.

"Can't sleep?" Mary asked.

"Oh, you're awake... No, too much on my mind."

"I'm sorry. What's bothering you?"

"Everything, I guess."

Mary gave him a hug. "Can I help?"

"You always help. But there are some things I must handle myself."

"How do your legs feel?"

"Much better, thanks to you. As I said, you always help." He pulled his boots on without bandaging his legs. "I have to go a short distance from camp. To be alone. Please don't worry, okay?"

"I'll try not to. Will you be gone long?" Mary suspected what her husband was going to do, and decided to respect his privacy.

"No, not long." Grabbing his rifle, he slipped out the back of the wagon and lowered himself to the ground. As he walked away from the wagon train, he waved to a guard posted nearby. *I should have taken my turn as guard last night,* he thought. *I didn't sleep very well anyway.* John had the important responsibility of arranging the hours and rotation of camp guards and was doing a good job of it. Steven walked another five minutes and found a secluded spot partly surrounded by trees. After looking around to see that he was alone, he placed his rifle against the trunk of a tree and knelt down to pray. He spent the next ten minutes telling God how inadequate he felt and asking Him to give him the strength and wisdom to lead Pioneer One the right way.

By the time he had finished, he felt much better and was no longer sleepy. He arose and descended a gentle slope toward the caravan until he could see the entire camp clearly. From that vantage point, he sat on a huge boulder and stared at the immensity of his responsibility. No wonder some of the people were starting to complain! Their lives were in the hands of an idiot who had no experience whatsoever at leading other people. It certainly wasn't a job he had asked for. His eyes full of tears, he thought about the Lord when He asked the Father to remove the bitter cup. Of course, his pain and burden didn't begin to compare with Christ's, but still his turmoil and fear were real. As he watched the first few people slowly exit their wagons and tents below, he thought he heard a voice close by. He looked around, but saw no one. He listened carefully and heard the voice again. It was louder now, and he discerned a few words.

"Who is there?" Steven said cautiously.

"It is I," the voice said clearly. It seemed to come from inside him and yet from the outside at the same time.

Steven remembered something he had read in the scriptures and replied, "I'm here, Lord."

"Fear not, my son," the soft, gentle voice continued, "for it is I who have chosen you."

Steven was so astonished that he couldn't say a word. The powerful words came as in a whisper, but they penetrated his heart.

"Pray to me always and I will guide you and go before you. Your enemies are now combined, but they shall not prosper."

As he listened, Steven's heart burned with healing fire and his mind was filled with joy! It was the strongest and most thrilling experience he had ever had.

Steven asked the invisible being other questions which were bothering him, and received satisfying answers. After some time, the soothing voice faded as He pronounced His final words, and Steven soon realized that his visitor was no longer there. He sat there another ten minutes, pondering the experience. Now, instead of fear, he felt happiness and self-confidence. Finally, he set out for the encampment.

As he approached camp, he saw the Cartwrights emerging from their huge tent. Since Douglas and Elizabeth had six children they usually slept in the tent instead of their wagon. He caught sight of Mary waiting for him just outside the ring of wagons. He saw her troubled face brighten suddenly when she saw him from a distance. Apparently, the children were still asleep.

"Steven, you were gone so long!" she exclaimed. "In another minute I would have sent Paul and his friends to search for you."

Steven looked at his watch and was surprised to see that it was 8:15. His interview with the invisible being had taken almost two hours. He took Mary into his arms and kissed her tenderly. He told her that he had heard the voice of a messenger from God and had received the help and inspiration he so desperately needed.

Mary burst into tears and embraced him earnestly. "I'm so happy," she declared.

Steven kissed her cheeks and dried her tears. They walked a short distance from camp and sat on some boulders at the edge of a gully. Mary couldn't control her curiosity. "Who spoke to you, Steven? Was it the Lord?"

"I feel that it was Him, but I'm not sure. I know that in the scriptures Jesus sometimes speaks as though He is the Father, and angels refer to themselves as the Son. Of course, they're actually speaking as agents for those higher in authority. I believe it's called the Doctrine of Agency."

"Is that why the angel in the first part of the Book of Revelation says that he is Alpha and Omega?"

"I believe so. The angel does nothing more than quote what the Son said." Steven stopped and faced Mary. "I suppose it really doesn't matter who spoke to me. Still, I'm convinced that it was the Lord Himself."

"Why?"

"Because I don't believe that any personage other the Lord or the Father could tell me so many intimate, personal things about myself or communicate such an intense feeling of love to my heart. No, I know it was Him."

They heard a voice calling from camp, and saw Paul waving them in.

"I guess it's time for breakfast," Mary said.

While they walked back to the wagon, Steven's three children ran to meet them.

"Uncle Paul is making pancakes," Jennifer yelled as she rushed up and seized her father's arm. "The Cartwrights are coming for breakfast too."

"Yeah!" Andrew added enthusiastically. "Big fat pancakes, covered with butter and maple syrup."

"Wow!" Steven shouted gleefully, trying to match their enthusiasm. He got the impression that his children were still treating this long trek through what might be some of the most dangerous places in America as a camping trip to Vivian Park in Provo Canyon.

"The trouble is, he wants us to drink milk with the pancakes!" William said. "I hate that milk!" William had refused to drink the cow's raw milk ever since they had acquired her a week before leaving Provo.

Mary laughed. "Well, we have Lucretia now and she gives us precious milk twice a day. So we have to drink it." William scowled, not in the least convinced.

"Besides, it's delicious," Steven said. "I'm sure you'd get used to it if you just tried it."

"Yuck!" William cried, sticking his tongue out.

"You guys should see Jarrad trying to milk our cow," Andrew yelled hilariously. Jennifer began to laugh, and William rolled to the ground giggling and holding his belly, paying no attention to the dirt sticking to his clothes.

"Sometimes...the stuff doesn't...doesn't even come out," Andrew went on, laughing so hard he could hardly talk. "And...and sometimes it sp...spurts and hits him smack...smack in the face!"

"That's right!" Jennifer hollered. "But all Jarrad does is give that silly little smile of his and keep right on squeezing those long things. I think he enjoys it." She laughed even louder.

As soon as they reached camp, they said a prayer, and Paul served pancakes. While they were cleaning up, John appeared and approached Mary. "Mary, I need your help," he said. "One of the brothers broke his ankle a little while ago. You're the only registered nurse in camp."

"But Quentin Price—"

"The good doctor's nowhere in sight. I suppose he's off fixing someone else. Will you come?"

"Certainly." Mary ran to the wagon and retrieved her medical kit. When she returned, she said to Steven, "Can you help?"

"I'd love to."

The children begged to accompany them. Steven looked at Mary, who nodded her approval. "Okay," she said to the children. "It'll be a good experience for you. But I don't want you to get in the way. Come on. Let's go!"

They followed John a quarter of a mile from camp to a small stream, where they came upon a middle-aged man lying a few yards from the water. He was in great pain. Mary was relieved to see that the victim was conscious and that a second man was kneeling nearby, talking to him and holding a cloth against the wound. A crowd had gathered, but had shown enough sense to stand back so the victim could get air. Mary knelt beside the injured man and removed the cloth. A bone protruded through the skin of his ankle and the wound began to bleed. Immediately she reapplied the cloth. She noticed the shocked expression on the children's faces. *It does look kind of scary*, she thought.

"You did a good job of slowing the bleeding," Mary said to the victim's friend. "What's your name?"

"Name's Wesley. Wesley Duke. This here's Judd Hawks."

"Why don't you rest for a while, Wesley? I'll take care of Judd. Does he have a wife?"

"Nope. He's an old bachelor. I've been trying for years to get him to repent and accept one of those beautiful ladies who are always trying to get him to the temple—in other words, to be exactly like me—but he doesn't seem to care if he goes to hell or not."

Mary smiled and said to Steven, "Will you help?" As Steven moved into position beside the patient, she took a clean bandage from her kit. She handed it to her husband and said, "We need to apply direct pressure to stop the bleeding. Are your hands clean?"

Steven checked. "No."

She nodded toward the stream. "You can wash them over there."

Steven ran to the water and washed. He returned quickly, and Mary poured rubbing alcohol on his hands. She handed him the bandage and said, "Take it from the wrapper."

Wesley spoke up, "We was climbing around on those rocks over there when Judd slipped and fell." He pointed to a line of rocks which extended several hundred feet along the side of the stream. "I guess they was just too slippery."

"Evidently." Mary said. "Did he hit his head?"

"I don't think so."

"We can be grateful for that." She looked at Steven. "Ready?" Steven nodded. After removing the cloth, she poured alcohol on the wound. "Okay. Now hold the bandage against the wound."

While her husband held it, Mary checked the victim's airway, his breathing, and his circulation. Next she examined him for other injuries. Steven was amazed at the speed and skill with which his wife worked. When she had finished these important checks, she examined the wound. Once again it began to ooze blood, so she reapplied the cloth with her right hand and pressed the fingers of her left hand into the victim's groin, about one-third of the way across. She felt the underlying pulsation of the femoral artery, the arterial pressure point, and pushed against it firmly. She called for the people standing nearby to bring blankets. Within minutes a woman brought several blankets, and Mary asked her to cover the top of the injured man's body with one of them. While Mary worked, she explained to Judd what she was doing and assured him that she expected Dr. Price to be there soon. Although he was still in pain, her kind words seemed to quiet him.

Six minutes later she asked Steven to hold the cloth against the wound because her right hand had started to ache. As she continued to apply pressure to the artery, she checked her patient for the signs and symptoms of shock. She continued to apply pressure to the artery another five minutes and then checked the wound again. She smiled when she saw that the bleeding had almost stopped.

"Things are looking good, Judd," Mary said. "All we have to do now is dress the wound and splint your leg. That should help with the pain."

After wrapping the wound with clean gauze, she checked the leg to see if it still had sensation and a normal pulse. Next she rolled up one of blankets tightly and gently placed it between his legs. It extended from his feet to several inches above his knees. After that, she tied the legs together with four lengths of cloth to stabilize the injured ankle.

"I think you can make a stretcher now to carry him back to his wagon.

Please make sure you don't move the ankle, if possible."

"Thank you, sister. You're an angel of mercy," Judd declared gratefully.

Mary smiled as she patted him on the hand. She gave Wesley some final instructions on how to care for the patient and turned to her husband. "That's all I can do for him. The doctor will have to repair the injury when he shows up. We can go now. Can you come and visit a while, John?"

John looked at his watch. "I suppose so, but Tania will be expecting me for lunch."

On the way back to their wagon, Steven put his arm around his wife and said, "He's right. You are an angel of mercy."

"Man! That was awesome," William exclaimed. "For a moment I thought that old guy was going to bleed to death!"

"Not with Mary around," Jennifer stated.

Steven detected a hint of pride in Jennifer's voice, and he was glad. His daughter was still jealous of the attention he showed Mary, but she seemed to be changing slowly. As for the boys, William remained reserved, while Andrew was already calling Mary "Mom." Steven noticed also that Mary had a pleased look on her face. As they approached the wagon, he caught sight of a second crowd. He sighed, figuring it must be another problem. Oh well, after the marvelous thing that had happened to him that morning, he felt strong enough to face any challenge!

Forty people had gathered around a large old man resting on a stump. Most of the listeners were sitting on the ground, but some had plopped onto boulders or logs. A few lucky ones used folding chairs. Steven noticed that Paul, Jarrad, Leonard, and the Cartwrights had found places close to the visitor. Everyone seemed transfixed by the newcomer, who appeared to be a mountain man. His clothes resembled something from an old western film, except that they were incredibly worn and filthy. His ravaged hat was turned sideways after the manner of George "Gabby" Hayes, the old-time movie side-kick of Roy Rogers, and his gray beard flowed half way down his chest. When he talked or grinned, which he did constantly, you could see that six front teeth were missing. In his left hand he grasped the barrel of a long-range Sharps buffalo rifle. Steven estimated that he was about fifty-eight years old. In spite of his age, his demeanor and rugged appearance suggested strength and vitality.

Paul and the other bachelors squatted close to the formidable old-timer. Seeing Steven and the others arrive, Paul announced, "This is my brother Steven Christopher, the leader of the wagon train, and his wife Mary." He nodded toward John. "And this is my other brother, John. He's second in charge. The kids belong to Steven and Mary."

The visitor pulled himself off the stump and said politely, "Nice ta meet ya. I'm Rutherford Johnston, Ruther for short." After shaking hands with

Steven and John, he rotated toward Mary, took her hand daintily, leaned over gracefully, and kissed the back of her hand softly with puckered lips. Steven heard a light smack as the man's toothless mouth touched the small hand. "And good morning to you, Ma'am. Now that I sees ya, I know why this day is gittin' so bright and sunshiny."

Steven and Mary looked at each other and grinned. Several of the people who sat nearby vacated their seats so Steven, Mary, and John could sit close to the guest. After they talked about the weather and other polite things for a while, the old man said, "So is it true that every last one of ya is Mormons?"

"Most of us, yes," Steven answered cautiously. He motioned to the Cartwrights. "However, Doug and Elizabeth here are Methodists."

Ruther shot the Cartwrights a toothless grin. "That's nice. I like the Methodists. But don't that beat all! So many Mormons traveling all together up the highway, purdy as ya please!" Steven figured the man had either watched them arrive the day before or had examined their tracks to see which way they were going.

"Well, you're more or less in Mormon country here. You know, the state of Utah. And Salt Lake City is only fourteen or fifteen miles west of here."

The old man replied, "Yep, I know that. Even though I been livin' a long time in the mountains a hundred miles east of here, I still know this here's Mormon country. But the reason I was so surprised is that there's a heap of danger in the wilderness these days, and it seems strange to see all you folks campin' up here and traipsin' around as if ya didn't have a care in the world. Where are ya all going? Don't ya know it gets worse and worse as ya go east?"

"What do you mean?" Steven asked.

"I mean, there ain't much food and water out there. This nice highway is broke up—you know, big gaps and sinkholes and sech—in a thousand places. So they tell me. But that ain't the worst, not by a long shot."

"It isn't?"

"Heck no. There's savages out there. Both men and women."

"You mean, American Indians?"

The visitor guffawed. "Shucks! The Indians is downright genteel in comparison to the savages I'm talkin' about. They's nothing but wild brutes, without a humane conscience. Didn't ya see what they done to the people in this valley, both Mormons and non-Mormons?"

Steven wanted to avoid this subject, but knew it was already too late. Douglas seemed to realize that also and said, "Yesterday we searched the communities east of here and found a lot of bodies. Were those people killed by the men you're talking about?"

"Well, first there was some bad floods which destroyed all kinds of

26

property and a heap of people. I seen the floods coming, so I headed this way ta see if I could help. But then I seen those creatures from a distance. I used my binoculars and I could see 'em a comin' down from the mountains north of here. Musta been at least two hundred of 'em. I got out while I could. Because of the disasters, the nice people livin' here wasn't prepared and didn't have a chance."

No one said a word for moment. Steven looked around. The fear of the crowd was evident. If only the old man had spoken to him about the massacre in private instead of making it public! Would the old-timer's report undermine the morale of the caravan? Or would it make the pioneers stop straying off into the countryside against the rules?

"Do you know who those people are?" John asked.

"The killers?"

"Yes."

"Yer durn tootin'. From what I see'd myself, and from what the mountain boys say, I've a purdy good idea! Some of 'em used ta be respectable people who lived in these parts. But most of 'em came from the cities west of here. Then, when all heck blew loose, and there was no control from the authorities, the people I'm talkin' about just went crazy. Like everybody else, they ran into every kind of trial and privation and they couldn't handle 'em. When the goin' got tough, and there was fewer restraints, their baser instincts took over. That's the way I figure it."

"Do you know where they are now?" Steven asked.

"Don't rightly know for sure, but I heard they set up their main camp near a mountain called Windy Knoll. That's about twenty-three miles northeast of here as the crow flies. But that's only one of their camps. It appears they move all over this region so they can plunder, murder, and rape anyone they can find. I understand they got some trail bikes so the leaders can move around real fast when they need to. I broke bread with an old-timer last week who swore he saw a storage tank in one of their camps. It looked ta him like they was drawin' gas from it for their bikes. He was too afraid of them devils ta git close enough ta make sure."

"Doesn't our road lead us close to the area of Windy Knoll, Steven?" Mary asked.

"I think so, but I'm not sure."

Ruther said, "Are ya stickin' ta I-80?"

"Yes, for nearly nine hundred miles, if we can," Steven replied.

"Ya don't say! I'll be a long-tailed bobcat! That brings me ta my first question. Where are ya all going to?"

Steven asked himself if he had blundered by revealing so much about their travel plans. "Maybe we can talk about that some other time if we get the chance. What about Mary's question? Do we go near the headquarters of the gang?"

"Purdy close. When ya goes through Echo Canyon on I-80, you'll be about four miles from their main camp...Come ta think of it, it might be smart for ya ta contemplate taking another route ta git ta wherever you're going if ya kin find one."

All eyes turned to Steven.

After hesitating, he said, "We'll consider your suggestion tonight when the leaders of the wagon train meet."

Ruther reached into his pocket for a chew of tobacco, but changed his mind and withdrew an empty hand. "Ya know, the idea keeps a comin' to me that I ain't got nothin' special ta do in the next little while, so if you folks would like a bit of company, I might travel with ya for a spell. You know, ta show ya some trails and maybe make a few wilderness-type suggestions."

Steven wasn't fooled. He looked into the man's eyes and saw his worried look. You never know what form human goodness might take. "I'm sure I speak for everybody when I say you are most welcome," he said. "However, what if we run into the gangs? Aren't you afraid of what might happen?"

"Yes siree! I'm scared plumb out of my wits, after seeing what they done." Then, with a twinkle in his eye, he added, "But sometimes a man has got ta take his fear into hand. Besides, I'm a hopin' ta get some of that thar women's cookin'."

Everyone laughed.

"But there's something else I was wonderin' about." Ruther's face took on a subtle grin.

"What's that?" Paul asked.

"Well, when I first got here, I saw a shockin' sight."

"A shocking sight?" Steven said.

"I don't know if ya noticed it, Mr. Christopher, but ya've got a lot of people here who look like they've spent some time livin' high on the hog. Those folks are sportin' on their very person enough vittles ta last them for the next three months. They shouldn't have ta eat a durn thing for the rest of your trip. The only trouble is, I wonder what will happen when they hit some really rough country or have ta run for their lives."

"This isn't rough country?" John asked.

"Shucks! It ain't nothin' here like it is up the road a piece."

Steven laughed. "Mr. Johnston, I have confidence in our people. They'll become fit as they travel and—"

"And the greenhorns!" Ruther continued as if he hadn't heard. "So many people wearin' the wrong clothes, and—"

"Maybe you can help us with these things," Douglas said.

Steven looked at his watch. "Listen. It's almost noon. Can you eat lunch with us, Mr. Johnston?"

"I'd be much obliged."

During lunch everyone delighted in the company of the mountain man, and it was clear that he enjoyed entrancing his listeners with his anecdotes about his experiences in the mountains. Mary left for fifteen minutes and returned to tell Steven that Dr. Price had reset the ankle of Judd Hawks, and the man was doing well. The only problem was that the resetting had been extremely painful because there was no way to put the victim to sleep, and the small supply of pain killers had been exhausted during the first three days of travel.

The rest of the day, the new pioneers relaxed and nursed their aching bodies. Although the children had shown signs of distress the previous day, it took only one night of sleep to renew their spirits and bodies. After they completed their assigned chores, they flew into action, organizing races and games like "steal the bacon" and "capture the flag." Steven was careful to make sure that John had posted a double guard to protect the camp.

Since Steven was concerned about the dangers ahead on I-80, he visited John's wagon in the afternoon in order to use the only transceiver radio in the camp. He played with the frequencies for a few minutes, and finally reached Salt Lake City. He waited until they brought the Prophet, Josiah Smith, to the set at the other end, then told the church leader his concerns. Josiah counseled him to go to God in prayer because he had the right to obtain revelation for his stewardship, which at this time was Pioneer One. The Prophet suggested that he not change the preestablished route of the wagon train, but that he should get the final answer on that matter from the Lord Himself.

Because of his conversation with the Prophet, Steven told Mary that he had decided to return to the secluded spot he had visited early that morning. She was deeply concerned for his safety, but said nothing. Steven became excited as he hurried to the place which was sacred to him now. He hoped that perhaps he might feel at least a small measure of the ecstasy he had experienced before. And he wasn't disappointed. After praying for some time, he arose and returned to the camp. He knew that he had received the answer he needed.

Chapter 4

Dr. Sarad Jalil, head of the Jalil Medical Clinic, in Calcutta, India, sat at his desk trying to wake up after a sleepless night. He had already consumed three cups of coffee, but his mind was still muddled. He poured himself another cup and drank it rapidly. Maybe a fourth shot of caffeine would do the trick. It was 8:00 a.m. and he needed to find the strength to face the nightmare once again. A lot of lives were depending on him. He heard the door to his tiny office open, and he looked up to see his secretary.

"Doctor?" the secretary said in Hindi. Even though she lived in a great city, the secretary wore the traditional sari, which was a straight piece of colored cloth draped around her body as a long dress.

"Yes, Sitara," he replied in the same language.

"It's time for your rounds."

"I know, I know," Sarad said wearily.

"Didn't you get any sleep last night?"

"I was in bed five hours, but I doubt that I got more than two hours of good sleep."

At 2:00 a.m. Sitara herself had insisted that Sarad leave the wards for some rest. She caught sight of the blanket and pillow on his couch. "But you didn't go home! How many times have I told you that you can't sleep properly on that tiny couch? And I see you've been drinking coffee again. As a doctor, you should know coffee will kill you!"

"I know, I know. I've heard this a thousand times before. You talk like my mother."

"Well, somebody has to watch out for you. You won't do it yourself!"

"Are there many new patients?"

"Yes, doctor! Dozens and dozens. And more coming in all the time."

Sarad sighed deeply. "How many deaths from last night?"

"The nurses report that twenty patients died after you left."

"How many does that make since the beginning of the plague?"

Sitara consulted a notebook she carried with her everywhere, made some quick calculations, and said, "Twelve hundred and ninety-six."

Sarad couldn't believe it. Twelve hundred and ninety-six deaths in one small hospital in less than three months, and the incidence of infection was increasing every day. He wondered how many people had died in the entire city of Calcutta, with a population of fifteen million people.

"Remember that the news people will be here at 9:00."

"News people?"

"Yes, yes. I told you about them last night when I made you stop working."

Sarad remembered she had told him something unusual last night, but he still couldn't get his mind to work right. "Uh, that's right... Why don't you go over it again? I was pretty tired."

"Like I already said, the government gave the BBC permission to send a news team here to cover the plague first hand."

"Why on earth did they pick my clinic?" Sarad groaned. "We're nothing but a tiny facility in the suburbs."

"Well, who else are they going to choose? Most of the big hospitals in the city still haven't recovered from that sneak air raid from Bangladesh last month. You know that!"

Every time Sarad thought about the air raid, he seethed inside. "Fifty thousand people slaughtered and billions in property damage! Those ungrateful Muslims! We helped them gain independence from their Pakistani brothers in 1971, and that's how they repay us!" Sarad hesitated as horrible scenes from the past raced through his mind... "Still I'm sure some of the big guys are back in service by this time. The reporters should go there."

"Frankly, I don't know why they're coming here... Are you ready, doctor?"

Sarad figured that the caffeine in his system had finally reached sufficient levels, because his mind was clearing and he was starting to feel better. "What's my staff for today?"

"Two RNs, four LPNs, and five or six volunteers. That's all I could round up."

Twelve people to help treat fifty or sixty very sick patients. "All right. I'm ready, I guess."

Sarad hurried to the first ward. Thirty patients were lying in four rows, taking up all the available space. Some occupied cots, but most had been laid on floor mats. The aisles which permitted access to each patient were no more than three feet wide. The noise and the stench were terrible! Sarad knew that by eleven the heat would reach more than a hundred in the room, and the situation would become almost unbearable. Even now the temperature was eighty-five. There were only two small fans, one at each end of the ward, and their effect was scarcely noticeable. The doctor saw that six of his assistants were busy laboring over six victims. They looked up when he entered the room, and one motioned to him. He rushed to her side, put on protective gloves, and began to work.

An hour later he had just finished clearing a patient's lungs of vomit when he heard a sudden commotion at the entrance to the ward. A tall man with red hair and a short mustache bore down upon him, followed by a woman and a hippy carrying a camera. *So this is the crack news team from the BBC?* Sarad thought.

"Dr. Sarad Jalil?" the tall man said in English.

"Yes."

"I'm Edward Courtland. The reporter from the BBC." He held out his hand. Sarad removed his right glove, and the reporter shook his hand warmly. As Sarad put his glove back on, he noticed that Courtland didn't bother introducing his assistants. The hippy lifted the camera to his shoulder, put his eye to the viewfinder, and started to pan the ward.

"Nice to meet you," Sarad replied, struggling to be friendly. He gestured toward the young RN standing nearby. She wore a white uniform and had short black hair. "This is Amy Jacobs, one of my nurses. She's an American."

Courtland glanced at the nurse. "Ah, yes. My condolences. No way to get home these days, is there? Not that it would be wise to go there." Without waiting for a reply, he looked around the ward and said, "So these people are victims of the dread cholera."

"Yes, they are," Sarad said irritably.

"Do you mind if we do an interview at this time, doctor?" Courtland said. One of the patients nearby began to retch violently. Courtland nodded toward the sufferer and said, "Dr. Jalil, why don't you tell us what is going on here?"

Sarad moved to the noisy victim. "Well—"

"Are you ready, Patrick?" Courtland said to the cameraman, who ceased panning and pointed the camera at Courtland. "Good. This is Edward Courtland," the reporter said into the camera, "reporting from a small hospital in a suburb of Calcutta, in India. Dr. Sarad Jalil and his small staff run this facility with almost no modern equipment or the medicines and supplies that we Europeans consider so essential for good medical care. Every day of their lives Dr. Jalil and his staff are faced with almost insurmountable problems as they struggle to snatch hundreds of unfortunate human beings from the clutches of one of the most dreaded diseases in the history of mankind—cholera. And they perform this labor of love at the very risk of their lives. Dr. Jalil is a modest man, but in my estimation he's one of the true heroes of our times."

Sarad was angry and wanted to tell these invaders that his facilities were not all that inadequate, that their lives were probably not at risk, and that he was certainly no hero. Then he stopped himself. It suddenly occurred to him that through this interview he might be able to inspire people from the West to supply him with the intravenous equipment he needed to treat his patients properly.

"Doctor, will you please tell our viewers what is going on here with this patient?" Courtland moved aside so the camera could get a good shot of a middle-aged man lying on the floor, who was struggling to vomit, but couldn't. The American nurse had pushed him upright and was trying to make him swallow a clear liquid from a bottle.

"Well, this is one of the symptoms of cholera. The victim vomits or retches continually."

"Why don't you start at the beginning, doctor? Tell our viewers what causes this illness."

"It is caused by a comma-shaped bacterium called *Vibrio cholerae* which is ingested by the victim in food or water."

"But how does the germ get into the water or food?" Courtland asked.

"Usually the water supply is contaminated in some way by human feces. In our area the sewer system was damaged in the recent wars with Pakistan and Bangladesh, and waste materials seeped into our wells and tap water. The hundreds of bombs and mortars have completely disrupted our essential services. You realize, of course, that a short time ago India and Pakistan attacked each other. Four nuclear bombs were—"

"Yes, of course," Courtland interrupted flippantly.

"That's why cholera is widespread in both countries."

The man on the mat behind them pushed the nurse's bottle away from his mouth and vomited a stream of liquid over the lower part of his body.

Visibly shocked and disgusted by this scene, Courtland's eyes bulged, and he struck his mouth with the microphone as he jerked it toward himself to speak. "Uh, no doubt. But, doctor, tell us what this deadly germ does in the body."

"If it is able to survive the natural acids of the stomach, it produces toxins which cause the intestine to secrete huge amounts of water and salt. The result is dizziness, sweating, severe diarrhea, vomiting, loss of body salts, and dehydration. The onset of the disease is very rapid. Because of the loss of body fluids, the victim loses weight and his skin hangs on his body as if he had aged fifty years in a matter of an hour or two. His body goes into spasms and he has severe pain in his limbs. The patient becomes desperately thirsty. But the retching and vomiting make it extremely difficult for him to drink. Eventually, many areas of his body turn blue, and then almost black. If he does not receive proper treatment, he will go into a coma and die. The entire process normally takes about twenty-four hours."

The nurse behind them was trying to put more fluid into the victim, but he retched so uncontrollably that she couldn't get the water to stay down.

Sarad noticed that Courtland looked ill, and the two assistants behind him were also very pale. "But there...there is a treatment?" Courtland stammered. "You can cure this disease?"

"Yes, in many instances. There has been a vaccine for cholera since 1893, but it is not effective against the mutated strain we face today."

"Mutated strain?"

"Yes. The bacterium *Vibrio cholerae* has mutated several times since it first came out of the Ganges River not far from here in 1817. The current strain is much more virulent."

Sarad saw that Courtland was less cocky and more nervous than he had been at first. "So how do you treat the disease?" Courtland said uneasily.

"In the time-honored way, for the most part. If we can. We dissolve a mixture of salt and sugar into a liter of pure water, and try to get the victim to ingest it. The government supplies us with hundreds of small plastic bags with the right mixture of ingredients. Sometimes we have to mix the basic ingredients ourselves. It is one teaspoon of salt to four teaspoons of sugar. The sugar is needed mostly to make the salts acceptable to the gut. We should give the patient roughly the same amount of liquid as he loses in diarrhea, but that's difficult for us to keep track of when we have so many patients. The problem is, the current strain of cholera causes so much retching and vomiting that we find it very difficult to give the patient sufficient liquids by mouth."

"But aren't there better ways to treat them? It seems terribly ineffective to try to force liquids down their throats."

"Yes, there are better ways," Sarad said. Seeing the Englishman's ignorance, Sarad wondered if it would do any good to say that India needed millions of dollars for intravenous equipment, new vaccines, and premixed solutions, without which 900,000 victims were in danger of losing their lives. He pointed to one side of the room where several patients were attached to tubes. "We could be more effective in saving these wretched souls, if we had the intravenous equipment we so desperately need."

"Well," Courtland said, partly recovered from his shock. "I'm sure that thousands of our viewers will respond to your terrible predicament, now that you've uttered such a passionate plea on international television... But, doctor, I see you are wearing gloves. Is that your only protection from the bacterium while you are treating your patients?"

"Yes, we always use plastic gloves. Also, we boil the water we use and we cook our food thoroughly. You see, our patients constantly pass stools which look like rice water, but it does not smell. That's one of the sure signs that the disease is cholera. The problem is, when the stool dries on the bedding and the patient's clothes, it becomes practically invisible. So it's easy for us to soil our hands without realizing it and ingest the dangerous contagion with our food. We have to be very, very careful."

"I can see the problem." After pausing a moment, the reporter continued, "Dr. Jalil, did you say that this plague was caused by damaged sewers leaking polluted water into the culinary water system?"

"No one knows for sure, but that's our best guess."

"Is it possible that there could be some other cause?"

"I suppose it is possible, but—"

"Yes, doctor, it is possible. And we have it from other sources—sources which have proven their reliability in the past—that it is not unlikely that this terrible plague was planted in the water systems of many Indian cities by entities who have shown themselves to be enemies of India." Courtland looked directly into the camera, "Now we hear from an expert in this field, Dr. Sarad Jalil, who confirms that such suspicions are possible, even probable!"

Sarad was startled. "But I—"

"Thank you, doctor, for that remarkable revelation! Now we return you to the offices of BBC news. This is Edward Courtland reporting from Calcutta on the deadly—and suspicious—spread of cholera in India." Courtland smiled with satisfaction as he handed the mike back to his female assistant. "Okay, people, that's a wrap." Without another glance at Dr. Jalil and the patients suffering around them, the crack news team rushed from the hospital ward.

Sarad watched them go. Once again, his belief was confirmed. The liberal news media were nothing but corrupt social and political activists. Nevertheless, he prayed that someone out there cared enough to help his fellow countrymen who were suffering from the terrible plague.

*****

It was dark and silent in Kansas City. Even in the daylight it was dangerous to venture forth, but at night only the most foolish or the hungriest dared to risk it. And the gang was very hungry. Led by Silas Kitch, nine shadows slipped noiselessly down Sixth Street, looking anxiously for prey. They could barely see where they were going because of a full moon. From time to time, Silas saw a dim light high up in some apartment. No use messing with that kind of stuff. The occupants had probably installed bars on the windows and had barricaded the door. Their kids would be lying around on the floors wrapped in dirty blankets, and the adults would be playing cards or reading some religious junk to give themselves a glimmer of hope for the future. And they always had plenty of weapons around to bolster that hope.

That was pretty much the way it had been the times he and the boys had blasted their way into those minifortresses and satisfied their hunger. But recently, it had cost them a lot of blood and two lives. No, what they needed were easier targets. Like those two fools they had beaten up about a year ago in Provo behind that market. Silas figured he should have killed those dudes, instead of just taking their wallets and their car. But these days nobody got off so easily, because the gang had much greater needs. He looked over the city and saw small fires burning everywhere and he realized that his fellow anarchists would soon burn everything. In a week or so the gang would have to leave Kansas City and seek better pickings elsewhere.

"Silas, where's that mark you was talkin' about," one of his boys whined. "I'm dying for a smoke, and if I don't get something to eat soon, my belly's going to hit my backbone."

"Shut up, Fats. It's not far now. You can eat when we get back." The gang called him Fats because he was six feet two and weighed a hundred and thirty pounds.

The going was rough. They had to fight their way through debris, clamber in and out of craters in the street, and crawl over smoldering vehicles and piles of twisted metal. *Kansas City sure isn't as pretty as it used to be*, Silas thought with amusement. Now and then they came upon a body and stepped over it without even checking to see if it was still alive. It was probably just another casualty of the war for survival where friends and family members murdered one another for a crust of bread. Or maybe the plague got him... They walked another ten minutes until they came to a four-story apartment building, which was partly demolished.

"This is it," Silas murmured softly. "Marny says the guy comes out of that building at 9:30 nearly every night. The girl's always with him."

After waiting fifteen minutes, Silas saw two figures at the entrance to the building. They stood in the doorway for a while, then moved around to the side of the building. They stopped at a Dumpster in the alley, and the girl climbed in. A short time later, she crawled out, and the two walked past the front of the building and down the dark street. Silas figured they had checked the Dumpster for food and, finding nothing, intended to get food another way. Silas waved his gang forward, and within a minute they had swooped down upon their victims.

"Hold it, buddy," Silas snarled at the man, who whirled to face the sudden threat. The little bald man, who seemed about fifty and was putting on weight, trembled with fear. The girl moved close to him for protection. Silas guessed that she was fourteen or fifteen years old. The man put his arm around his daughter and said, "What do you want? I have nothing of value."

"Of course you do, old man. You've got the girl."

"No, please!"

"Look, we know you lend her out just about every night to any guy who can give ya a bit of grub."

"No! I'd never do such a thing."

"Don't lie to me. I hate it when people lie to me. One of my boys seen ya do it." The little man acted as though someone had hit him with a two-by-four, and the girl began to weep. "Take it easy, both of you," Silas said, "we ain't going to hurt nobody. We want to make ya the same deal. The girl for food. Look, man, you can trust me. I'm the only one who'll touch her."

"No, no, I beg you. This isn't right!" It was clear that the father didn't believe Silas for a moment.

Several of the gang members pulled out knives and guns to intimidate their victim. Fats seized him by the collar, and screamed, "You ain't got no choice! We're taking her."

Silas handed the man a sack of food and pulled his daughter from his grasp. "Don't worry, old man, I'll return her when I'm done."

Silas dragged the girl down the street, and his boys swaggered after him, whooping with delight. They knew they would have their chance with the girl. They had done the same thing many times before, and when they grew tired of their victims, they murdered them without mercy. The father cried out pitifully and tried to follow them, but Fats knocked him out with a blow to the side of the head.

"Why did ya give him the groceries, Silas?" one of the hoods said to the leader, as they headed for their hideout on the outskirts of town.

"Hey, man, I got my integrity to think about. A deal is a deal. Maybe I'll even return this little girl after a few days, if I can keep you slobs from killing her. Marny says the old boy's got another daughter and a wife who ain't all that bad."

*****

Because Kansas City had become such a dangerous place, three decent families desperately hoped to reach Wyandotte County Park, seven miles west of the city, before daylight. They knew it would not be easy to escape without risking their lives.

By Wednesday morning, April 19, the families had decided to leave the city together.They had to find food and a refuge from the violence. Since the six adults and eight children lived in the same apartment building, they had come to know and trust one another. During the daytime on Wednesday, they had pooled their supplies and weapons, determined to leave as soon as night fell upon the city.

Jared Luce was excited and relieved that they were finally doing something. At nineteen he was a young man of action, and he hated to sit around and do nothing but—as he saw it—whine about their situation. And he certainly wasn't afraid. After all, he was six feet tall, weighed a hundred eighty pounds, and had a black belt in wado-ryu karate.

The families waited until 10:00 p.m., and then slipped out of their building. Jared acted as the lookout for the fugitives and was sure that no one had seen them leave. He felt marvelous to be outside at last after being holed up so many months in the tiny apartment, sneaking out occasionally with one or two of the men, at great risk, to seek the essentials of life. Lugging heavy bundles, the fourteen people headed immediately for the outskirts of the city. They stopped and hid when Jared informed them that danger was near, and they started off again when he indicated that it was safe to move on.

This worked well enough until a pack of animals wearing leather jackets and baggy, faded Levis surged around a building not far from them. Jared urged his charges to move back behind a nearby fence, but it was too late. With a shout of triumph, the hoodlums rushed forward and surrounded them, brandishing knives and guns. The fathers quickly trained three rifles on the intruders to keep them at bay.

"Well, well, what do we have here?" one of the savages said, as he waved a twelve-inch hunting knife back and forth. He was tall and skinny and the only tough wearing a black T-shirt instead of a leather jacket. His long unkempt hair, dirty teeth, and bushy face made a disgusting sight. Jared was amazed to see that his skinny arms were covered with tatoos of snakes and naked women. Then another thug, the leader of the band, waltzed through the ring of killers, pulling behind him on a tether a fragile, tear-stained girl.

Silas Kitch eyed the weapons in the hands of his would-be victims and said, "I see you've found some new friends, Fats."

Jared's father, Anthony Luce, pointed his rifle at Silas. "Back off now, and no one will get hurt."

Silas raised his left hand in the air as a gesture of peace. "Hey, man, we don't want no trouble. Give us food and a few packs of cigarettes, and we'll move on. To show our good will, and to make sure there ain't no accidents, we'll throw our weapons on the ground. Right, boys?" The gang members grunted their agreement. "And then you do the same. You look like good Christian people to me, and I'm sure you don't want to see your fellow man starve." The girl standing next to Silas said nothing, but her eyes revealed her terror.

"Don't trust him, Dad," Jared cried.

"Hey! What's this world coming to when people can't trust each other?" Silas said fawningly. "We're victims of the circumstances too. Look, man, if you don't help us, we ain't got no choice. We'll do what we must to survive. Even if it means a little violence. You know how it is." While Silas was talking, one of his cronies moved behind the family group, who focused their attention on the leader. A father stood facing toward the rear to watch their back, but from time to time he turned his head to the front, straining to hear Silas.

After consulting in whispers with the other parents, Anthony said, "We can give you a small amount of food and four packs of cigarettes, but that's all. However, we intend to hold on to our weapons."

"Dad, don't listen to him!" Jared said. "Don't give them anything!" He couldn't believe his father was so gullible.

His face devoid of emotion, Silas stared into Anthony's eyes as he took a pistol from his belt with his left hand and laid it on the street. His friends did the same at once. Each had several weapons, and in seconds the street surrounding the families was littered with rifles, knives, pistols, two numbchucks, and one Uzi. Seeing this apparent display of sincerity, Mr. Luce cautiously collected the packs of cigarettes and several small bags of food. Next he stepped forward to place them in front of Silas, lowering slightly the muzzle of his rifle.

At that moment, the gang member who had moved up behind the families leaped forward and slammed into two fathers standing close together. Instantly three other thugs pounced on the men, and Silas sprang toward Anthony, reaching him before he could raise his weapon. He forced the rifle barrel downward and punched his knee into the man's groin. Anthony dropped to the ground like a stone, groaning in agony. Gloating happily, the toughs scooped up their weapons and trained them upon their helpless victims. During the melee, the kidnapped girl bolted, but one of the thugs grabbed her.

Silas glared at his prisoners with hatred. "Now you'll all pay!"

"Please let us go," one of the fathers said. "We'll give you everything we have."

"Listen, man, all we have to do is kill you and take what we want. Nobody stands up to me and gets away with it." He looked at Jared's thirteen-year-old sister and grinned wickedly. "Maybe if you people beg, we'll take that sweet young thing with us instead of killing her." Then he noticed the anger in Jared's eyes. Slithering up to him, he leaned into his face. "And you, pretty boy, I'm going to cut you up into little pieces!"

Faster than the eye can see, Jared reached out with both arms, grabbed the thug by the head and neck, spun him around, and applied pressure to his Adam's apple. It was a killing hold that Jared had learned in karate, and applied even partially, it dealt excruciating pain to the victim. Since Jared was extremely strong, Silas was helpless in his arms. The gang leader's stifled groans and ghastly appearance showed everyone that his life was in serious danger.

"Come one step closer, and he dies," Jared said to the gang. None of them budged. Next Jared spoke to Silas. "In a second I'm going to release my grip a bit on your throat, and you're going to tell these creeps to leave. If you don't, I'll kill you. Since you were going to murder us anyway, I have no choice."

When Jared relaxed his grip, Silas began to struggle and croak. Instantly, Jared tightened his hold, and his captive uttered a muffled screech, squirming like a fish out of water. "You can't escape, tough guy. You'd better believe that I can kill you with one motion if I want to. So let's try it again. And you'd better do it right this time. Here's the rules: your boys leave now, without weapons, hostages, or food!" He shouted this for all the toughs to hear. Jared's family and friends were too stunned and afraid to help him.

Jared loosened his hold. Silas choked for a while, but at last said to his friends, "Do like...like he says. Go—quick!"

After gawking at each other in confusion briefly, the thugs slipped away. When they had disappeared, Jared released Silas. He fell to the street, moaning, choking, and struggling for breath. The others surrounded Jared and shouted their gratitude and praise. Then, afraid the gang might return, they hurried away. One of the mothers put her arm around the rescued girl and led her to the place of safety.

Chapter 5

After supper, Steven and Mary read scriptures with the children. At 8:00 Steven met with the other caravan leaders. They held this meeting several times a week in order to resolve problems in the wagon train. Tonight, however, Steven also invited the three bachelors and Ruther Johnston. He hoped the mountain man might be able to give them valuable insights. Mary and Dr. Quentin Price sometimes attended the meetings because of their medical training. After they had discussed routine matters, Steven brought up a problem which concerned him greatly.

"I'm worried about the health of our people," he said. "Many have several ailments and are in poor physical condition. Mr. Johnston here said something today which made me realize how serious the problem is. At the time we were planning this trek, the Prophet warned me to tell the people of Pioneer One to prepare themselves spiritually and physically. That's why the leaders, with the help of Dr. Price, gave them general ideas on how to improve their health and fitness. We left it up to them to decide exactly how they should do this. Now I fear that we made a mistake in not providing them with more detail."

Dr. Price said, "I think the counsel we gave was good. The people knew what to do, but many didn't do it. Now the only thing we can do is repeat the advice we already gave. They should eat nutritious food, and avoid junk food and treats. Even though these things are hard to find these days, I saw many people in of our pioneers in Provo eating homemade foods which were not much better than refined, manufactured foods. The second thing they can do is to cut down the amount of good food they consume. That will also help ration our supplies. My last suggestion is that they should exercise. Of course, they'll get that automatically on this trip."

Steven replied, "Okay, I'll present your suggestions to the company as soon as possible." He hesitated. "You mentioned rationing. The problem of our general food supply has worried me as much as health and fitness. It would be a disaster if we ran out of provisions before we reach Missouri. But when I travel through our camps, I see people eating huge quantities of very good food." Steven felt a twinge of embarrassment. "I have to admit, however, that I'm not a very good example. This morning I had pancakes smothered in butter and maple syrup."

"That was my fault," Paul admitted.

Mary put in, "What about our nursing mothers? I don't see how they can go on a starvation diet."

Quentin replied, "I didn't say people should starve themselves. Just reduce their calories. Nursing mothers, of course, need special consideration."

Jasper Potter, one of the company's colonels, indicated, "We may have to gather the food supplies into specific wagons and ration it out like the early pioneers did."

Steven placed another log on the fire. "The presidency of Pioneer One discussed that idea months ago and decided that our wagon train was so huge that such a procedure would be impractical."

John spoke up, "Still, it may become necessary to implement some form of rationing soon if our people don't take themselves into hand. As you remember, Steve, I was in favor of rationing from the beginning."

"Yes, I remember, and you may be right. I suppose I turned the idea down not only because of the size of Pioneer One, but also because it sounded too much like controlling the lives of other people. That's completely against my nature. I have always believed in Joseph Smith's statement that if we taught them true principles, they would govern themselves. I know the guidelines teach true principles."

"What you say is true, Steven," Brother Potter replied, "but when they refuse to follow good principles, it may be necessary to take firmer measures. God does this frequently with His children."

"Yes, laws must be enforced sometimes when we know for a fact that it is God's will, but I'm not sure this is one of those times." Steven looked at the mountain man. "What do you think we should do, Mr. Johnston?"

"Well, it ain't really none of my business. But if I was in charge, I'd probably tell them what's what, and if they wasn't smart enough ta watch out for theirselves, they'd just have ta go on ta their Maker all alone. I would have done my job. But I suspect ya cain't look out it that way, Mr. Christopher, so you'll have ta do the obvious."

Steven felt a sudden liking for the rough old hillbilly. "Which is?"

"Firstly, read 'em the gospel of vittles. Threaten a tad. Secondly, watch 'em a few days. Thirdly, start rationin' if they don't shape up."

Everyone laughed, and Steven said, "That seems like a wise course, Mr. Johnston. Do the rest of you agree?"

"Yes," came a chorus of voices.

"Okay, is there anything else we need to take up?" Steven asked.

"Yes," John said. "What about Mr. Johnston's suggestion this morning about taking another route to Missouri? You know, to avoid the gangs in the mountains?"

They discussed different routes for a while, but there were important reservations regarding all of them. Still, several brothers held the position that it was vital to take almost any available route to avoid the creatures who would murder their fellow human beings so callously, as the gangs had done to the citizens of this mountain valley.

Finally, Steven said, "I appreciate your ideas. But it seems to me that the alternate routes which have been suggested are either impassable or would involve days or weeks of delay. So I've decided to continue on I-80. I want you to know that I've prayed a great deal about this... Any questions?... No? Okay, I guess that's it for tonight. Please circulate the message that the morning bugle will sound at 6:00, and that at 8:00 I would like everyone to gather in the center of this circle for announcements. Good night, brethren."

The meeting concluded at 9:00 after a prayer. Steven, Mary, Ruther, Paul, and the two bachelors remained at the fire to talk. Before long, Douglas and Elizabeth Cartwright joined them.

"Can I ask you folks a question?" Ruther said, after a moment of silence. Several of those present indicated their approval. "Let's see. How can I put this delicate like? Ya sees, I'm an old-time Baptist. Of course, I ain't been ta church in years, unless ya consider these mountains ta be a kinda church. But every time I run into other Baptists in these parts, they somehow end up talking about the Mormons, and it ain't always what you'd call flattering." He paused, evidently not knowing how to proceed.

"Go on, Mr. Johnston," Steven said.

"Well, what those Baptists always seem ta say is that Mormons really ain't Christians."

"You mean they think Mormons aren't good Christians?" Elizabeth asked.

"No! They say Mormons ain't Christians at all, not one little bit."

The others, shocked, glanced around the circle. Steven saw that Ruther's face took on a mischievous look, and he wondered how much this man really accepted the Baptists' point of view.

"What I want ta know is what I should tell my fellow Baptists when they talk like that."

No one said a word. Steven smiled and looked around. "Well, folks, what should he tell them?"

After a moment of silence, John said, "Mr. Johnston, I've always liked the Baptists because I think they're good people, and most appear to love the Lord. However, I have to point out that churches and individuals have been saying all kinds of things about our religion from the very beginning, and most of those things have been misrepresentations. Yet nothing they've said has ever stopped the church from growing and accomplishing its mission. So

43

please don't think me rude when I ask you why we should care what the Baptists think."

"I understand what you're saying, young man, and ya make a good point. But fer my benefit, what should I tell my fellow Baptists?"

Steven answered, "Before these guys answer your question, Ruther, I'd like to ask you a question."

"You betcha."

"Why is it that some Baptist writers profess to expose the errors of Catholics, Jews, Jehovah's Witnesses, and Mormons out of Christian love, but at the same time they use erroneous evidence and unfair arguments in an unkind spirit?"

Ruther squirmed. "I see what you're gittin' at." Steven guessed that Ruther had noticed the same faults in the books of Baptist authors. "Believe you me, I'm plannin' on makin' yer points ta my friends the moment I sees 'em. I sure expect they'll squirm some! Listen, ya don't have ta answer that Mormons-not-being-Christians stuff if ya prefer. I understand completely."

"No, we want to answer," Steven said, "but I hope we haven't offended you."

"Heck no! Takes more than a little kick in the pants ta make me run."

When the laughter died, Paul began his answer. "Let me say that the Baptists are right. Mormons are not Christians."

Everyone was startled, and most of all Ruther. "What! You say they're not?"

"No, we are not Christians according to the way the Baptists define the word 'Christian.' But we are Christians according to how we define the term."

"Okay..." Ruther said, confused.

Paul continued, "So what is your definition of a Christian?" Steven was amused at how Paul made Mr. Johnston answer for himself instead getting away with pretending he was relaying the words of a third party.

"Well, let me see now. A Christian is somebody who believes in Christ."

"Okay, we do that."

"And he tries ta follow Christ's way of life."

"Okay, we do that. So are we Christians yet?"

"No, ya have ta believe in the true Christ. Ya have ta understand his real nature." Ruther was getting warmed up now. "Ya have ta believe He's an aspect or a manifestation of the one God. Ya have ta believe men can only be saved by His divine grace, and not by works lest any man boast."

"I see. You mean we have to accept the doctrines of the Baptists in order to be Christians."

"Well...yes! How can ya be a true Christian if ya don't believe in the true Christ?"

"What would you say if I told I can prove that those doctrines are false? If I can prove the Baptist doctrines on the nature of Christ and on grace are not scriptural, will you let us be Christians then?"

"Uh, well yes, I suppose. But that might not be easy."

Steven said, "That's one of the reasons we hope you stay with our wagon train as long as you can. We can have fun trying to change your beliefs."

The group roared. Even Ruther got a gleam in his eye. "Yes siree, it might be fun at that! Of course, there's always the danger I might convert you instead."

Steven broke into a grin. "You'll never know unless you stick around to find out. And, Mr. Johnston, even if we could prove to you beyond any doubt that the Baptist doctrines regarding the Lord are false, we'd still accept you as a Christian, and you wouldn't even have to become a Mormon!"

Ruther gave Steven a toothless grin. "Why that thar is downright neighborly of ya, Mr. Christopher. How is it that ya kin do that?"

"Because our definition of the term Christian is fairly general. We believe that anyone who sincerely believes in Jesus Christ is a Christian, no matter what church he belongs to."

Steven saw that Ruther became silent suddenly, and he wondered if he had touched the old man's heart.

After the friends talked another hour at the fireside, they got up and went to their own wagons. Paul had invited Ruther to sleep in the bachelor's wagon. At first Ruther refused outright, declaring that he'd prefer to sleep under God's stars. But when Paul had promised him some good religious debates, the old-timer chuckled and accepted immediately. When Mary and Steven climbed into their wagon, they saw that the children were still awake. It took another half hour to get them to sleep.

"We sure don't have much privacy in this wagon, do we?" Steven said with a touch of irritation. "Newlyweds deserve to have privacy!"

"Sweetheart, do you want to sleep under the wagon tonight?"

"Yeah right! Hey, I have an idea! Why don't we put the kids under the wagon, and we stay in the wagon?"

Mary let out a muffled laugh at her husband's little joke. "I know. We could leave the kids here and set up the tent."

Steven madly searched for the tent. Ten minutes later they had erected the tent and were snuggling together in privacy.

"This is great," Steven declared, sighing. "But I wonder how long it'll take for the kids to realize we're gone and storm our position."

"Not long, I'm sure."

Steven grumbled, "Do you really think it's dangerous to sleep out in the woods?"

Chapter 6

The bugles sounded at 6:00 a.m. on Thursday. Even though the pioneers would only travel six hours a day for a week, Steven did not want to spoil them too much. He hoped that by the end of the week the people who had been having trouble with their legs and feet would be able to increase the hours of travel until they could tolerate ten hours a day. Later he would extend the travel time to eleven, then twelve hours a day.

By 9:00 the Saints had gathered in the center of the first circle of wagons. There were one thousand and four people. After six days, Pioneer One had already lost the twenty people who returned to Salt Lake City. Because of the great multitude gathered in one spot, Steven had difficulty quieting them down. Finally, he stepped onto a folding chair and raised both hands high in the air. The crowd gradually became silent. John, who seemed to think of everything, handed him a homemade megaphone.

"Thank you, brothers and sisters," he said into the megaphone. "I just want to make a few announcements. As you know, we will be on a reduced travel schedule for a few days to help us adjust. That means we will travel from 9:00 to 12:00 in the morning, and 1:30 to 4:30 in the afternoon." The crowd cheered and clapped. "Afterwards, we will increase our travel time until we can walk for twelve hours a day." Steven heard a few groans, but went on. "Twelve hours a day seems like a lot, but we will have to make up later for the time we lose now."

After answering a few questions about the hours of travel, Steven continued. "As you know, the leaders of Pioneer One have asked you to manage your own food supplies. However, we have noticed that many are consuming more food than is necessary. This is extremely dangerous, because we may run out of provisions before we reach our destination. For that reason, we urgently caution you to ration your food carefully. Choose nutritious food, and eat only enough to keep you strong and healthy. Above all, we must begin to use the edible plants available around us. We ask you to increase gradually the quantity of edible wild foods you eat until they constitute the bulk of your diet. Be careful about what you pick, because some of the plants are poisonous. If you have any doubts concerning the safety of a plant, please consult the people who have been trained to identity the safe plants along our route. You will find a list of their names in the guidelines."

"But if we ration our food and eat that many wild plants, we'll die for sure anyhow," shouted one of the brothers who was standing close to the front. Many in the crowd indicated their agreement.

Steven smiled, then said, "I'm afraid we have no choice. In any case, please don't worry. Dr. Price assures me that the new diet will not harm you, as long as the plants are safe and you increase their use gradually. Of course, if you begin to feel sick, dizzy, weak, or have gastric disturbances, you need to see one of our medical people. Besides the doctor, we have a registered nurse, Mary Christopher, and two practical nurses, Gertrude Jones and Karla Millman. I would like to emphasize that if we cannot learn to ration our food, the presidency will have to take more stringent measures to insure the well-being of all of the pioneers." Steven was surprised that no one seemed to object to that statement.

"The next point concerns our safety. We learned yesterday that we may face danger from certain gangs farther along this route. There is very little more I can tell you at this time, so it's useless to ask questions. We ask only that you use common sense and obey the guidelines we gave you before we left Provo. Be especially alert to any possible threat. We expect the men to keep their weapons loaded and close to hand at all times. And if any of you sisters have a weapon and can shoot, please do the same... Okay, that's all I wanted to say." Steven looked at John and Paul. "Is there anything you wish to add?" His brothers shook their heads. "Okay, let's move out now!"

The Saints trudged back to their wagons, carts, and converted vehicles. Ten minutes later they moved slowly onto the highway in a double column. Steven watched them from his horse as they went by. They looked weary already, and some could hardly walk. He knew that many would have to ride before long, but at least now they were trying their best. He was proud of them and admitted to himself that they had courage. He suspected that in the months ahead they would need every ounce of courage they could find. Steven's feet and legs were swollen and gave him a lot of pain, in spite of Mary's treatments, but he knew that others were worse off than he.

*****

After he had finished reading the report, the President of the church, Josiah Smith, sighed and looked up at his counselors. "Well, brethren, what do you think? Is there any truth to this?"

Bennion Hicks, the Prophet's first counselor, spoke first. "In my opinion, the report seems largely based in rumor, and is simply too crazy to believe. A Mexican Army of Liberation gathering and preparing to travel on foot and horseback to invade Utah. It's ridiculous!"

"How far away is this army supposed to be?" Josiah asked, searching through the report to find the information.

"About two thousand miles," Bennion offered. "It's impossible!"

Josiah smiled at his counselor's reactions. It was always a mistake to dismiss something too rapidly just because it sounded fantastic. "What do you think, Samuel?"

"It's certainly hard to believe," President Law observed. "Why would these people risk their lives and their property to make such a long trip? And why attack us?"

Josiah replied, "The report doesn't speculate on that, but it's obvious, isn't it? These wicked men, supported by criminal governments, desire everything we have: our land, our possessions, our wives, and our lives. My guess is that the bandits *are* the government."

"So you think the report is true?" Samuel Law asked.

"I don't know for sure, but we cannot afford to ignore the possibility. A few nights ago, when I thought I was asleep, I saw a vision in which a huge man in uniform stood over me with a sword raised above his head. Then the vision disappeared, and I found myself sitting up in my bed. I don't remember many details, except that my pajamas were soaked with sweat."

Samuel said, "So you believe this vision might be a warning that we will be invaded by some terrible enemy."

"I learned long ago to trust the dreams and visions which the Lord gives me." The Prophet got up and stretched. His arthritis had been giving him trouble, and stretching helped ease the pain. "Therefore, Samuel, I want you to make sure the General Authorities know about these rumors. Next I want you to gather a group of men you can trust to investigate this report. The men you send should be Mexican Saints, who can travel in Mexico with greater safety."

"What if it's necessary to send them as far as Mexico City, where the report says the army is gathering?"

"Then do it. And, Bennion, I want you to warn stake leaders to prepare for the possibility that we might be attacked. I don't want them to alert the people at this time, but simply to make plans on how the Saints in their areas might defend themselves in case of attack. If these reports are true, we may have to gather our own army. I know the Lord wants us to defend ourselves."

"It won't be easy, President. Most of the stakes don't have radio communication with us," Bennion said.

"Do the best you can. Send men on fast ponies if you have to. As soon as possible, bring me a list of the regions you were not able to reach."

"All right. I'll get on it today."

After his counselors left, Josiah got to his knees, determined to ask the

Lord if the Saints were truly in danger. He knew that if they were, he would have to take more drastic measures.

*****

They headed east on Boulevard Blanqui in Paris, moving slowly in the 5:00 p.m. traffic. Pierre Laborde was frustrated. The fuel pump on André's Citroën Evasion minivan had stopped working, and the vehicle had been in a downtown garage until 4:00. As a result, they had not been able to leave earlier, and they had been forced to travel in the city at rush hour.

However, Pierre felt grateful that his friend still had the van. He turned to see how the women were coping with the kids. The four children were obviously frightened by the sudden escape through the city, but they were holding up well under the stress. The two younger kids, a boy and a girl, belonged to him and Diane.

Yesterday evening Pierre and André had visited André's stake president to receive counsel on how to respond to the government's demand that all Mormons register with the authorities within three weeks. They had been stunned to see that the president and his family had already packed their car and planned to leave the city the next day. The leader had informed them that he had just received confirmed reports that UGOT was imprisoning Mormons in great concentration camps and confiscating their property. It was official government policy. There were even ugly rumors that some Saints were being executed, but this could not be confirmed. As a result, church leaders in Europe were advising members to go into hiding in any way they could.

"Pierre, do you really think we can be safe with your friends?" André asked in French.

"I'm certain. They're not Mormons, but I've known them for years. They're good people. Their son fell into the Marne River one winter years ago, and I saved his life. They'd do anything for me."

"How far did you say it was to their farmhouse?" Mireille said.

"It's forty-five kilometers to the city of Meaux. At that point we turn off the main road and follow a country road for a mile. Their home is a quarter of a mile south of the Marne."

As they approached the Place d'Italie, the vehicles ahead came to a complete stop. An ambulance flew by on the right with its siren screaming, but it was forced to halt two hundred feet ahead. Pierre decided that this was the biggest traffic jam he had ever seen in his life. The helpless ambulance continued to wail as if to mourn the passing of its occupant, but none of the other Parisians paid the slightest attention. Pierre figured that the only way the ambulance was going to get to the hospital was for a gigantic helicopter to swoop down and pull it out of this mess. However, if any helicopter appeared, it would no doubt be the military police of UGOT hunting for his family and friends. Instinctively, he checked out the square and the side streets, looking for those ugly green uniforms, which in the last few months had replaced the familiar blue outfits of the Paris police.

It took them a full hour to move across the Place d'Italie, but finally they began to make progress. Before long, they left the city heading east on an excellent highway. They picked up speed as the traffic thinned out, but they were terrified that at any moment they would be stopped. Pierre got the impression that many of the other travelers stared at them when they came abreast of their van. For a while, he wondered if there was a sign on the top of the van which read "Mormons."

*****

David Omert leaned back in his chair in his office in Jerusalem. "I'm very concerned over how Israel will survive. What happened last year will be nothing in comparison to what we will have to face." He and his friend, Chaim Yehosua, were having lunch in David's office in the Knesset Building, home of Israel's parliament. Both men were members of parliament.

Chaim frowned. "Do you really think we're in that much danger? I don't see any real proof that UGOT wants our blood. What I see is the same old thing from the Arabs: refusal to accept the Jewish state, threats of eternal destruction, guerilla warfare, and manipulation of the world press. It doesn't seem to matter how many times we defeat them in war, or how many pieces of land we concede later. They still won't give up. I'm afraid we'll have to continue warring with the Arabs until the end of time, or until your Messiah comes."

"It seems that way, doesn't it? I seriously doubt that there will ever be a permanent resolution to the Arab-Israeli conflict, because the claims to the ownership of Palestine on both sides date to the time of Abraham, and the hatreds are too deep. It will take more than diplomacy and treaties."

"I agree," Chaim said. "There are too many people on both sides whose reason for living is to hate their traditional enemies."

"Of course, not every Jew is like that."

"Oh, you must be thinking about that new group. The Coalition for— What is it?"

"The New Coalition for Reconciliation... But there are others too."

Chaim smiled broadly. "I know! Certain political leaders like David Omert."

"And Chaim Yehosua!"

"Yeah, I suppose so, but I'm not as dedicated to love and brotherhood as you are."

David laughed. "You are too! You just hate to admit that you're one of the good guys. But we're not the only ones. There are a growing number of Christian Jews who want genuine reconciliation."

"Hah! Not here in Israel!"

"Yes, here in Israel. Chaim, I've told you before that you need to pay more attention to what the media is saying. Sometimes it can give you better and more recent news than government channels."

Chaim groaned. "Yeah, yeah, I've heard it a million times. So these people are Jews who used to be faithful to Judaism, but have turned to Christianity."

"Some of them."

"Liberal or conservative Jews?"

"I don't know! Does it really matter? I do know, however, that some of these Jews were descendants of the victims of the holocaust. Because of the horrible tales their parents related, they became agnostics or atheists in their youth. But later they converted to Christianity. Now they proudly claim to be both Christians and Jews."

Chaim said, "Some Jews believe that the term Christian Jew is a contradiction in terms."

"I know. That's why they often reject the Christian Jews as traitors to their race."

"Have you ever had the occasion to talk to any of these converts?"

David put his feet upon the desk. "Yes, a few times. I found them to be proud of their Jewish heritage and yet to possess a strong faith in Jesus Christ. They believe He was the promised Messiah who came to bring salvation to the world more than two thousand years ago, and that He will return again some day."

"Whew! I'll bet that goes over big with other Jews. What do they say about the fact that the Jews were responsible for crucifying this Messiah?"

David paused as if he were trying to remember actual conversations. "Well, they don't condemn their ancestors... They feel it was all part of God's plan."

"How do they explain the two thousand years of pain, suffering, and exile that we Jews have gone through?"

"They blame it on Satan, who used the wicked nations of the earth to fight against the Jews because they're the race who gave the world salvation through the Son of God."

"So you think these Christian Jews are increasing in number?"

"From what I read, Jews are converting to Christianity by the thousands now, both in Israel and in other nations. But one point I have heard them stress is that the Jews as a nation will only turn to Jesus Christ when He appears to them at Armageddon and shows the physical signs of his crucifixion. At that time, He will save the Jews from the mighty armies of Gog."

"Brother! I hope they're wrong. How crushing, how humiliating it would be to stand there on the Mount of Olives in front of the great Messiah, and suddenly realize that your ancestors had murdered him from fear and jealousy."

David grinned. "I see you've been reading the New Testament."

Chaim looked at his friend sheepishly. "Oh, I check it out a little now and then. Nothing serious, you know. So what do you think about the claims of the Christian Jews?"

"I'm not sure what I think. Right now I'm carefully searching the Old Testament for every word which might pertain to the Messiah."

"So where do the Christian Jews get the idea that the Messiah will appear on the Mount of Olives?" Chaim asked.

"That's how they interpret Zechariah, chapters twelve through fourteen," David replied.

"And this happens during the great war called Armageddon, where all the nations of the earth gather to wage war against Israel?"

"Not all nations. The wicked ones," David corrected. "Why?"

"Well, I was thinking about what you were saying a little while ago about UGOT. It has almost become a worldwide dictatorship."

"Yes, an oligarchy," David added.

"So if UGOT is plotting against Israel, as you suspect—"

David interrupted, "It may be that the great power called Magog in the scriptures is none other than UGOT."

"Yes! The wicked power ruled by Gog, the great dictator."

David teased, "You are remarkable, Chaim. The truth is, I've been entertaining the same idea for months now."

Chaim scowled and hurried to explain. "I didn't say I really believe this stuff. I was simply exposing to the light of day the crazy things you've been imagining."

David laughed warmly, then became serious. "This brings me back to my alarm concerning the future of Israel. If UGOT continues to undermine our reputation and security in what is left of the world community, as I believe it's doing, how can we possibly defend ourselves against such overwhelming forces? We would be like a mouse defending ourselves against an elephant."

"But soon we will be better prepared to defend ourselves than ever before! Our army is much stronger than it was a year ago."

David shook his head sadly. "We are completely alone in the world. The

United States can no longer help us, and no other nation seems to have the strength or the desire to do it."

"David, you're far too pessimistic. After all, we have the great Minister of Defense, Menachem Hazony, and soon we will have a new prime minister. A forceful young man of exceptional talent and intelligence."

"Funny, Chaim."

"No, no, it's pretty certain that our party will gain the most seats in the election in May, and that it will choose you as the prime minister. With you and Hazony, we have nothing to fear." David and Chaim were members of the Likud Party, which was an alliance of small parties. It believed in limited government control over the economy, a hard line against the Arab states, and retaining the territories captured from the Arabs in previous wars. Their chief rival was the liberal Labor Party, which believed in strict control of the economy and, in hopes of finally obtaining a lasting peace, compromising with the Arabs over occupied lands.

"The chances are slim that they'll elect me. Frankly, if they did, I have no idea how to protect Israel."

"But you're forgetting your Messiah. The Jewish Messiah, that is. When the going gets tough, He'll descend from heaven and save our bacon."

In spite of Chaim's ironic statement, which revealed his lack of faith, those words had the remarkable effect of filling David's heart with peace. "You're also forgetting something, Chaim," David said calmly.

"Which is?"

"I told you last year that God would some day clear the Temple Mount of Islam's holy shrines, and you couldn't believe such a miracle was possible."

Chaim's face froze.

"And now we're rebuilding Jerusalem, and have already set the foundations for the Third Temple."

"You've made your point, David. Please don't rub it in."

*****

The President of the Republic, Alejandro Calvino, was adored by the people and had been elected to his office by a landslide vote. He turned from his map of Venezuela, which covered a third of the south wall of his office in Caracas in northern Venezuela, and sat on the front edge of his gleaming mahogany desk. His face was lined with worry and lack of sleep. He looked at the two men sitting on padded chairs in front of him. Ramón Sánchez was the President's top advisor and a longtime friend, but the second man was another matter. He considered Diego Romero, the new Minister of Defense, to be an evil little traitor who would sell his own mother for a profit. UGOT had forced him to place the man in his high office three months ago for one purpose only: to make sure Venezuela's leaders did what they were told.

And since Diego had entered the administration, the government had been forced to do many things to curtail religious freedom in Venezuela. Now it was forbidden to display the cross or religious icons in public. One could no longer give public prayers to any deity, and religious holidays had been canceled. The normal use of cathedrals, churches, and temples was in grave danger. The President had even received reports that the green coats and the regular police, under the authority of the office of the Minister of Defense, had secretly invaded private homes to destroy religious images, Bibles, and other sacred writings.

The President was ashamed to think of what he had been compelled to do to the former minister of defense, another friend, in order to make room for UGOT's toady. Through his own office he had leaked false charges to the press accusing the previous minister of being involved in drug trafficking, and the media had spent two weeks rehearsing every possible angle of the sordid story.

Secret agents from the new world government had already arranged some timely "accidents" for ten of the most prominent leaders in the National Congress, and had threatened to kill other national leaders, and Alejandro himself, if they did not fall into line and accept the pawns sent by UGOT. As President, he could have ordered the military police to arrest the foreign agents, but most of them worked under cover like terrorists, and he had not been able to discover their identity. And when he had resisted orders as they were given, he had received another threat directly from UGOT headquarters in London: if he didn't become more agreeable, UGOT would send an army to Venezuela to enforce compliance.

Alejandro had sought the aid of neighboring countries—Guyana, Colombia, Bolivia, Ecuador, Peru, Brazil, and Chile, but they had been too afraid to intervene. Peru, Chile, and Bolivia had already complied with the rules of the new world order, and the other four countries declined to interfere. Since UGOT had not yet bothered them, they considered themselves safe.

"How can you expect me to do this terrible thing?" he said to Diego Romero in Spanish. "If I required the members of this church to register with the government, to the exclusion of other religions, it would cause a popular uproar. Especially since Venezuela has had a long tradition of giving religious freedom to all its citizens." Alejandro glanced at Ramón to see how his friend was reacting to the terrible news. Ramón showed no emotion whatsoever.

Diego smirked. "There'll be no uproar because you'll not make it public. The Mormons have a lay clergy which is highly organized. I understand that

their church can get messages to its entire membership within hours if neces
sary. All you need to do is pass my instructions to their leaders, and the public
will hear little of it. And if someone asks questions, we'll simply deny it. The
main thing is, you must make the Mormons think this is a routine census of
religious groups in Venezuela, and that the government will require the other
churches to register in succeeding months. You should make it clear that it's
the only way the Mormon church in Venezuela can maintain its tax-exempt
status. If you do as I say, the Mormons will come running because they've a
history of obeying their government." Diego took hold of his briefcase and got
up slowly from his chair. "I must go now, for I have other things to do. Mr.
President, I want your message to reach Mormon leaders by Wednesday,
April 26, five days from now. Their members must comply by Friday, May 5.
Are we agreed?"

"Yes."

"Don't be so glum, Mr. President," Diego said. "As I told you before,
when we accomplish the great things I have planned, Venezuela and the world
will be the better for it. You must have faith in that and in nothing else." He
inclined his head. "Good-bye for now."

Alejandro and Ramón said at once, "Good day."

When the door closed behind Diego, the President turned to Ramón
and cried, "The things he has planned for Venezuela! The arrogant little
weasel. He's nothing but UGOT's dog. Ramón, my friend, you must go to your
people and tell them to resist this registration at all costs."

"But why? Diego is just expressing his innate desire to lord it over
others. I'm sure he simply wants to stick his nose into the church's business
once again, or to make us Mormons pay higher taxes."

Alejandro shook his head urgently. "No, I have reason to believe it is
much more serious than that. UGOT is far more interested in eliminating
obstacles to its plans for total power than to increase its revenues."

Ramón was visibly shaken. "What makes you think that? What do they
want with us?"

"This morning I received a report from people loyal to me in intelligence. They say that Romero and his henchmen have taken control of three of
our major prisons in the last four days. I'm powerless to stop it! As Minister
of Defense, he's head of the National Guard and has used this authority to
replace the regular prison personnel with soldiers from the Guard. It seems
that after he seized control, he released 50 percent of the condemned prisoners."

"Why? It's crazy."

"That's what I've been asking myself all day. But when Romero
announced his plan a half hour ago to register the Mormons, it all fell into
place."

"You don't think—"

"Yes, I do! He intends to throw your people into prison and confiscate their property. It explains the reports I've been getting some time now from abroad."

"What reports?"

"Reports that UGOT is incarcerating rebellious religious factions in many other countries. I didn't think much of it at first because I figured the new world government was using that tactic to insure order. You know, get control of the violent cults so it could promote its programs in peace."

"What do you think we should do, Alejandro?"

"As I said, resist the registration at any cost."

"But will that be enough? I'm sure Romero has access to computer records and will come after us when we don't show up to register."

"Then you must go into hiding. Like the ancient Christians in the Roman catacombs. I believe it's a matter of life and death for your people to disappear as soon as possible. At least for now." Alejandro lowered his voice suddenly as if he remembered that his office might be bugged. "I want you to know that I'm doing everything I can to regain control of this country. But it will take time."

"When should we act?"

"Today!"

"All right, I'll take your message to church leaders. I'm sure they'll follow your advice. And, Alejandro, Mormon leaders in Utah encouraged us two years ago to set up a special settlement about sixty-four miles southwest of Caracas, just south of Maracay Lake. We built thousands of homes, most of them underground, and gathered all types of supplies, including weapons and ammunition."

"Yes, I knew you were doing something unusual in that area. But why are you telling me this?"

"Because I trust you completely and I want you to know what some of your fellow countrymen are doing to preserve their freedom."

"Thank you, Ramón, you've always been a good friend."

"We also have six other isolated colonies in other parts of the country. We didn't fully understand why the leaders asked us to prepare like that, but we did it anyhow. Now I know the reason. The Venezuelan Saints don't believe in violence, but we will defend the lives of our wives and children."

Alejandro touched Ramón's hand. "You may have to, my friend. You may have to."

Chapter 7

André Renan saw the French police car behind them in the rearview mirror when they were half way to Meaux. It was nearly a mile back, but over-taking them rapidly.

"The cops!" he shouted.

Pierre looked back and said, "They're gaining on us, but having trouble with the traffic."

"I didn't hear any siren," Mireille exclaimed.

"That is unusual," André replied. "What do I do? Speed up, get off the freeway?"

"This van has a lot of power," Pierre said. "We might be able to outrun them."

"We don't even know they're after us!" Diane cried. "And they're the regular gendarmes, not the green coats."

"She's right," Mireille said earnestly.

"But you never know which of the regular police are taking orders from the green coats anymore!" Pierre stated frantically.

André suddenly realized what he had to do. "Calm down, all of you. I'll handle this."

He maintained his speed and watched the approaching patrol car care-fully. When it was two hundred feet behind, André heard the nerve-racking wail of its siren. He continued his pace until he saw his pursuers move up almost to his bumper and stay there. Then he immediately slowed down and pulled to the right side of the highway. The police car stopped ten feet behind, its siren silent, but its lights still flashing.

"I hope you know what you're doing," Pierre said, as they waited for the policemen to walk up to the van. André rolled down his window.

"Get out of your vehicle," the officer growled. "All four adults. Not the children."

Mireille told the four children what the officers wanted and reassured them that there was nothing to worry about. As the adults got out of the car, the second officer, who was standing behind the van on the passenger side, called out sharply, "Step to this side of the vehicle, away from traffic."

André was terrified, but tried not to show it. He noticed the same fear in the eyes of his companions. The policemen acted as if they were dealing with common criminals. After demanding their driver permits, the first officer walked back to his vehicle.

While the patrolman checked their licenses on the government's central computer, André said to the other officer, "Did I break some law? What's going on?"

The policeman rested his right hand on his gun holster, but did not draw the weapon. "You will not ask questions. You will wait."

After fifteen minutes, the dread in André's heart was so great that he could hardly breathe. Why was the first cop still sitting in the car? What were they waiting for? Then all at once the terrifying idea came to him that the man in the car must have radioed for the green coats to come. That had to be it. It was only a matter of time before a military truck arrived and carted them off to the concentration camp. André desperately wanted to warn his wife and friends, but was afraid to do it with the patrolman nearby.

While he was entertaining these gruesome thoughts, another patrol car appeared and stopped in front of his van. The officers in the second car did not get out. Now André was confused. Perhaps he was wrong. Maybe they had called for backup because somehow the computer messed up and listed them as dangerous criminals. He felt a little better now because the policemen he was dealing with were fellow countrymen, dressed in the normal uniforms of the French Highway Patrol. No doubt it would take only another minute or two for this matter to be straightened out.

"Why is this taking so long?" Pierre asked ten minutes later.

"As I said before, you will not ask questions," the officer replied.

André had begun to think about the green coats again when a third patrol car arrived on the westbound side of the freeway. It continued a few hundred yards past them, pulled to the left side of the freeway, and turned across the meridian. As it pulled up behind the first patrol car, the patrolman who had made the radio call exited his vehicle and marched up to them.

"You are all under arrest," he announced.

"But why? What did we do?" Pierre cried. André wondered if they were under arrest because Pierre had opposed UGOT on television talk shows and documentaries.

The policeman turned a cold eye on Pierre. "We will not respond to your questions. They will be answered in due time by the proper authorities. You will get into your vehicle and follow the patrol car in front of you. The driver will turn across the meridian and return to Paris, and you will follow him very closely. If you try to escape, we will have to use deadly force to stop you. Do you understand?"

"Yes, sir," André said meekly.

André and Pierre hopped into the front seat of the van, and the two women got into the back with the children. They waited for the car in front to move. There was a great deal of traffic on the freeway, and it was more than five minutes before a gap came in the eastbound traffic. Finally, the car took off abruptly, heading for the meridian. When André hesitated an instant, the driver behind leaned on his horn. André jerked the van into motion and slammed to a stop in the center of the meridian, behind the leading patrol car. He glanced through his rearview mirror and saw that the cars following him were lined up close behind on the meridian.

"So much for safety!" Pierre yelled. "We could have been killed pulling such a stunt!"

"Under the circumstances," Diane said, "it might have been much more dangerous if they had tried to stop the traffic."

"Yes, this traffic is brutal!" Mireille observed.

Since the westbound traffic was also heavy, it took another five minutes of waiting before the four vehicles could move safely onto the freeway. The first car moved into the right lane and sped up to a hundred kilometers an hour. André followed about fifty feet behind, and the second car almost lay on his bumper. The third police car moved up on the left side and stayed there, blocking him in, but also forcing the freeway traffic to follow their caravan at the same speed. Obviously, the police had no intention of letting them escape.

"Talk about overkill," Pierre complained. "Three cop cars to escort one little minivan."

"André, we can't let them take us in," Mireille said tearfully. Her emotion caused the children to cry. Seeing what she had done, Mireille struggled for control and dried her tears on a sleeve. She and Diane shushed the children and encouraged them to be brave.

"She's right," Diane said. "They'll treat us like the Nazis did the Jews. I'm sure of it."

André himself was almost in tears. "But I don't know what to do. They have us boxed in."

"Think, everyone," Pierre exclaimed. "There has to be a way!"

"Dear Father in Heaven," Diane said in a clear, loud voice, "We, Thy faithful children, ask for Thy help in this desperate situation."

Everyone was surprised to hear Diane, Pierre's wife, openly appeal to God in such a simple, fervent way. The other adults and the children said "amen" almost instinctively. André's face burned and he felt a peace and confidence he had never known before. He constantly glanced into the rearview mirror as the miles passed, and soon a plan came to him. It was wild and dangerous, but it just might work. Since they were only seven or eight miles from the city, he had to act quickly.

"Listen, everyone," André said. "In a minute or two I'm going to do something shocking. You can prepare yourselves by making sure your seatbelts are tight, and by hanging on to something to steady yourselves."

"Tell us what you're going to do, s'il te plaît, please!" Mireille pleaded.

"I'm sorry. There isn't time." André had decided not to scare them. He saw the turnoff two hundred yards ahead.

Pierre exclaimed, "But we may object to your plan!"

André paused, then declared, "That's right!" At that instant, he jerked the wheel to the right and slammed on the brakes. The van skidded and nearly rolled over from the sudden turn, and everyone screamed. As André accelerated down the off-ramp, he stole a glance through the mirror, but could not see what had happened. His only impression was that the patrol car which had been following them had not made the turn after them. While the women and children continued to cry, Pierre strained to see the freeway. At the end of the off-ramp, André braked once more and made a sharp right turn without stopping. He gunned the powerful motor as he headed north. Checking the mirror again, he glimpsed a pile of wrecked cars buried in fire and smoke.

"What happened?" André hollered.

Pierre let out a whoop. "They crashed into each other! The patrol cars." He looked at passengers in the rear and said firmly, "All right, everyone, quiet down. We're okay now."

A few minutes later, after the adults had succeeded in calming the children, André said, "I didn't see it, Pierre. What happened?"

Pierre replied, "When you yanked the van off the freeway, the car in front slammed on his brakes. It's clear he wasn't thinking about the results of such a reckless move. The car behind us didn't even seem to notice you had turned off and, still speeding merrily along, piled into the rear of the lead car. At the same time the character on the left must have figured that since you made the ramp, he could do it too, because he swerved violently to the right and struck the second car just as it collided with the lead vehicle. The gas tank in the first car exploded, and all three caught fire."

"What a terrible way to die!" Mireille moaned.

"Yes, it's horrible!" Diane agreed. "I feel so sorry for those poor officers."

Pierre turned and looked at them with a level gaze. "Yes, but we have to remember that those 'poor officers' were taking us to slavery or death, and didn't seem especially unhappy about it."

"Do you think they knew what was going to happen?" Diane asked.

"I'm sure of it," Pierre said. He examined the road ahead. "Do you know where you're going, André?"

"Not really."

"Well, I know this area like the back of my hand. Turn right at the next road. I can take you there by the backroads. Unless you people prefer not to go to our original destination." Everyone agreed that they should still seek refuge at the home of Pierre's friends.

After a minute of silence, Pierre looked at his friend and said, "André, what I'd like to know is what possessed you to do such a crazy thing back there? What made you think they wouldn't simply slow down, turn around, and come after us? What if the car behind us had been able to make the ramp like we did? What if the van had rolled over? There was so much risk. Frankly, I don't get it."

"Well, I noticed that the driver behind us was having trouble staying awake. He was following so close that I could see his face through the mirror. I figured that if I could make the ramp, he wouldn't even see it until too late. As for the lead driver, I didn't know for sure what he would do. But something told me there was a good chance he would panic and brake too hard."

"It turned out great, and I'm proud of you. But I still think you were possessed," Pierre said.

Diane replied, "He was possessed, all right! By the Holy Ghost."

*****

Gerald Galloway admired the exquisite beauty of the sunset from the terrace of his mansion in Hampshire, England. He had spent many remarkable hours in this spot and others on his vast estate, expressing his soul through painting. And he was a master at it too, for many of his masterpieces had sold for substantial sums on the world market. Recently, the critics had increased the crescendo of their adoration, and Gerald wondered if it was because of the improved merit of his work or because they feared his growing power.

"It's a splendid sight, isn't it, Gerald?" Lucienne said as she followed his gaze. "And all the haze and dust from so many disasters in the world have only increased its beauty."

"Yes, what arises from pain and degradation is often more beautiful than anything man has seen before. They are the flowers of evil as Charles Baudelaire put it."

"True, but usually someone of superior genius must control the growth of the new beauty. Just as we did in our meetings the last three days."

Gerald laughed. "Yes, some of our associates are not fit to rule themselves, much less the world. One must always guide them and control them."

"I agree. They're nothing but sheep. Maybe that's why the Bible calls the true believers 'sheep.' Like our stupid comrades, the believers have no intelligence of their own, but must be led like dumb beasts."

"That's why I asked you to come with me to share the sunset and a glass of sherry. I would like you to give me a personal report on your progress in controlling the world's religious communities."

"What exactly did you have in mind?"

"Well, since you've taken charge of your new assignment as head of the Ministry of Religion and Spiritual Welfare, I believe we've made great progress in nullifying the authority and influence of the churches."

Lucienne frowned as she took a sip of wine. "Thank you, Gerald. I admit, however, that I definitely prefer my old job of associate to the United States. It was much more challenging and rewarding trying to outwit political leaders whose primary goals were to enlarge their own power and fortunes. I understand such people. They're so much more intelligent than these gullible fanatics I have to deal with now." Lucienne pouted.

Gerald felt the urge to kiss her beautiful red lips. He laughed and said, "Well, maybe some day we can return you the States, when the smoke clears away, and there is something for you to govern."

"You want me to govern the United States!"

"Why not? You could enjoy the same intrigues and mind games as you did before, but this time as Chief Executive."

"Oh, thank you, Gerald. You are definitely my favorite world dictator!"

They laughed heartily at Lucienne's little joke.

A moment later, Gerald said, "But for now, you have this religious assignment. How is your project with the Mormons proceeding?"

"Very well. However, I must admit that it hasn't been easy. There are about thirteen million of them worldwide, excluding the United States, of course, and they're found in every country in the world. Their population is especially dense in Central and South America."

"How is your registration going?"

"Fairly well. We've registered almost a million."

Gerald was not happy. "One million out of thirteen. That's not many after all these months. What's the problem, Lucienne?"

"Well, they're an independent and rebellious people. Most have refused to register."

"Round them up and put them into prison camps!"

"It's not that easy. As soon as they hear about the registration, they go into hiding."

"But Colton Aldridge told me once that Mormons believed in—how did he put it? Oh yes, in obeying the law of the land."

It was Lucienne's turn to laugh. "Gerald, they believe in obeying what they call the constitutional law of the land, not in a dictatorship which seeks to control them, make them renounce their God, and—well—you know the rest!"

"Yes. But how do they know we plan all that for them?"

"I've asked myself that many times. In spite of my excellent security, they just seem to know. Someone told me once that they claim to get personal messages from their God."

"Every one of them?" Gerald said, shocked.

"Yes, every one who really wants it."

"Curious concept! But some day our laws will be the constitutional law of nations. I'm writing that constitution now. Will the Mormons obey the laws then?"

Lucienne yawned. "Somehow I doubt it."

Gerald got up and took another bottle of wine from a nearby cooler. "Then ferret them out, and if they resist, kill them."

"That's what I intend to do. But, Gerald, what about the Mormons in the United States? There must be seven million of them, concentrated mostly in the Rocky Mountains. What should I do about them?"

"Most are children, I understand," Gerald said ironically.

Lucienne sneered. "Yes, it's disgusting. All those mouths to feed, and the screaming! But what should I do about them?"

"Nothing for now. We must wait until the Americans finish each other off, and until we have assured our power. Then we'll send armies to the Rocky Mountains. Of course, we don't want that to interfere with our prime objective."

"Destroy Israel!" Lucienne declared with passion. "I pray to God that we can do that soon!" Lucienne strived to do a good job of acting. Unlike Gerald, she was relatively indifferent about destroying Israel.

Pleased with her fervor, Gerald said, "We're getting closer to that goal every day... But now I want to hear about the other religions. You know, the Christians, Taoists, Buddhists, and so on."

"Generally speaking, they're not as hard to handle as the Mormons. We deal with them in many different ways, but we have only begun our work. I have used Colton Aldridge to advantage in some of my visits to governments which are greatly influenced by the biases of a dominant religion."

"Yes! That's what you said in some of your reports, but you didn't provide many details. Please explain."

"Well, for example, when we visited India, Colton went around for a few weeks doing miracles, and soon the news of the great new prophet spread like wild fire. The believers of Hinduism thought he was the incarnation of one of their many deities, and they were ready to listen to anything we had to say." Lucienne put her hand to her mouth to suppress a laugh. "They saw him as even more sacred than their cattle. So when we went to the government to encourage them to accept Colton's guidance—that is, UGOT's guidance—

there were no serious objections. That's how we placed some good people next to the Prime Minister as his special advisors."

"I knew it would happen. What kind of miracles did our favorite prophet do?"

"He healed the sick, blind, and lame in nearly every country we visited. He caused it to rain in India, brought down thunder and lightning in Korea, made statues bleed in Italy and Spain, and even led the police to a kidnapper in Taiwan. He has done so much that I can't remember it all. The truth is, he scares me sometimes. When he does a miracle, his body vibrates all over, and his eyes seem to turn into burning coals." Lucienne was mesmerized by the memory of Colton's incantations.

Gerald touched her shoulder and said, "Lucienne, Lucienne, are you all right?"

"Yes... I'm sorry. I got carried away."

"You must control yourself. After all, Colton is nothing but a tool."

"I know, but you should see him."

"He actually does the things you said?"

"Yes. I don't know where he gets his power, but I know it works... Listen, Gerald, you must be careful with Colton. He's very dangerous."

Gerald sat on a chair next to his mistress. "Don't worry. I know how to control him."

"I hope so. I truly hope so."

"I'll simply instruct my medical staff to put him to sleep some day and insert a biochip. Just to be safe."

"You mean, like the American Government did when they were having so much trouble with anarchists and paramilitary groups?"

"Exactly! Listen. I have a secret to tell you. I haven't announced it to the Committee yet, so you're the first to know. I've initiated a program to implant every human being on the planet with a biochip. We've found ways to do it which are so subtle and quick that the victim doesn't even know he's been implanted."

"You say everyone will get it. Does that include the Twelve?"

"No! The Twelve and our close operatives are a secret society. They've made sacred vows and know that if they violate those vows, the penalty is death. Colton is not really a member of our society, and so I've decided to control him with the microchip."

"But I thought the chip was no more than a sophisticated identification card, which allows you to locate a person anywhere in the world and access his personal data. In other words, it only provides partial control of the carrier. Is that right?"

"Normally, that's the case. But the new chip is something special. It contains a tiny amount of a deadly compound which can kill the carrier within seconds. You only need to push a button on a master control. Obviously, we'll only use this chip in people we consider a potential threat. We're also working on a biochip which can explode in the brain of the bearer."

"What wonderful news! Gerald, you do think of everything. I hope you stick one of the new chips in Colton as soon as possible." She gave a low laugh. "I also have good news. News from our trip to India."

"What?"

"Soon there will be millions of people who won't need a biochip."

"Meaning?"

"While Colton and I were in India, we learned that a new pandemic of cholera is sweeping the subcontinent. They expect it to spread throughout half the world within a year. A hundred million people will perish."

"Oh, yes. The BBC gave a minireport on it a few hours ago. You realize, however, that this type of thing helps our cause in another way. These plagues usually take their greatest toll on the poor and uneducated of mankind. Such creatures are a burden to the world community, and we'll find it easier to govern if they're eliminated. How can we ever have a perfect society if it's full of dross and refuse?"

Chapter 8

The wagon train moved slowly along I-80, covering slightly more than one mile each hour. No breeze cooled their bodies, and no clouds protected them from the scorching sun. The temperature climbed quickly to ninety-two degrees by noon, and every traveler was soaked in sweat. Steven felt that the heat was almost unbearable, and when they stopped for lunch at noon, he rolled under his wagon and lay on the road to rest. Only one thin blanket separated him from the hard surface. His legs throbbed, but he dared not look at them. He felt guilty for not having the strength to be a bold hero, like Moses, who could walk among the wagons when they stopped to encourage his people in their suffering. He knew that some must be worse off than he, but he feared what they might say when they saw him. He silently cursed himself for his laziness in leading such a sedentary life in the city.

"Steven, are you all right?" Mary called, squatting beside the wagon so she could see him.

William kneeled on the road beside her. "Hey, Dad, what are you doing? We need to make lunch."

"Okay, I'm coming."

He pulled himself from beneath the wagon and sat on the folding chair Mary handed him. He noticed that Jennifer and Andrew were exploring a ditch not far from the highway.

"How are your legs?" she asked.

"Painful, but I'll survive."

"I'll check them after we eat lunch. Then I'm going to make sure you ride for a while, either on your horse or in the wagon."

"But—"

"No buts, Mr. Hero. The other men are doing it, and you should too!"

Steven was going to protest when he saw two men and a woman heading toward them. The woman and one of the men were obviously married. He was not especially happy to see any of them because he figured they were bringing complaints.

"I've got a problem I need to discuss with someone," one of the men said, looking at Mary.

"It's the same with us," the woman declared.

Steven replied, "I'm sorry. I can't remember your names. I guess it'll take me awhile to get to know everybody."

"I'm Joshua Hale," the first man said.

"And I'm Hannah Baldwin." She nodded toward the second man. "This is my husband, Victor. We're friends with the Hales, so we got Joshua to come with us."

Steven said, "Look, why don't you talk to your leaders and ask them to bring the problems to us at the review meeting tonight."

"I'm afraid it can't wait," Joshua said.

Hannah agreed, "I have a personal medical problem, Brother Christopher. I need to talk to your wife. I tried to see the doctor, but he's got a line of people at his wagon. Besides, I can't stand the arrogant—" She stopped short when she saw her husband's sharp look.

"Steven, would you please make lunch so I can talk to these people?" Mary said. She handed him the materials to make sandwiches. "Let's talk about things under the trees over there." Mary pointed to a few scraggly trees not far from the highway. "We'll take these folding chairs with us."

Steven wearily began to prepare lunch as he watched the visitors walk away with Mary. What was so important that they had to talk to Mary now? Why couldn't it wait until tonight? He shouted for the children to come and help. Twenty minutes later, he was pleased to see Mary returning so soon from the sessions with her patients.

"What was that all about?" he asked.

"Health problems. One had a caffeine addiction. He had a huge cache of caffeine pills, but ran out two days ago. I gave him advice on how to handle his withdrawal. The other person has ulcer pain. I suggested she take natural remedies. I promised to help them all look for burdock root and Brigham tea when we stop for the day."

"You're wonderful," Steven said.

"I don't know about that, but I do know I'm hungry. Did you save me anything?"

"Yes, two sandwiches and a glass of milk."

While Mary was eating, Paul, Jarrad, and Leonard arrived with three young women. Paul was doing his best to escort all three women at once, as if they belonged to him. Andrea Warren, Anastasia Borisovich, and Rachel Crell, the third bachelorette, played along with Paul, laughing and joking in spite of their sweaty and bedraggled appearance. Mary dropped the rest of her sandwich into her plate, sprang from her chair, and embraced her old friend.

"Where have you been, Andrea?" Mary said. "I went to your wagon ten times in the last few days, and you were always gone! Are you trying to avoid me?"

"Heck no! Whenever we stop, I wander around checking out the available men. I'm almost thirty-two now and don't have time to waste. I'm tired of mothering these two female brats, and I want someone—a man—to take care of me for a change. Besides, I need to prove you wrong." The other young people loved to hear Andrea's banter and gathered around her anxiously.

"Prove me wrong? I don't know what you mean."

"Look, dear, you once told me that I gave a hard time to every available male I met, and I'm determined to expose your faulty thinking during this trip."

Mary replied in the same tone, "Well! It's about time. You know the old Mormon belief: every woman needs a man to make her life complete!"

"Yeah, right... No, Mary, the real reason you haven't seen me is that I saw you coming and I hid. I was afraid you might drag me to your wagon when Steven was there. The temptation to run away with me might simply be too great for him!"

Mary laughed, but Anastasia smiled subtly. "Heavens!" she exclaimed. "Steven would never be interested in another woman when he has one as beautiful and intelligent as Mary."

Paul searched around a moment and said, "Hey, where's the grub? You didn't save anything for us?"

"Sorry, little brother," Steven replied, "but you need to feed yourself more often. Our supplies are limited, you know... Now there's something else I need to chastise you for. Don't you think you should be a tad more circumspect? You're one of the leaders of the caravan, and this fooling around might give people a bad impression."

"Shoot! Everyone knows how much I'm really suffering. They're fully aware that my happy-go-lucky demeanor is just an act to cheer them up and give them courage."

"Yes, I forgot." Steven wondered how it was that his brother could look so good and have so much energy, when he wanted to crawl into bed and sleep a week. He was only thirty-seven, but he felt like ninety!

"But, Steve, the real reason we brought the flower of Pioneer One—the lovely ladies you see before you—to visit, is to let you hear them relate in person the rumors they've heard. Anastasia overheard a new rumor this morning which I want you to hear."

Steven said, "Why don't we get off this freeway before we burn up?"

While Mary remained at the camp with the children, the others headed for a cluster of trees which grew sparsely on the north side of the highway. Since many pioneers had had the same idea, they found it necessary to walk several hundred yards before they found a band of shade. They sat in a circle, and the three young women related the rumors they had heard. Since Paul had already given him the same information two days ago, Steven was not surprised. He knew, however, that the three bachelorettes traveled in the same wagon and had plenty of time to discuss these intrigues, and he wondered whether or not they had embellished the stories for effect.

"Okay, Anastasia, tell him the new gossip you heard," Jarrad said.

Anastasia smiled coyly and caressed Steven with her eyes. He wondered why it was that whenever she spoke to him, he got the impression she was flirting. Maybe it was the way she had with all men, and she didn't mean anything by it.

"Well, this morning I visited my parents and overheard a man—I don't know his name—talking to my father. He said he was on guard yesterday and came across a group of men talking by a stream not far from the wagon train...I hesitate to repeat this because it's probably nothing except empty gossip."

"What did the guy say, Anastasia?" Paul said impatiently.

"I think he said that they said the leaders of Pioneer One have a hidden agenda..."

"And?" Paul prodded.

"They said Steven really wants to lead us to North Dakota—or was it Canada?—to set up his own kingdom and rule over us. I'm pretty sure that's what he said they said." Steven couldn't believe his ears.

"It's the silliest thing I've heard in a long time," Jarrad said.

Paul added, "It's amazing how many nutty things people can imagine. I doubt any sensible person would believe it."

"But I sort of believed it—at first, that is," Anastasia admitted.

"Do you want us to chase it down, Steve?" Leonard asked.

"Oh, I don't know. Keep your ears open, but don't waste a lot of time investigating. You've more important things to do." Steven glanced at his watch. "It's almost 1:30. We'd better get back to our wagons. By the way, Paul, where is Mr. Johnston? I haven't seen him since this morning."

"He took off on his mule right after your talk this morning. Heading northeast. He told me he wanted to check out the road ahead, but should be back in time for supper."

Steven was disappointed. For some reason, he felt safer with the old Baptist hanging around.

The caravan couldn't start by 1:30 p.m. During the morning, several wheels on different wagons had begun to seize up, and the owners and wheel-wrights were still busy repairing them. It seemed that whoever had made the wagons had forgotten to put grease in some of the hubs. During the remainder of the trek to Zion, the pioneers learned that the wheel hubs were the weak spots in the construction of the wagons, in spite of the modern grease and roller bearings that were commonly used. The "Moderns," or "Converters," as the wagon builders called them, gloated. They had no problems with their modern vehicles and saw the wheel repairs as proof that they had been right all along.

During the lunch period, they had spent most of their time promoting two basic ideas. First, Pioneer One should no longer be referred to as a "wagon train," because it was not comprised solely of "ancient" wagons. They suggested instead terms like "conveyance train," "carriage cavalcade," or "buggy column," which got the most votes, because these terms could refer to any vehicle, old or new. Later in the journey they presented this suggestion at a regular meeting of the caravan leaders, who shook their heads sadly and said they'd take the proposition under advisement. For some reason, however, none of these terms ever really caught on, in spite of the machinations of the "Moderns."

On the other hand, their second idea became more and more accepted as Pioneer One continued its long trek. It was that the pioneers should watch for wrecking yards along the highway, so that they could gradually replace their broken-down wagons with a selection of modern vehicles, which the "Moderns" claimed they could convert in the blink of an eye.

Finally, at 2:30 p.m. the caravan set out again in the terrible heat. After driving his wagon for a while, at Mary's insistence, Steven mounted his mustang and walked him down the road to check on his people. He was pleased and surprised when many pioneers gave him a friendly wave. Several people who were traveling on foot came up and declared how much they appreciated his concern for the hard time they had been having. By the time he returned to his wagon, he was elated. He climbed up next to Mary, threw both arms around her, and kissed her hard on the mouth.

"Yuck, Dad! That's gross!" Andrew exclaimed.

Steven turned and grinned at his son. "Oh, I didn't see you, Andrew. I thought you were walking with the other kids. Yes, it's gross, but it sure is fun!"

Mary said sweetly, "Thank you for the kiss, dear husband. I'm sorry I didn't check your legs at lunchtime."

"You didn't have time. Besides, they feel better now. Pretty soon, I'll try to walk again—with your permission, of course."

An hour later, Steven hopped off the wagon and began to walk. The initial shock was bad, but soon the pain subsided and he could move more easily. The caravan continued laboriously along the highway until it came to the end of the valley. At that point the road narrowed to two lanes and turned to the northeast. There were many ups and downs in the freeway, but the overall upgrade was negligible. The mountains on both sides gradually moved closer until the road ran through a narrow gorge a few hundred yards wide.

The heat was still intense at 4:30 when the pioneers pulled off the highway half way between Exits 148 and 152. After they had formed the wagons into three large circles, the pioneers found any shady spot they could to escape the heat. They lay around exhausted, too tired to do anything but doze and nurse their aching bodies. Only a few bothered to pitch tents this early. After checking that John had posted a double guard, Steven climbed under his wagon with his family and fell asleep immediately. A half hour later he was awakened by shouts.

"Brother Christopher, please wake up! I really need to talk to you. It's an emergency!"

Steven rolled from under his wagon and looked around with sleepy eyes. He finally recognized one of his colonels.

"Who is it, Steve?" Mary called.

"It's Seth Crowell. He wants to talk to me. You can go back to sleep."

Steven staggered to his feet and said, "Can I help you, Seth?" He could see that his visitor was very agitated.

"You've got to do something about Brother Hamilton! He's driving me crazy!"

"Frank Hamilton?" Frank was one of Seth's captains.

"Yes! He never cooperates. No matter what I ask my people to do, he invariably ignores me and does his own thing. It's hard enough to handle the things I have to do without having to put up with him. All I'm trying to do is follow the guidelines and do a good job!"

Steven was astonished to see how angry the colonel was. "But why are you so mad, Seth?"

"You ask me why? Well, it's obvious, isn't it? That guy seems to do it on purpose. He enjoys torturing me. I've never seen such willful disobedience. The truth is, I think he refuses to cooperate because he doesn't respect me. Or maybe it's just a personal dislike. This afternoon I told him I was going straight to you about his behavior."

Steven was certainly awake now. He put his hand on Seth's shoulder and pointed to some boulders a short distance from the camp. "Why don't we sit over there and discuss it?"

"Good! We need to solve this problem right now."

They walked to the boulders and found a seat. The area was not protected from the sun, and the late afternoon glare intensified Steven's headache.

"Why don't you tell me some of the things Brother Hamilton does that causes so much trouble?" Steven said.

"Hah! The list is endless. I have to remind him constantly when it's his turn for guard duty. Then he always insists on taking his wife with him, or he tries to exchange watches with someone else. He refuses to obey the rule about families quieting down at 8:00 p.m. When we're traveling, he some-times moves his wagon alongside that of another young couple so they can joke around together. They make so much noise that an Indian tribe could attack and they wouldn't even know it." Seth paused to catch his breath.

Steven pulled his hat down to cover his eyes better from the sun. "So you think that what he's doing is dangerous?"

"It certainly is," Seth said angrily. "When he pulls that trick, he's trav-eling triple file instead of double file like the rules say. Also, I reminded him today that the men in our group were going to have a brief meeting tonight to report on their weekly visit to their assigned families. This will be our first meeting of the trip, and it's important that everyone be there. But Frank said he didn't feel well and wasn't coming. However, I know for a fact that he's as strong and healthy as a bull. So it boils down to one thing. He's giving a terrible example to the other brethren."

"Is that all?" Steven said.

"Let's see. He doesn't keep his campsite clean and he—I don't know. The things I've already mentioned are probably the most important."

"That's a long list after only seven days. Let me ask you some questions, Seth. How well do you know Frank Hamilton?"

"All I know is, he's about twenty-four years old and got married two weeks before Pioneer One began this trip. It's difficult to get to know someone when you feel he doesn't like you."

"That's true. However, the fact that he's so young and recently married might explain some of his behavior. It's understandable that a newlywed hates to be away from his wife even for a moment. I got married ten days ago, and it's very hard for me to leave Mary for one hour. Also, you said he constantly moves his wagon into triple file to talk to the other young couple?"

"Yes."

"Well, we probably should consider that behavior to be typical of young people who are full of excitement about life and want to share their feelings with people their age. The dirty campsite might also be explained by Brother Hamilton's youth."

"Being young is no excuse for being stupid!" Seth exclaimed.

"But that's my point. Is his behavior really stupid?"

"I don't get your drift."

"Does Frank water his animals when and where you suggest?"

"Yes, he does."

"Does he do what you ask when you call on him to help members of your group repair wagons or do other important tasks?"

"I suppose so," Seth said reluctantly.

"Does he obey most of the guidelines such as keep his weapon at hand, drink plenty of water, stay close to his family, and ration his food?"

"Yes, he obeys those rules, but he breaks others. What about him not quieting down at 8:00?"

"In what way does he not quiet down?"

"I hear him and his wife chattering until nine or ten. You can hear them a mile away."

Steven smiled a little. "And the other pioneers are completely quiet and trying to sleep?"

"Uh, no..."

"They're talking too?"

"Yes, I guess they are," Seth admitted.

"Well then, maybe we shouldn't blame Frank for doing what everyone else is doing... The reason I asked you about the good things Frank is doing is to point out that he seems to be obeying the guidelines which really count. For example, take the problem of him traveling triple file instead of double."

"Yes."

"The reason for traveling double file instead of single file is so the Saints would be bunched closer together in case of attack. So if Frank travels triple file, isn't he really obeying the purpose of the guidelines?"

"Except you're forgetting that those two couples make a terrible racket traveling next to each other," Seth objected.

"I know, but most of the Saints make too much noise as they go along. It's a problem everybody has. Hopefully, we'll solve that weakness in the next few days."

"Okay, okay, I understand. You want me to ease up on Frank a bit."

"A lot."

Seth picked up a boulder and heaved it in an arc, crushing a black beetle six feet away. "All right, a lot. But what about his refusal to come to the report meeting tonight?"

Steven was disturbed to see Seth's pleasure in killing the bug for no reason at all. "Yes, I wanted to ask you about that meeting. What do you intend to do there?"

"I'll go around the circle to check on whether or not they're doing their assigned visits. Then we'll discuss any serious problems their people might have. It's kind of like a meeting on home teaching."

"So you'll go around the circle and ask each man there to report on his activity in front of about forty other men?"

Seth replied, "Yes, it's a good way to get a report quickly without having to contact each man separately."

"Have you questioned Frank about his activity in front of people on other occasions?"

Seth paused. "Yes, but only in front of his wife and some of his friends. I had no intention of embarrassing him."

"I see. Well, I counsel you not to do it that way."

"But why? It's very effective."

Steven frowned. "Because it employs social pressure to get the men to do their duty. It's really a form of intimidation and manipulation, which are actually the same thing as compulsion. I prefer you don't use compulsion to influence the behavior of the brethren."

Seth raised his eyebrows as he declared positively, "But the brethren like that technique! I've used it many times in the past, and no one has ever objected. A lot of leaders do it that way."

"That's because they care mostly about what is convenient for them. Their main desire is to get that report, no matter what. Obviously, they're not sensitive to the men who might be exposed in public as negligent in their duties. And what is the result? The exposed individual is deeply humiliated and, since it's done out of convenience and not in the true spirit of love, he resents such treatment and may be tempted to rebel."

"No. I assure you that I do it in love."

"Maybe, but the method of public report is a terrible way to motivate anyone to do the Lord's work in the right spirit. The people who depend on it also tend to use excessive persistence, veiled threats, and even anger to intimidate the Saints to perform. In my opinion, they've no idea what they're actually doing. They need to study and memorize the words of Doctrine and Covenants, section 121, especially verses thirty-six through forty-two."

Seth got a triumphant look in his eye. "Yes! But verse forty-three says 'Reproving betimes with sharpness, when moved upon by the Holy Ghost!'"

"I'm afraid that's one of the most misunderstood verses in scripture," Steven said. "The sharp reproof it speaks of, which is inspired by the Spirit, cannot include anger as we know it, because the Holy Ghost never moves man to anger. There are other scriptures which say that anger is always evil. Also, the angry brothers who think they're using the Lord's 'sharp reproof' are usually too mad to remember the second part of the verse which declares that the reprover must quickly show an 'increase in love.' If you're increasing your love, that means your reproof involved love, not anger. I'm afraid no one can immediately show love after being angry."

"However, God sometimes uses 'righteous indignation' when He deals with man. It's an example for His children."

"I realize that, but we are not righteous like God, and our so-called indignation is quickly corrupted by negative anger."

Seth arose and said, "Well, Brother Christopher, I see you have strong opinions on how to deal with people. Listen, I'll give your words some serious thought, but it's hard to stop doing things the time-honored way simply because one person thinks you should. I know the old methods get results. The work has to be done, and we need those reports!"

"That's right, but at what cost? I suggest you forgive Frank Hamilton his weaknesses. Show him kindness, patience, and gentleness, instead of sternness and impatience. Show him you truly love him and care about him, and he'll come around eventually. Also, I believe that instead of focusing on getting work done, you might find out why he does what he does. After all, this is a community of love, not a business for profit."

"What do you mean by that?"

"Well, three months ago I interviewed Frank in connection with the journey to Zion. During our discussion I discovered that Frank's father had been an alcoholic. To make a long story short, the sick man brutalized his son. Instead of showing the boy love, he used threats, anger, and intimidation to control his behavior. So it may be that today Frank sees you, to some degree at least, as just another abusive adult."

Seth looked crushed. Tears came to his eyes as he struggled to say something. Steven waited patiently, his own eyes filling with tears. Finally, Seth said, "I had no...no idea, Brother Christopher. Look, I promise you I'll try to do better."

Steven watched as Seth returned to his camp. He decided that his crabby old colonel was basically a good man, and would probably always do the right thing once he knew the truth.

Chapter 9

"Where's Mary?" Steven asked William when he returned to camp.

William was preparing a fire for the evening meal. "She went up the road a little way with some people. Doug and Liz and most of the kids went too."

Steven remembered that Mary had promised Joshua Hale and Hannah Baldwin that she would take them on an herb walk to find Brigham tea and burdock root. Steven walked a hundred yards toward the road and finally caught sight of them not far away near the highway. Everybody had baskets and seemed to be finding many good plants. Douglas was guarding them with a high-powered rifle. Steven noticed that Hannah and Joshua had brought their spouses with them.

He returned to his wagon, unwrapped his legs, and rubbed them with cayenne ointment. He was pleased to see that the swelling had gone down. A half hour later the plant pickers returned.

Mary giggled as she ran up and kissed her husband. "We found so many medicinal herbs! My patients have enough to last them a week. I even remembered to tell them how to prepare and use them. Aren't you proud of me! And look at what else I found!" Giggling louder than ever, Mary shoved a basket under his nose.

Steven gave it a sour look. "Nice! What are the weeds for?"

"Supper."

Steven swallowed hard and caught the other plant pickers laughing at him as they placed their baskets brimming with forage close together near the wagon.

He gazed at his wife in disbelief. "Tell me you're kidding."

Mary suddenly stopped giggling. "Not at all, young man, you told every person in Pioneer One that we had to live off the fat of the land, and that's what these weeds are."

"I told them that?"

"Yes, in your speech and your famous guidelines."

"Oh."

"Aren't they wonderful?"

"Yes, of course! So what's for supper?"

She began to giggle again. "A lovely salad of dandelion leaves and thistle stems, uncooked, of course. Also, we'll have bean soup seasoned with wild onions. It's all very healthy." Mary waved good bye to the Hales and the Baldwins, who started to leave. They had been listening to Mary and Steven's conversation with amusement.

"Sounds delicious," Steven replied ironically. Although he wasn't looking forward to eating the new forage, he was very proud of her ingenuity. "I have a good idea, Mary."

"What's that, dear?"

"Tomorrow, instead of preparing a meal, why don't we just walk out into the fields and graze like the cattle?"

Instead of getting angry, Mary put her hands on her hips and thought hard. "Mmm, that might not be a bad idea. At least we'd be a lot healthier than we were when we bought our food at the grocery store in the city."

The women finished preparing supper at 7:00. The usual crowd was there: Steven and Mary's family, the Cartwrights, and the three bachelors. Rutherford Johnston returned from his excursion in the mountains in time for the meal, which he ate with relish, as if it were the most normal food in the world. Steven loved the soup, but hated the salad. From the look on their faces, he guessed that the other "civilized" people in the group shared his opinion. All except Mary, of course. After they had cleaned up, they sat around in a circle and stared at the fire without saying much.

"I kin understand why you Mormons is so sad and ain't got much ta say," Ruther said with a sparkle in his eye.

This remark stunned everyone, and every eye turned upon the mountain man. Steven smiled and said, "What makes you think we're sad, Mr. Johnston?"

"Call me Ruther. I hate that formal stuff."

"Okay—Ruther. Why do you say we're sad?"

"Well, it's probably because ya all know you'll probably end up sittin' here chewin' yer cud, or doin' somethin' else inconsequential, when the Christians—excuse me, the other Christians—are carried up to bliss. Now, I don't intend ta get yer dander up sayin' such a shockin' thing, because I'm really startin' ta like you folks. But the truth is the truth."

Steven suspected the old man was deliberately baiting them, and was purposely using the worst English he could to make them believe he was just a hick. But was the old coot as ignorant as he acted?

Steven took the bait, "I'm not sure what you're getting at, Ruther."

"Well, the scriptures teach that the true believers in Christ will suddenly disappear from the earth. Poof! Just like that. Millions of 'em gone. And the other folks who was talkin' to 'em will look around ta see where the heck they went, and they won't find a durn thing! The wunnerful thing is, those true believers will be taken up ta meet Jesus before the great tribulation hits the earth. It's called the rapture. Then, after the tribulation, Jesus will come in wrath and punish the wicked. Do ya remember that scripture which talks about the two men in the field? One will be taken and the other left. That there refers ta what I'm talkin' about."

"What about the other true believers?" Paul asked.

Ruther appeared confused. "What other true believers? There's only one church of true believers. They belong to different denominations, but they're all part of the one great church."

Paul kept going, "But some of those believers say the rapture comes after the tribulation, and others believe it comes during the tribulation. Even those who accept what you say, that it comes before the tribulation, are constantly fighting over the details of the sequence of events. Are the true believers who reject your point of view going to be raptured anyhow?"

"Oh, I suppose so. The believers disagree on details, but they'll still be raptured when the time comes."

"What about the Latter-day Saints?" Elizabeth asked.

Ruther replied cautiously, but with the same grin. "I wish I could say yes, but you folks don't believe in salvation by grace alone, and ya don't believe there's only one God."

Steven wanted to challenge him on those two doctrines, but decided to wait until another time.

Paul replied, "So you're saying the same thing you said before. Yesterday you said we aren't Christians because we don't believe the way you do, and today you say we can't be caught up to meet Christ for the same reason."

"Yep, that's purdy much it. But it's not really because ya don't believe the way I do. It's because ya don't accept what the Bible clearly says."

Jarrad Babcock said, "Mr. Johnston, we love the Bible, but it's not as clear as you say. That's why so many true believers—as you call them—can't agree on when your rapture is supposed to take place, and why there are so many different Christian churches."

Douglas added, "And history shows that those different sects often hated one another and fought to the death over the details of their beliefs. Doesn't that seem strange to you when they based their beliefs on the same Bible?"

"Well, ya got me there," Ruther said. "Let me think about it a few days before I answer that point."

"I have a question, Ruther," Mary said sweetly.

"Yes, Ma'am?"

"What happens to the people who aren't raptured?"

Ruther struggled to maintain his composure. "They go through the tribulation."

Mary dug in. "Does that mean they're damned?"

"Mmmm, uh, yeah, I suppose so."

"So what you're saying is that millions of believers are saved, but billions of unbelievers are damned."

"Well, uh—"

"And that includes millions of good people who have never had the chance to hear about Jesus, and millions of babies who are too young to believe?"

"Well, I don't know about that! You better give me a chance ta discuss this with some of my Baptist friends."

Steven said, "Ruther, you are a good man, and I'm sure you don't want anyone to suffer the tribulation. That's probably why you're trying to warn us. However, I'd like to know where you find the idea of a rapture in the scriptures."

"Okay. I learnt where those scriptures are by heart." Ruther pulled out a tattered Bible from inside his coat and found a passage. "Here in First Thessalonians, chapter four, verses sixteen and seventeen, it says Jesus will come from heaven, the holy dead will rise, the living believers will be caught up with the dead ta meet the Lord in the air, and all of them will live with Him forever. And in First Corinthians, chapter fifteen, verses fifty-one and fifty-two, it says we—meanin' the true believers—will be changed in the twinkling of an eye at the last trump. So ya see, the scriptures prove our belief in the rapture."

"But, Ruther," Leonard Reece said, "didn't you say at the beginning that Jesus will descend from heaven after the tribulation?"

"Yep, I did."

"I'm confused then. The verses you summarized in Thessalonians says that He will descend before the rapture. That means before the tribulation."

Ruther answered, "Well, actually Jesus comes from heaven more than once. He descends at the rapture, then again to punish the wicked."

Jarrad jumped in, "But isn't the rapture supposed to be a secret, quiet event that only the raptured recognize?"

"That's right."

Steven was concerned that the Mormon defenders were ganging up on the old man. Still, everyone continued to discuss the ideas with a good spirit, and Ruther seemed to love it, so he did not come to Ruther's rescue.

Jarrad continued, "Then why does First Thessalonians say that the Lord shall descend with a shout and the trump of God? That doesn't sound very silent to me."

"That there has a spiritual meaning. It isn't a physical event. Ya got ta read all these here scriptures in context."

Jarrad smiled and let it drop. However, Paul had something else to say. "Okay, let's put it into a context of other scriptures. Mark, chapter thirteen, and Matthew, chapter twenty-four, seem to put the three events we're discussing into the same order: first the tribulations, then the Second Coming, and finally the gathering of the elect from the four corners of the earth. Doesn't this contradict your idea of the rapture occurring before the tribulations?"

"Yes siree, Mr. Paul, I've read them scriptures and I cain't figure 'em out. So until I does, you'll have ta wait ta git my answer."

Steven was relieved to see John and the four colonels heading toward his wagon. "Well, the leaders are coming for our meeting at 8:00. Thank you, everybody. It's been an interesting conversation!" He looked at Ruther. "We certainly appreciate you keeping us on our toes, Ruther!"

"Glad ta be of help, Steve."

The meeting with the leaders of Pioneer One lasted a half hour. The item which caught their interest most was the report which Ruther gave at Steven's request. The mountain man explained that he had spent the day exploring the country ten miles up I-80 for signs of the gang which had terrorized the entire region. He discovered nothing except a few indications that members of the gang had passed over that area a week earlier. Steven told him that he was grateful for his concern regarding their welfare.

After the leaders returned to their own wagons, Steven and Mary sat around the campfire discussing the events of the day with their friends. Later that night, Steven and Mary had their own conversation by the light of a lamp as they lay in their beds.

Mary asked, "So Anastasia said she overheard gossip that you're going to lead us to Canada so you can rule over us as king?"

"That's what she said."

"But it's so weird! How could anyone believe it?"

"I don't understand it. Still, I have to admit that I've seen people believe some pretty strange things in my life."

"That woman bugs me!" Mary said angrily.

"Who?"

"Anastasia, Steven!" she said impatiently.

"How does she bug you?"

"The way she looks at you all the time. She puts on that little-girl act of hers, puckers up her yummy round lips, and sighs deeply as she gazes longingly into your eyes."

"Mmm, I haven't noticed."

"Liar!"

"Who? Me?"

"Yes. You know perfectly well what she does!"

"Shoot! She does it to every man in camp below the age of fifty."

"I know, but she really turns it on when she sees you! I'd sure like to know why."

Steven couldn't resist the feeling that Mary was preparing a trap for him. Maybe a test. "I have no idea."

"Maybe it's because you're so friendly to her," Mary probed.

"Of course. I try to be friendly to everybody."

"Well, maybe you're trying too hard when it concerns her."

"Whew! That sounds like jealousy."

Mary suddenly changed her tone of voice. "Don't be silly! I'm not jealous at all. Jealousy is a weakness which is beneath a mature woman. A woman who truly loves and respects herself does not feel a trace of jealousy." It sounded like a line memorized from a book on modern psychology.

"Yes, I've heard you say that before."

Mary went on, "All I'm trying to say is, when you're so friendly to Anastasia, she prefers to interpret that to mean you're interested in her personally."

"I am interested in her personally." Steven didn't intend to help Mary out.

"I mean, she interprets your friendliness as a sign that you're romantically attached to her."

"That's her problem then, not mine. What do you want me to do, grump and frown every time she comes near me?"

"Nooo! All you have to do is be a little less friendly."

"Okay, sweetheart, I'll try to follow your guidelines."

"Remember, you're the spiritual and temporal head of Pioneer One, and your behavior must be above reproach."

"I'll try to remember."

After a minute of silence, Steven said, "Did we just have our first argument?"

"Of course not! We simply engaged in a mature discussion about relationships."

"Boy! That's a relief."

Still later, Mary said sullenly, "I certainly wish that hussy would get her own husband."

Steven chuckled. "Mary! Hussy?" He waited for her to take it back, but when she didn't, he went on, "It seems that's what she's trying to do."

Mary was surprised. "What do you mean?"

"Paul tells me she's been spending a lot of time helping one of our available men pull a handcart. Apparently, she's working herself half to death doing it."

"Who?" Mary said hopefully.

"I'm not sure you know him. His name is Pierce Hudson. He's about thirty-three, tall, blond, good-looking, quiet, and has three children. His wife was killed last year by some thug. He has a wagon, which his twelve-year-old son usually leads, and a handcart."

"I believe I treated him for blisters. So is it serious?"

"Well, according to Paul, I may have to perform a marriage in the near future. Paul, as you might expect, pretends he's outraged that she would pick someone besides him."

Mary's voice revealed her delight. "Instant motherhood. I know what that's like. It'll be especially good for Anastasia."

"I'm glad you have her best interests at heart, dear," Steven said, giving her a very wet kiss on the mouth.

Several minutes later, when Steven was half asleep, Mary said, "Why was Brother Crowell so angry today?"

"Uh, well, one of his men gives him trouble once in a while, and it really upsets him. He's a colonel, you know. The details aren't important."

"It's probably good that he came to you and was able to express his anger."

"Perhaps you're right," Steven said. "However, I suggested to Seth that he wasn't using his authority properly when he got so mad. The truth is, I'm coming to the conclusion that anger is always bad."

"I'm not sure it's always bad. There are schools of psychology which teach that venting your anger acts as a catharsis and dissipates the emotion."

"I've heard that before. However, some people believe that catharsis stuff is nothing but theoretical mumbo jumbo. Let me tell you my own theory on anger."

Mary rolled toward him and put her leg across his legs. "Okay. I usually like your ideas."

"I compare how people handle anger to the three degrees of glory. On the lowest level, the telestial, the angry person seeks revenge. He's so full of anger and hate that he purposely seeks to hurt his enemy in some way. Eventually, he puts his desire into action. On the terrestrial level the angry person vents his feelings, but doesn't act upon them. However, these releases of emotion often become little more than practice, and so there is a danger that the anger may consume his life and poison his relationships with others. Of course, if he expresses the anger directly to the people he's mad at, they end up hating him. On the highest level, the celestial, the person is so full of the Holy Ghost that he doesn't feel anger in the first place when provoked. He has the power to see the truth in the situation and always reacts with love instead."

"I'm not sure I buy all that, Steven, but it's worth thinking about."

"Well, the scriptures say we should put away anger. They don't say we should express it, to relieve stress or for any other reason. Other scriptures say we should be slow to anger. If our final goal is to have the constant companionship of the Holy Ghost, what place will anger ever have in our hearts if we achieve that goal? The fruits of the Spirit are love, gentleness, kindness, patience, and so forth, not righteous indignation."

Mary observed quietly, "The goal of being so good that we never feel anger might be similar to the goal of perfection. It's an ideal we can strive for, but never really obtain in this life."

"Yes, you're probably right... But to get back to Seth. I also suggested something else to him. Apparently, it was a revolutionary concept he'd never heard of before..."

"Which was?"

"I counseled him to find out why people do what they do, instead of harping on nothing but performance."

"Hah! If you keep talking like that, you're going to make a lot of enemies."

Steven gazed at her curiously in the dim light, admiring her intelligence. "I suppose you're right on that one too." He felt a great fatigue come over him. "Well, we'd better get some sleep." A few minutes later, he murmured, "Something tells me that the future holds hardships we can't even imagine today, and that we'll need all the strength we have to handle them."

Chapter 10

During the next few days Pioneer One continued to move along at the same rate as in previous days. The travelers made every effort to live off the land in order to conserve their food supplies, and some began to experience gastrointestinal disturbances. Dr. Price had great difficulty handling the long line of people who gathered at his wagon whenever the caravan stopped. His advice was that they should increase their intake of the new fare more gradually, and make sure the plants were not toxic. Since he knew nothing about natural pharmacology, that was the only advice he could give.

The thing which puzzled him the most was the fact that many of the Saints were beginning to complain of severe diarrhea, nausea, and vomiting. To some degree, he attributed these problems to the plants they were ingesting, but the intense and constant diarrhea seemed unusual. Unfortunately, not only did he lack antibiotics, but he also had no lab facilities and could only guess as to the cause of the ailment. He figured the pioneers had drunk polluted water from one of the streams, but couldn't be sure. Hoping that the problem would resolve itself naturally in a week or so, he encouraged the victims to avoid dehydration by drinking plenty of water which they should purify by boiling.

The pioneers faced another serious problem when it came to taking care of their natural needs. Their meager supply of toilet paper had run out a few days after the trek had begun, and they had been forced to use the leaves of plants to clean themselves. This presented certain unique difficulties, because the supply of plants which bore leaves long enough and broad enough and soft enough to do the job, were sometimes hard to come by. Often the pioneers chose the wrong plants and ended up with stinging rashes in very inconvenient places. The herbalists in the company encouraged them to be patient and look forward to May, the month when nature's toilet paper—mullein—begins to push forth its broad downy leaves.

In any case, after they finished their task, they had to dig a hole and bury the fruits of their labors with the soiled leaves. Before long, they learned to use a special board, which they carried with them whenever they wanted to commune with nature. It was eighteen inches wide and thirty inches long, and the round hole in the center had a diameter of seven inches. As soon as they reached an appropriate secluded spot, they dug a deep, narrow hole, placed the board across it, and used it as a portable toilet seat.

Some of the sisters insisted on raising the board a foot or more above the ground so they could be more comfortable and not soil their clothes. It didn't seem to matter that their outfits were already covered with layers of grime and smelled horribly of sweat. They elevated the boards by propping logs or stones under both ends, or by having their husbands build supports, so that these contraptions ended up resembling lap boards that people use when they wish to eat or read in bed. The great thing was that a dozen people could use the same board over the same hole and come away perfectly clean.

Some husbands made solid boards with sturdy supports, but it took two women to carry one. Other husbands, motivated by love and respect, were particularly diligent and created boards which were light and elegant so that the women might have less trouble carrying them to the relief site. In the second instance, however, some of these favored sisters, demonstrating unusual confidence in their husbands' skill, plopped too vigorously on the boards and immediately plunged deeply into the smelly holes as the boards snapped in half.

In spite of the convenience of the boards, it was often embarrassing for the sisters to handle the natural need. In order for them to go to the rest room when the wagon train stopped, they had to gather into small groups of four or five women and, accompanied by their daughters, search for a spot out of sight of camp, but not so far that they were in danger. At least one of the women carried a weapon to protect the group. Unfortunately, it was not always certain that those bearing the arms actually knew how to use them. Every time Steven saw a troop of them heading away from camp equipped with a shovel, a special board, and a rifle, he had no doubt as to what was going on.

The problem became even more grave when the pioneers learned that violent savages, who did not hesitate to rape and murder women, lurked in the nearby wilderness. At that juncture, going to the toilet became more diffi-cult, because many women refused to leave camp without a man or two in escort. After they procured the assistance of some reluctant male, the sisters set out to brave the rocky wasteland, carrying the necessary equipment. When they found a suitable location, and the armed escort disappeared from view, the women and girls did what they came to do, fully assured that they had secured both their privacy and their protection.

But when other sisters heard what some were doing, they knitted their brows in disgust and marched off alone, declaring that they didn't need any man to take care of them. Steven let them go, figuring that if any savage was foolhardy enough to mess with those sisters, he deserved what he got.

The greatest problem came, however, when the Saints had to go to the toilet while the wagons were moving. Most of the males handled the problem quickly, but the females had a more difficult time of it—at least at first. At the beginning of the journey, the women and girls had secreted themselves in their wagons and had solved the problem with the aid of special plastic containers they had brought for that very purpose. But soon they had discovered that they ended up with the disgusting job of emptying and cleaning the containers, or disposing of them, when the wagon train stopped.

The situation became especially disagreeable for the sisters who had squeamish husbands, because they declined to relieve themselves in the open. Following the example of their wives, they also hopped into the wagons to do their duty. Unfortunately, however, by some strange quirk of the male mind, a number of the finicky brothers had inadvertently used a family utensil instead of the designated containers. When this happened, the discord erupted so violently in some families that news of the event spread rapidly through the entire caravan. In spite of everything the sisters could do, the smell stuck to the utensils like flies on flypaper, and most grumbled and glared as they worked to purify the utensil.

So as time progressed, most sisters resigned themselves to following the example of the shameless males. As soon as nature's urgent call struck, they made a beeline to the nearest bush, squatted until the work was done, then hurried to overtake the moving caravan. They soon learned that this simple technique had a double advantage: they could always claim, when questioned by some insensitive observer, that they had only gone to pick a lovely flower or a rare edible plant. However, a few determined sisters insisted on fighting nature's call until they though they would die, or until the caravan finally stopped.

On Friday, April 21 the wagon train pulled in for the night just south of the town of Wanship on the Weber River. Steven sent a group of armed men to investigate the town, and they found nothing to indicate violence—only a hasty departure. It was a mystery as to what had become of the town's citizens. Later, as Steven walked through the camp to check on the Saints, he was shocked to see that the dysentery which had struck several days earlier was becoming widespread. In nearly every wagon there was at least one person who was down with severe fever, vomiting, weakness, and diarrhea. The disease seemed to attack people of all ages and conditions. Steven consulted with Dr. Price and Mary, but they were at a loss to explain the cause of the malady or suggest an effective remedy. Dr. Price assured Steven that the sickness was probably not fatal and would soon run its course.

The next day, Ruther rode out of camp again, declaring he wouldn't return until he located the gangs. The travelers set out at nine in double file. Soon they saw the road turn directly north and open into a wide, flat valley surrounded by low hills. The valley was full of farms, pastures, and long sheds. Once again, search parties explored the area and found that everything was where it should be, except the people. Even the animals were in their cages or grazing contentedly in the fields. As Steven double-checked one small community close to the road, the ridiculous idea came to him that the people had been raptured, just like the old Baptist had said would happen to the true believers.

News of the missing inhabitants spread like a plague in the wagon train, creating consternation in the hearts of the pioneers. Steven saw terror in every eye, and some could not control their sobbing. The leaders did their best to assure the people that the Lord would not forsake them, and that Pioneer One had the strength to deal with any threat which might arise. Steven secretly asked himself many times if that were really true.

The pioneers reached the southern tip of Echo Reservoir by the end of the day. In spite of their fear, many of the sisters could no longer bear the smell of their bodies nor the filth of their clothes. Nearly every female in the company gathered into one group and agreed to go together to the water for a bath. After explaining their plan to the men and warning them to stay in camp until they returned, they hiked down to the reservoir three hundred yards away. They spread out along its banks, threw off their clothes, and washed their bodies.

As soon as they had finished that task, they washed the clothes they had been wearing. Afterwards, they put them on wet, unless they were fortunate enough to have a fresh change of clothes. Then they washed the bundle of dirty clothes they had brought. A number of sisters brought rifles to protect the bathers. When they returned an hour and a half later, they were smiling and looking much happier. Some of the men were so impressed by what the bath did for the females that they decided to do the same thing. When they reentered camp after an hour, it was beginning to grow dark.

Even though the pioneers were now able to smile and talk pleasantly, a feeling of impending doom still lay heavy upon the camp. As they went about their chores, the travelers stopped frequently to search the growing shadows for any sign of danger. After asking John to increase the guard even more, Steven walked through the entire encampment to encourage the people, smiling and showing a confidence he didn't feel. Then he remembered the powerful words of the voice which had spoken to him in secret, and the smile came more easily.

The following day was Sunday, and the Saints used the day to rest and renew their spirits. In spite of the fact that nearly one-fourth of the Saints were sick with the new disease, the members insisted on having church services. The colonels organized and directed four separate meetings so that the people would not be gathered into one place. In the initial session everyone received the sacrament, heard a short speech, and sang several hymns. Afterwards, they divided into small classes to hear a lesson on the Lord's dealings with Lehi and his family in the deserts of Arabia. The entire service took no more than an hour and fifteen minutes. Most of the people sat on the ground during the meetings.

That night Steven insisted on taking a watch, in spite of the protests of John, who felt that the leader of the caravan should not put himself in peril. John also admitted his fear: if Steven were injured or killed, the task of leading the wagon train would fall upon him. As he stood guard, Steven tried hard to remember the lessons Ruther had taught him two nights ago... Oh yes. Keep your eyes open but, above all, penetrate the dark with your ears. Learn to recognize the normal sounds of the wilderness. Then, when he listened, he would recognize the sounds that shouldn't be there, and he would know that danger might be near. Steven had to admit that simply having the old Baptist around gave him surprising reassurance. Where was he now and what had he discovered?

On Monday the wagon train traveled near Echo Reservoir, which stretched for three miles beside the highway. The two parts of the freeway divided and continued on separate levels. A high ridge on the left shadowed the lanes they followed. Steven was constantly concerned that it would be easy for an enemy to wipe out the entire company from that vantage point with little danger to itself. Soon he could bear it no longer. He gave instructions to a contingent of men to climb the rise and follow the caravan along the top. He looked up the road ahead and was relieved to see the scouts, who were checking the path a half mile in front of the main body. Then he noticed the road itself and was troubled to see that the number of fissures and gaps was increasing, making travel more difficult. The Saints boiled under the hot sun, and many trudged along awkwardly. And yet the fear of what lay ahead seemed to make them forget their present pain for a time.

By mid-afternoon Pioneer One had reached the junction of I-80 and I-84, where the road turned sharply northeast and led to Evanston, Wyoming. Shortly after they made the turn, John, Paul, Jarrad, and Leonard came riding up to Steven as he walked beside the lead wagon.

"Steven," John called. "Aren't we getting close to the area Ruther warned us about? If the headquarters of the gang is near Windy Knoll mountain, I figure it's only six miles from here."

"That's what I was thinking," Steven replied. "What do you suggest?"

"I'm not sure. Where on earth is Ruther? We could sure use his advice."

Paul said, "He left two days ago to check on the bandits and isn't back yet."

"I suggest we bring the wagons up three abreast," Jarrad said. "Also, we could instruct the drivers to stay as close together as possible. Look at them. They're kind of strung out right now."

"Good suggestions, Jarrad," Steven observed. "John, would you tell Murray Hutchinson to sound the danger signal?" Steven glanced at his wagon and saw the worried look on Mary's face.

"You got it!" John shouted as he trotted his Morgan horse down the line of wagons.

Steven turned to Paul. "Who's driving your wagon?"

"A teenage kid we bribe when we need to take off together."

As they continued to move with the wagons, Leonard declared, "This highway is a problem at times like this! It's so high above the surrounding terrain that it makes us sitting ducks!"

Paul examined the sides of the road. "Steve, there's another problem. A big one. The terrain is so rough in this area that we couldn't get the wagons off the freeway and into circles."

Steven looked around. "You're right. Trees and ravines everywhere... Think, brethren! We need to decide what to do if we're attacked."

They heard a bugle sound two short blasts, followed quickly by two additional blasts. After a short pause, the same warning was repeated again. A minute later they heard an identical signal repeated more faintly farther down the wagon train. They understood that the alarm would be repeated by several buglers the entire length of the caravan until every pioneer heard it. Quickly the drivers moved into triple file and drew their wagons closer together. John did not return, but Steven knew he was taking charge of the caravan's rear guard.

Steven smiled at Mary, and called, "That makes me feel better." She waved him a kiss.

Steven said to the bachelors, "Okay, guys, what else can we do?"

Paul said, "What choices do we have? If the bandits attack, we have to stop the wagons and return fire."

Jarrad scowled. "What if they attack from both sides of the road?"

"Yes, of course," Paul replied. "I must be off my nut. Somehow I got it into my head that they would attack from the cliffs on this side." Paul gestured toward the Canyonland-type bluffs several hundred yards away on the north side of the highway. "If they hit us from both sides, we're dead."

The bachelors tied their horses to their own wagon, the third wagon in the caravan, and spread out in a line on the left side of the road not far from the lead wagons. Before long, they were joined by other men armed with hunting rifles. When the time came for the wagon train to pull in for the night, Steven urged them on because there was no place to stop in safety. Even though the travelers were consumed by exhaustion under the hot sun, and the grade was steeper, they sensed the urgency of the situation and increased their pace. In the next hour they covered almost two miles.

Steven was anxiously studying the land south of the road for an open spot, when he heard a resounding whack not far away. He whirled around, searching for the source of the sound. He heard the shouts of men and the cries of women and children, but he couldn't see what was happening.

Just then Paul and Jarrad appeared. Paul seized Steven by the arm and shouted, "It came from the cliffs on the left."

Jarrad added, "The bullet smashed into the side of a wagon, but no one was hurt."

At first Steven wondered why no one had returned the fire, but then the thought flashed his mind that his men probably couldn't see the enemy rifleman any better than he. Followed by Paul and Jarrad, he moved to the extreme left margin of the road. As he scrutinized the bluffs, he heard another shot and thought he saw a movement half way up the hill. At the same instant, one of the young men on his left, Murray Hutchinson, the bugler, dropped abruptly to the ground, his head blown half off. He heard a woman give a bloodcurdling scream. Steven angrily raised his .30-06 to shoot back, but saw no one to punish.

Paul screamed in Steven's ear, "We've got to stop the wagons and take cover!"

For a moment Steven panicked, knowing that so many lives depended on him. Then all at once he knew what he had to do. "Double time! Now!" he shouted.

The men around him obeyed without question, and urged the people to pick up the pace, following the action of their leader. They continued at this stride for two minutes.

"Faster," Steven yelled.

They began a slow jog. During the next five minutes, they heard additional shots ring out from the bluffs, and bullets slammed into wagons and ricocheted off the pavement. Several Saints were injured by flying debris, but no one was struck by gunfire. The Saints were struggling so hard to maintain the pace that none bothered to return the fire. It was even more difficult now, since there were so many, including grown men, who had been attacked by the new illness and were too weak to do anything except lie in the wagons. During the desperate run to safety, a chubby brother, red of face and gasping for breath, suddenly crumpled to the pavement. The wagons veered around the unconscious man as his wife and children ran to his rescue. Steven figured the pioneers had jogged at least a half mile and he knew they couldn't continue much longer. The terrible thought hit him that perhaps his inspiration had been nothing but his own imagination.

Then he saw it. "Over there," he shouted, pointing to the south.

It was an open area on the right which was reasonably smooth and accessible. He ran across the road in front of the caravan and began to direct the wagons into the field. The men who had been trotting beside him followed his example.

Steven called to his helpers, "Tell them to put the wagons into two circles, one inside the other."

Steven and Paul watched by the edge of the road as the line of wagons rolled off the freeway and into the field. A man who prodded his oxen into the gully at the side of the road crumpled abruptly. Steven saw a bloody spot spread across his back. Because of the rumble of the vehicles, he hadn't even heard the report of the enemy weapon. His heart ached as he wondered how many others along the line had been injured or murdered by the devils in the hills. Realizing then that their current position made them easy targets, he grabbed his brother's arm and pushed him into the ditch.

Steven looked to his left under the passing wagons. Through the dust he saw other brethren spread along the gully, facing the enemy. He recognized the face of Byron Mills, the "scriptorian" from the Grandview Second Ward. Most were firing their weapons. Steven and Paul trained their rifles on the cliffs and shot at the slightest sign of movement. After a few minutes, they fired repeatedly into the ravines as a matter of course. They had little hope of hitting what they couldn't see, but knew that their fire would force their attackers to stay down. Steven asked himself why the enemy gunfire wasn't much heavier if the bandits numbered several hundred.

The fifteen minutes required to form the caravan into two circles seemed like an eternity to Steven. As soon as the drivers moved into position, they unharnessed their animals and drove them into the nearby countryside. Next they pulled the wagons close together until the wheels interlocked. The inner circle was formed perfectly, with two small gaps on opposite sides. The outer circle was too large for the number of wagons making it up, and there were six large openings. The men filled the gaps with boulders, brush, and tree limbs. The shots from the bluffs ceased as the pioneers completed this task. The women and children took cover inside the inner circle, while the men, older boys, and the women who could shoot, found defensive positions in the space between the two circles. They waited for the enemy to attack in force, but the charge didn't come.

"Where are they?" Paul asked.

"You've got me, brother," Steven replied.

"Do you think they took off?" Leonard said.

Jarrad answered, "I doubt it. They're probably trying to decide on how to take us."

"I wish Ruther were here," Steven said.

John replied, "I'm not sure he could tell us what to do in this situation. Still, I'd feel safer with that Sharps rifle nearby. Ruther told me he has used that thing to hit targets the size of a man as far away as a mile."

After a moment of impatient waiting, Paul said, "If there are so many bandits, why wasn't there more shooting from the cliffs?"

"I've been trying to figure that out," Steven said. "It's possible that only a few members of the gang were there. The advance guard of the main group."

"That may be," Jarrad observed. "In any case, I bet they'll come in force when they make their next attack."

The bandits struck an hour before sunset. A hundred heads suddenly popped up from the ravines and depressions to the east of the pioneer enclosure, and a heavy fusillade of gunfire fell upon the Saints. Steven was astonished at the intensity of the assault. The defenders were forced to drop flat on the ground, as bullets whizzed over their heads and pounded into their wagons, showering them with painful splinters. The barrage was so great and constant that few of the defenders dared rise to fire back. And those who did were wounded or killed instantly. The initial attack lasted four minutes, and then there was silence.

"We're dead," John declared, his right cheek buried in the dirt. "There's no way we can stand up to that. They have automatic weapons."

Jarrad agreed, "If they storm us, we won't have a chance of resisting them."

Steven had the same thoughts, but was afraid to discourage the others by expressing his fear. He prayed to God with all his heart, but heard no comforting voice to reassure him. From time to time, John peeked out to check on the enemy. Steven moved to a sitting position and looked around. He saw two men lying in pools of blood, and a half dozen wounded. He remembered the grotesque condition of the corpses at Summit, and an overwhelming dread struck him. If these evil men overcame them, what would save the Saints from torture and death? He sat there trembling, when he heard someone call his name.

"Steve! Steve!"

Steven glanced up. "Yes?"

"It's Leonard. Over here."

Steven spotted Leonard crawling toward him. When the young man was ten feet away, he said, "Some guy around the circle told me that the gang is gathering on the other side of the highway. About two hundred of them."

"Thanks, Leonard," Steven replied. He turned to the man next to him. It was Frank Hamilton, the young man Seth Crowell had come to complain about. Because of the intensity of the assault, Steven hadn't even noticed that Frank was close by. "Go south around the ring and tell every third person to move to the north side."

Frank nodded and hurried away. Steven and Paul arose and slipped past their comrades until they reached the northern section of the defensive line. The freeway was a hundred yards away, and Steven could see a multitude of heads just over the crest of the road. There was little movement except that the heads increased in number as he watched. He yelled for the defenders to hold their weapons ready and fire on his command. He was pleased when he saw other brothers and sisters arrive to take positions against the protective wagons.

A short time later, he heard a fiendish scream from hundreds of throats, and the heads began to bob and grow larger as they advanced. At the same time, he heard the thunder of guns east of the double circle, and he knew that the bandits in that sector were firing again, no doubt to provide cover for the charge of the main body. He guessed that the same thing was occurring on the west side of his company. Steven waited patiently until he saw the enemy swarm to the top of the freeway, and then he yelled "fire."

The defenders fired as rapidly as they could, and the bandits began to take casualties. But as they drew near, voicing that same awful scream, dozens of them fired assault weapons from the hip, and the barrage became so intense that the defenders had no choice except to retreat behind the second row of wagons to avoid being slaughtered. Some didn't make it.

As soon as they swarmed into the inner circle, the beleaguered pioneers turned frantically and fired upon their enemies, killing many. As he fought, Steven felt helpless in the tumult, the smoke, and the violent movement of hundreds of people in conflict. The Saints fought as gallantly as they could, but the bandits, even the females, were experienced warriors. They came from every direction and fell upon their prey, forcing them to the ground. Steven was surprised to see that the bandits didn't kill their captives outright, but disarmed them and intimidated them with their weapons.

Then two men came from behind and attacked Steven. In the struggle he managed to kill one with a shot to the head. But the second bandit, a hulk of a man, hit him in the chest with the butt of his weapon, slamming him to the earth and knocking his rifle away. Steven watched helplessly as his enemy, who seemed infuriated by the death of his buddy, snatched a short sword from the scabbard lashed to his back. His eyes red with hate, the man raised the sword and moved to strike. As Steven stared at the instrument of death, which began to arc toward him, an awesome force suddenly struck the brute and hurled him backwards into the air. Nine feet away he dropped to the earth, lifeless. A second after the bandit fell, Steven heard a loud boom above the din of the struggle around him. It came from the wilderness south of the circles.

The struggle was over in less than ten minutes. The attackers pushed the Saints at gun point to the center of the inner circle, where they commanded them to huddle together on the ground. Steven searched for his family, fearing they might be injured or even dead, but saw them nowhere. Many of the pioneers around him were sobbing, and a few looked at him with accusing eyes.

Minutes later the bandits brought Ruther in. He wasn't carrying his Sharps. The old man sat next to Steven and said softly, "You okay?"

"Yes. That was you?"

"Yep. Couldn't let that runt kill a friend of mine, could I?"

Steven guessed that the old man had sacrificed his freedom to save him, but he didn't ask. "Thanks, Ruther."

"No problem, as they say. You'd do the same fer me."

In a low voice they continued to talk for a while about the attack. Steven was particularly frantic concerning his family, and Ruther did his best to reassure him. Finally, three bandits stepped past the guards watching the captives. They pushed John Christopher ahead of them.

One of the thugs walked up to Steven, carrying an automatic pistol in his right hand. "This guy tells me you're the leader of this outfit. Get up."

Steven got to his feet. "That's right."

"My name's Good, Isaac Good. I'm the leader of this pack of wolves." Steven didn't answer. The leader went on, "What are you carrying in these wagons?"

"Clothes, bedding, provisions, tools, personal possessions. Things like that. Nothing more."

"We can use it all. Got any gasoline?"

"Very little."

"We're always looking for gas." Isaac showed a mouth full of rotten teeth. "You forgot to mention your weapons and ammunition. And all those fine animals."

"Take it all, but let us go. We don't mean you any harm."

The gang leader sneered. "Oh, we'll take it all, all right."

"Are you the ones who killed those people at Summit?"

"I don't answer questions—I ask them. Look, Guddy, it's getting late and I'm tired. You've cost me a lot of time and some good people. So you're going to pay. I'll spell it out for you. We're taking your females with us. That kind of commodity is hard to come by these days. And we're going to kill the rest of you. We spared your lives so far because we want to have a little fun with you tomorrow. It's one of the few enjoyments we get out of life these days. A few exciting games, a bit of torture. You know, that kind of stuff."

"You'd better git while the gittin's good, my friend," Ruther said matter-of-factly.

Isaac turned toward the mountain man. His eyes were cold and his face expressionless. "What did you say, old man?"

"I said you'd better git while the gittin's good. It may be too late already."

One of the leader's lieutenants advanced with his hunting knife drawn. "Why you—"

The leader stopped him. "Get back, stupid, and keep your yap shut." He faced Ruther again, licking his lips. "Why do you say that, old man?"

Ruther looked as calm and peaceful as if he were basking on a sunny beach at the French Riviera. He pulled a twig from the corner of his mouth. "Well, have ya ever heard of the plague?"

Isaac froze, paralyzed by the word which had struck terror in the hearts of men for hundreds of years. "Sure," he said uncertainly. "Everybody's heard of it. So what?"

"Well, this here company's got the plague—the black death—and it's only a matter of time before everybody suffers the worst death you can possibly imagine. Not only the people, but the animals too. And if ya all want ta croak with 'em, I'd advise ya ta stick around—just a bit longer."

At first Steven couldn't figure out what Ruther was doing, but then he understood.

The lieutenant who had threatened Ruther snarled, "If that's so, you old coot, why ain't you worried?"

Ruther looked at him with calm resignation. "Oh, I'm a dead man too. I stuck around these folks a mite too long without realizin' it, and I've got the infection in my blood. It takes a few days ta show up, but it's there all right, eatin' me up." He glanced at Steven. "Ain't that right, Captain?"

"Yes, it's only a matter of time." Steven tried hard to mimic Ruther's tormented resignation, but he fully expected the thug to burst out laughing at any moment. But the man didn't laugh.

John wiped his nose and his eyes filled with tears. "My wife died three days ago."

Isaac trembled, but couldn't suppress his natural cynicism. "I don't believe you dirt bags for one minute, and I'm going to slice you up right now for trying to con me." He took out an eight-inch knife from its sheath.

Ruther laughed. "Go ahead! That kinda death would be pleasant compared ta what we're facin'. Look, partner, if ya don't believe me, look in those wagons over there. You'll see black death starin' back at ya."

The thug eyed the closest wagon, hesitated, then said to Steven, "Show me."

They walked to the wagon, followed by Ruther, John, and two of the thug's lieutenants. Steven pulled back the rear flap, and Isaac peered in, trying to see in the dim light. He pulled back instantly and swore viciously.

"The smell!" he exclaimed. "The guy's puking like mad, and there's blood all over his blankets."

Steven had no idea who was in the wagon. "Yeah, he came down with it two days ago."

The outlaw chief was terrified, but he still wasn't convinced. He stopped at another wagon, but heard nothing. At the third wagon, he heard retching and pulled back the flap. Almost immediately he reeled backward, holding his hand over his mouth. He checked three more wagons and found sick people in two of them.

Steven said grimly, "It's like that everywhere in the camp. All you need to catch it is to get a little too close."

"Let's get out of here, boss!" one of the lieutenants wailed.

The three bandit chiefs paused for a moment. Then they bolted for the safety of the wilderness. Fifty other gangsters, who had watched Isaac check the wagons, followed the example of their leaders. They rushed from the camp screaming "plague." News of the sudden evacuation spread quickly through the army of outlaws, and in seconds they fled from the Mormon camp. Many were so desperate to escape that they dropped their weapons and ammunition as they fought their way through the lines of wagons.

Ruther chuckled and turned to Steven, "Kinda shows what ignorance can do fer ya, don't it?"

Steven gave him a bear hug. "Thank God you came, Ruther!" The noise in the camp was so great that they had to practically shout these words.

"Well, we Baptists ain't all bad, ya know." John grabbed his hand and shook it vigorously. Ruther grinned and said to John, "As fer you, young man, ya done a right smart job of actin'. Ya almost made me bawl when ya talked about yer wife dyin' of the plague."

"Yeah, brother, I didn't know you had it in you," Steven said. John beamed.

Ruther got serious. "Listen, boys, you'd better go and locate your families. They'll be worryin'."

Steven and John hurried away to search for their families. The noise and the confusion were unbelievable as the mob of Saints jostled one another and staggered around looking for loved ones. Most had no idea why the band of criminals had fled in terror, but many released their pent-up anxiety by weeping. Some of the men recovered the weapons abandoned by the frenzied gangsters and took defensive positions at the outer ring of wagons.

Steven ran to where his wagon had been parked and found his family waiting for him. With joy they kissed and embraced each other. They asked him excitedly what had happened, and he related the ruse that Ruther had used to get rid of their enemies. The children clapped their hands in delight while their father acted out the entire scene, taking the role of each partici- pant in turn as if he were a child. Soon Paul and the bachelors appeared unharmed, except for minor scratches and wounds. Steven told them the same story again. But soon their joy turned to sadness when the colonels appeared and reported that they had found twenty-five Saints dead and dozens with serious wounds.

That night the Saints built a few fires to warm their bodies and their hearts. But they didn't feel like eating and they couldn't sleep. Instead, they spent the night comforting those who had lost loved ones or nursing the sick. Now more had the dread illness. Steven feared that before daylight, he would have to place their bodies next to the slain, whom the pioneers had covered with blankets near the center of the camp. He spent the night on the outer camp perimeter with Paul, Ruther, Douglas, and the two bachelors. He said a silent prayer to God, thanking Him for blinding the minds of their enemies.

Chapter 11

Steven vomited for the third time. His head was burning and hurt terribly. He had to go to the toilet so bad that he could hardly stand it. He looked at his watch. Five o'clock. Maybe he should follow the example of the other brothers who had hurried to the ravine fifty yards out to relieve themselves, and had returned looking much better.

Paul said, "Steve, you look awful! Why don't you go back to your wagon? Maybe Mary can help you."

"I doubt it. She's been working on people all night, but can't do much more than hold their hands. Besides, some of you guys are sick too."

Jarrad pushed his fist into his stomach, and said, "Naw! Just a little pain in the gut."

"From the looks of you boys," Ruther said, "maybe I was right about that black plague stuff."

Steven smiled in spite of his discomfort. "It might be an infection of some kind, but you know perfectly well it isn't the bubonic plague."

"No, but my story sure 'nough fooled them bad guys. We ain't seen hide nor hair of 'em since."

Everyone laughed. They had rehearsed Ruther's deception several times during the night and still couldn't believe the stupidity of their enemies.

Paul said, "I bet they're still running for their lives."

"I hope they do get a deadly plague," Leonard said sourly. "They're nothing but cold-blooded killers."

"What is this sickness we have?" Jarrad asked.

Paul replied, "Doc Price told me he believes we may have picked up some common bacterial infection or perhaps a parasite from polluted water."

"Oh, I see. No big deal," Jarrad observed.

"What I can't figure out is why Paul and Ruther aren't sick." Steven said.

"I don't know about Paul," Ruther said, "but I'm too durn ornery ta get sick. Just let those little bacterias or parasites get up enough nerve ta wiggle down inta my belly, and they'll get burnt to a crisp by my powerful stomach juices."

Paul grinned and patted Ruther on the shoulder. "I can believe it!" He turned again to his brother. "But seriously, Steve, you really look sick. Go rest awhile. We can handle it."

The others backed Paul up, insisting that Steven do as he was told. Reluctantly, Steven agreed, but first visited the ravine. Then he wobbled to his wagon, feeling very weak. He crawled into the wagon and saw with relief that his children were sleeping peacefully. A half hour later, Mary returned.

"I see you're a lot sicker than the last time I talked to you." Mary had visited her husband at 1:00 a.m. to see if he wanted a sandwich. He had refused, feeling too queasy to think about food.

"Don't worry. It's nothing serious. Probably a little infection."

"Steve, three people died from that 'little infection' last night."

Steven was thunderstruck. "Three?"

"Yes, and there'll be a lot more if we don't find a cure!"

Steven threw up and almost fainted. Mary held his head in her lap while she tried to clean up the vomit. Within a minute he felt better and crawled to the entrance.

"Where are you going?" Mary cried.

"I'll be back in a few minutes. I'm going to get the answer."

Mary didn't try to stop him. She believed in her husband and felt confident that he would receive an answer. Steven walked slowly to the south side of the camp, climbed through the outer ring of wagons, and headed for some huge boulders two hundred yards away. Curious eyes followed him as he staggered across the rough terrain. When he reached the boulders, he walked around them and fell to his knees. Tearfully, he pleaded with the Lord to help him know what to do to save Pioneer One. After repeating his simple prayer five times, he lay on his back and waited for the answer. A few minutes later, he heard a voice. It was almost imperceptible at first, but grew progressively louder.

"Ask your brother," a mild voice said.

"What?"

"Ask your brother." Now the peaceful voice was clear and penetrating.

"I don't understand!"

"Ask your brother," the voice insisted.

Steven asked for clarification again and again, but got no further response. For a long time he lay there, too weak to rise and too confused to reflect on the message.

Then Mary, who had decided to check on her husband, walked around the boulders. "Steve!" she called. Seeing him on his back, she cried in alarm and ran to him. "Are you all right?"

Steven lifted his head. "Yeah. Just weak and dizzy."

She sat next to him and put his head in her lap. "Isn't it dangerous out here?" she asked.

"No. I'm...sure they're gone...I got an...answer."

"I knew it!" she said excitedly. "What is it?"

"The Lord said, 'Ask your brother.'"

Mary frowned, perplexed. "But what does it mean?"

"I'm not sure. I have two brothers. Which one do I ask? And what do I ask?"

"The answer can't be complicated," Mary said. "The Lord doesn't play games."

"I know. Simple answers. But I...always...think things to death."

"What is there about your brothers which is different from the rest of pioneers?"

"I don't know. I guess it's an enigma."

Mary stared into the distance. "Yes, it is... Maybe the Lord wants us to do at least a tiny amount of work in this too. To solve the problem of the sickness, I mean."

"Great," Steven moaned. "I have to...think at a time like this." His head swam and he felt like fainting.

"So how are your brothers different?"

They discussed the matter five minutes. That is, Mary discussed it. Steven vomited several times, but Mary continued to prod.

Then Steven's face brightened a bit in spite of his nausea and fever. "I've got it! They don't have the sickness like the other pioneers do!"

"John came down with it early this morning," Mary said.

"Oh...I guess that's not the answer."

"No, silly, that is the answer. Paul's the one you must talk to."

Steven was just too exhausted and dizzy to think. "What do I...ask?"

"You ask him why he isn't sick. He must be doing something to prevent it. Come. Let's get back to camp."

Mary helped him back to the wagon and went to find Paul. Steven sat against a wagon wheel and waited. After vomiting again, he felt better and his head was clearer. A few minutes later Mary returned with Paul.

Sitting next to Steven, Paul said, "Mary tells me you want to know why I'm not sick. Believe me, I have no idea why I haven't caught this disease like everyone else."

With Mary's help, Steven questioned Paul concerning everything he did during the day, and everything he ate.

"That's it!" Steven said at last, full of joy and relief.

Mary was skeptical. "You mean those three little pills he takes every day prevent him from getting this terrible disease?"

"I'm sure of it!" Steven said. "Now I remember what Mom said before we left Provo. Take two or three of these tablets every day to protect yourself from a lot of problems."

"Yeah, Mom swears by grapefruit seed extract," Paul agreed. "Usually she's right, so I popped those little green babies every day, as a matter of course."

Steven said, "She gave each of us a huge bottle of the stuff, but I forgot to take it."

"Not only a bottle of the pills," Paul said. "She also stashed a gallon of extract liquid in all three of our wagons. The morning before we left."

"I wondered what was in that container," Steven said. "I've been so busy that I didn't even look."

Mary said hopefully, "Where are the pills, Steven?"

"I don't know."

Mary climbed into the wagon. She searched ten minutes before she returned with a bottle labeled GSE and a canteen of water. Among other ingredients, the label read 250 milligrams of grapefruit seed extract.

"Paul, how many should I give him?" Paul had worked from time to time in his mother's herb shop, and Mary knew he had some knowledge of her products.

Paul examined the container. "Well, it doesn't say what to do if you get a deadly case of some unknown infection, but I figure Mom would say to take two tablets at the start, and one every five or six hours until the patient gets better. That's for serious cases. For those who aren't sick yet, I'd guess two tablets each day. The stuff isn't toxic, so we have a lot of leeway in the dosage."

Mary was in a hurry. After giving Steven two tablets, she said, "Paul, go get your bottle of tablets and some water." Paul dashed to his wagon a short distance away and returned within minutes. "Now we'll start around the caravan. You take the outer circle, and I'll take the inner. Treat everyone you find. Two tablets for those who are sick. One for everybody else. If you run out of pills, find John and get his bottle. I'll catch up with you if I finish first. In five hours we'll do it again."

As Mary worked, she was surprised to find that Sarah, Steven's mother, had also talked several other families into taking bottles of grapefruit seed extract tablets with them on the trip. When she and Paul met at Steven's wagon at the end of their work two hours later, they discovered that they had gathered a total of fifteen bottles of pills and several gallons of liquid.

Mary shook her head in amazement at the ingenuity and foresight of her feisty little mother-in-law. Even though they had a great deal of the natural medicine, Paul estimated that they would be lucky to have enough of it to last the entire company one week, unless the illness could be overcome quickly.

The company remained in the same spot for the rest of the day. They buried the dead, both pioneers and attackers, not far from the encampment and performed a short service over the graves. They spent the rest of the day nursing the sick and wounded and trying to recover physically and spiritually from the battle with the bandits. By the end of the day, most of the sick were already showing signs of recovery, and there were no additional deaths. Steven felt well enough to visit a number of wagons and to consult with company leaders.

Since John was recuperating, Steven asked him to get on his ham radio to report to the General Authorities. Elder Jason Widtsoe, a young apostle, received the transmission. John told him about their battle with the savage bandits and warned that Pioneer Two might face the same peril. He also described the disease which had attacked the Saints and the remedy which had saved them. Jason was delighted to hear that the pioneers were safe and promised to inform the Prophet.

Jason also made a report to John. First, he informed him that Robert and Sarah, his parents, were well and happy in Provo. The apostle always made sure that the elderly couple received the news John transmitted to church headquarters. Next, he told John everything he knew about the rumored threat of an attack against Utah from an army of Mexican renegades. He instructed John to inform the pioneers of the danger, but to encourage them not to worry, for the situation was completely in the Lord's hands. He added that the church might have to postpone the departure of Pioneer Two.

Within an hour every pioneer in the caravan learned of the trouble in Utah. Some took the news well, but others surrendered to despair. At 6:00 p.m. Ruther sauntered out of camp on his big mule to search the surrounding wilderness for the location of the bandits.

*****

It was 5:30 p.m. when Elder Jason Widtsoe visited the Prophet's office. He waved at the President's secretary and said, "Is he still in?" When she nodded, he continued past her desk and knocked gently on the door. He heard a muffled voice inside telling him to come in. He opened the door and saw Josiah at his desk examining maps and papers.

The Prophet looked up and smiled. "Jason! Come in and sit down. I haven't seen you for days."

The apostle sat in a big armchair in front the Prophet's desk. "I've been pretty busy, President Smith. Still working on the Mexican problem?" The General Authorities had come to speak of the reported threat from the south as the Mexican problem.

"Yes. I'll tell you where it's at in a minute. But first, have you heard from Pioneer One?" The apostle had an office in the Church Office Building and consulted regularly with the President on the progress of Pioneer One.

"Yes, I just received a message from NB7EU." This was John Christopher's radio call sign, and many of the church leaders knew it by heart.

"Great! What is it?" the Prophet said eagerly.

Jason summarized what had happened to the pioneers in the previous week. The Prophet listened intently, asking questions now and then for clarification.

When the apostle had finished, Josiah said solemnly, "The Lord has truly blessed and protected them. And the leader He chose was the right man for the job... Jason, we need to see if we can procure a supply of grapefruit seed extract for the other wagon trains who'll travel to Missouri. Would you be so kind as to look into that for me?"

"Yes, of course. But what about the mountain gangs? They may still be in that area and present a grave threat to future caravans."

"I realize that. Also, they may be the reason we haven't heard from our Mormon communities along I-80 for so long." Both men were silent for a moment. But Josiah couldn't bear to dwell on the scenes which suddenly came to his imagination. He went on quickly, "What do you suggest we do?"

"It seems we have only two choices. We postpone the departure of Pioneer Two, or we send an army into the mountains to handle the gangs."

"I'm afraid you're right... Are you coming to the emergency meeting tomorrow?" The President had called a meeting with the First Presidency and the Twelve for 7:00 a.m.

"Yes, of course."

"We'll discuss this matter and the Mexican problem then. After the meeting tomorrow, I want you to arrange for a party of men to go into the mountains to see if the gangs are still a threat. The men you choose must know the region thoroughly and be trained in wilderness operations. And they should carry weapons to protect themselves.

"I'll make sure it's done."

"Thank you. Now, let me update you on the Mexican problem. The scouts we sent south to investigate the threat haven't returned yet. Haven't had time. But we've intercepted radio transmissions from Mexico which make it fairly certain that they're gathering a sizeable army and do intend to move northward in the near future."

After discussing the Mexican problem another half hour, the two church leaders went home to their families. The following morning the Prophet discussed the two basic problems with the other church leaders. They decided that Pioneer Two should be postponed temporarily, until they had better information on the mountain gangs. They also concluded that they needed to continue gathering facts concerning the size and the intentions of the so-called Mexican Army of Liberation.

*****

The exiles stood on a rise and gazed at the flames which consumed their hopes and their dreams. The inferno seemed to lust after the very sky itself as it devoured Kansas City. And in the darkness around them the refugees heard the constant sound of gunfire, and the screams of exquisite torment. They shivered and wept and held on to one another for comfort. Then they turned as one and headed back to their camp near the peaceful lake.

After Anthony and Jared Luce had found a comfortable spot near the family campfire, Jared said, "Dad, they want me to do the midnight watch tonight."

"No. It's too dangerous," said Rachel Luce, Jared's mother.

Anthony replied, "Don't worry. Jared can handle himself. And we really need every man we can get." Anthony had been chosen as one of the leaders of the Wyandotte Colony.

Rachel looked to her daughter Kimberley for support, but the thirteen-year-old girl stared silently into the fire, her face besmirched with dirt and tears. Anthony knew that what he had said about his son was true. Jared had saved their lives six days ago as they escaped from the city, and his father was proud of this son who had suddenly become a man.

The refugees now numbered in the hundreds at Wyandotte County Lake Park, located west of Kansas City, but the danger was so great that they had to stand guard twenty-four hours a day. Anthony and the other fathers who had fled from the city with him would be on watch during the early hours of the morning. One fourth of the men and boys in the encampment were needed around the periphery of the park at all times because they were under ceaseless attack. The assaults came from small gangs and individual rogues who sought frantically to satisfy their evil desires and needs.

After seeing the indescribable terrors of the last few months, Anthony was grateful that he and so many others had rejected the ignorant clamor of the gun-control crusaders and the self-seeking arguments of politicians who had used every subterfuge in their efforts to convince America to surrender its weapons.

Things became especially hard to bear when other exiles tried to enter the park. Sometimes they made it, but often they were ambushed—just before they reached safety—by the creatures who lurked on the outer edges of the park. Through his binoculars Anthony watched what they did to their captives until he could bear it no longer. His greatest worry was that the anarchists would some day gather together and attack the park in force. He avoided mentioning this fear to his family and friends, but he prayed in secret that

God would somehow prevent their enemies from combining.

Another serious problem which the exiles faced was how to obtain food and supplies for 264 people. By Monday, April 25, Anthony and the other park leaders decided that their provisions would be exhausted in less than a week. Then the problem of survival would become critical. After consulting for several hours, the refugee leaders decided to send out regular armed detachments late at night to find supplies. Using information from the citizens of the new little community, Anthony and Jared made up a list of the most likely places to find the provisions.

*****

The small French farmhouse was dark and still. The fugitives—Pierre, Diane, André, and Mireille—had watched it an hour in the protection of a small grove of trees. They had seen no movement in the shadows, and no suspicious vehicles. Afraid that the green coats might track them down, or even be waiting for them at the farmhouse, they had spent the last five days hiding in the French countryside and sleeping in the van. But finally, hungry and desperate, they had driven to the farm of Pierre's friends and, with their lights out, had slowly driven the van toward the main building. Leaving their sleeping children in the vehicle, they had walked the short distance to the grove.

"I think it's safe," Pierre Laborde said in a low voice. "Let's go in."

Mireille Renan whispered, "I'm afraid! The authorities knew we were heading east on the highway. Maybe they knew where we were going!"

"But how could they know?" Diane Laborde asked.

The friends had debated this over and over the last few days and couldn't agree. Pierre argued that someone might have seen them leave Paris and informed on them, but there was no way anyone could know their ultimate destination. They had not told anyone, except the people who owned the farm! André and Mireille had to admit that Pierre was right, but still something told them that they were in grave danger.

"It's impossible, I tell you," Pierre insisted a little too loudly.

Diane frowned and shushed him. "Pierre! If they're out there, they'll hear you," she whispered.

In a lower tones, Pierre said, "Listen, I have an idea. You guys wait here, and I'll check it out."

They agreed, and Pierre moved toward the farmhouse, which was a hundred yards away. He kept to the shadows and made as little noise as possible. After watching her husband for a while, Diane said, "I can't let him go alone." She left the trees and hurried to Pierre. Together they approached the house.

Mireille and André watched them fearfully. As they strained to see their friends, who had disappeared against the darkness of the building, their eyes were blinded all at once by glaring lights. Green uniforms sprang from hiding places everywhere and surrounded Pierre and Diane. Gasping from fear and shock, Mireille and André pulled back into the obscurity of the grove and dashed to the van. The enemy knew that Diane and Pierre had been traveling with another family and might pursue them at any moment. The fugitives slipped into the vehicle and backed down the road until they came to a spot wide enough to turn around. Then they drove away slowly with their lights out.

The green coats pushed Pierre and Diane into the house, now glaring with light. Pierre's middle-aged friends stood huddling together in their night clothes on the far side of the room.

"I'm sorry, Pierre," the man said. "They said they'd confiscate our farm and throw us into prison if we didn't tell them you were coming. We had no choice!"

Pierre and Diane were stunned and could not respond. The captain of the green coats ordered them to sit on a couch. When Pierre hesitated, the officer slugged him across the side of the head with the butt of his rifle. When Pierre came to a few minutes later, the officer questioned him and Diane for a half hour. At the end of the interrogation, he angrily accused them of being mortal enemies of the state. Then the soldiers forced the captives from the house and into a prison truck hidden behind the building. The middle-aged couple held each other tightly and sobbed bitterly.

*****

Ramón Sánchez, Chief Advisor to the President of Venezuela, looked to the north and saw the arrival of the Venezuelan National Guard. The guardsmen bivouacked between Maracay Lake and the Mormon settlement fifteen miles south of the lake. Several miles behind the Guard, the Mormon Militia was hidden in the hills directly south of the great lake. Ramón counted forty-one armored personnel carriers, which carried twelve guardsmen each, and about five hundred men on foot. A total of a thousand soldiers. Behind the troops he could also distinguish two Abrams tanks, purchased from the United States, and ten pieces of artillery.

Ramón turned to Elder Gutierrez, and said, "Looks like they mean business. You'd think we were a foreign army instead of their fellow citizens." Carlos Gutierrez was a regional representative who had charge of the military operations of the Mormon settlement.

"They're driven by the green coats against their will," Carlos replied, lowering his binoculars.

Ramón raised his eyebrows in surprise. "There are green coats out there?"

"Most definitely. Use your binoculars. Study the men in the personnel carriers more closely."

Ramón followed his friend's suggestion and, after examining several APCs, caught sight of green uniforms. "So they're beginning to come out of the woodwork."

Carlos said, "They won't have it as easy here as they do in many foreign countries."

"What do you mean?"

"Well, in Europe, Africa, Asia, Japan, Malaysia, and many other countries our fellow Saints have been thrown into concentration camps or have gone into hiding. But here we number a half million members and have far more power and influence. They won't find it so easy to intimidate us. And it's not only Venezuela. We're very strong throughout South and Central America. A mighty army, if you will!"

Years earlier the Prophet had warned church members in foreign countries to prepare for a worldwide attack against the Saints, and without hesitation church leaders in Venezuela had quickly organized their people and had made preparations. The Saints had stored provisions of every type, including weapons, and had created special communities in rural areas as places of refuge. There were seven of them in Venezuela alone, and the community south of Maracay Lake was the largest.

This settlement had nineteen thousand permanent residents, and space for another thirty thousand. After accumulating supplies enough to last two years, the citizens had built a concrete irrigation trench completely around their town. The reason given to the government for the trench was to supply the community with water from the mountains, but the builders had made it ten feet deep and forty feet wide, much larger than was actually needed. Of course, the citizens of the community knew that the ditch, and the chain-link fences which bordered it, actually served as protection against those who hated Mormons.

But the Venezuelan Saints knew that their special refuges could only give them limited protection. If the government became their enemy and brought its armies against them in earnest, they would be in great peril. So they depended mostly on God and the hundreds of thousands of Saints and friends who held positions in every institution in the country, including the government and the military.

After hearing his friend's review of the world situation, Ramón's face became tight with frustration. "How do you know all this, Carlos? I'm top advisor to the President, and I have scarcely heard of it."

Carlos replied, "You've had much work to do with internal problems, especially since UGOT's cur, Diego Romero, arrived. And these things are of recent development. Within the last few months. Fortunately, we have several ham transceivers and have been able to monitor world events."

Ramón looked at the troops again. "Do you think they'll really attack?"

"Not yet, not with so few soldiers. The Mormon Militia includes three thousand well-trained soldiers, and we have another thousand guerrillas hidden around the lake behind the government army."

Ramón grinned. "And that's not all. At least one in six of the Guard out there is a Mormon too. They're Mormon infiltrators, so to speak."

"Hah! You forgot the officers."

"Oh yes! One in four perhaps."

In spite of the danger, Carlos teased, "Yes, Ramón, there are so many infiltrators. For example, the President's Chief Advisor."

"Mmm, that gives me an idea. Maybe I should go over there and tell them who I am, and that I'm visiting this community. Would they avoid attacking if they knew those things?"

Carlos laughed. "I'm sure the green coats know you're a Mormon and the President's advisor. And they may know you're with us today. In any case, your presence here wouldn't stop them from attacking. In fact, it might encourage them even more."

"You may be right. I hope most of the Saints in this country can hide better than I."

"It's much harder for them to track us down now. Church officials in Venezuela have deleted computer records of church membership in this country. If UGOT confiscates our computers and diskettes, it will find nothing. Only a few carefully hidden hard copies remain."

Ramón was pleased. "I have good news for you too. I had some of our best computer specialists—LDS specialists, of course—check government records to see if UGOT could identify church members through computer files. They deleted everything which might even begin to help our enemies detect the Saints."

Carlos grinned as he slapped Ramón on the back, and the two men raised their binoculars once again to observe the movements of the National Guard.

Chapter 12

On Wednesday, April 26, the immense pressures that had accumulated for more than a century and a half finally reached the critical point, and the eastern boundary of the gigantic Pacific Plate suddenly lurched to the northwest in relation to the North American Plate. The results were unbelievably catastrophic along the entire San Andreas Fault, which extended eight hundred miles in western California. The offset in the southern section of the Fault reached a maximum of forty-two feet, by far the greatest ever recorded. This was followed seconds later by similar slippage along the northern section of the fault. There had been no foreshocks to warn the people that the Big One was coming. Within one day tsunamis caused great destruction throughout the entire Pacific Basin.

Seismic monitoring stations around the world measured the magnitude of the earthquake at 9.6 on the Richter scale. The great cities of Los Angeles, San Diego, San Francisco, San Jose, Long Beach, Oakland, Sacramento, and Fresno were completely flattened during the forty seconds that the quake lasted. Almost a fourth of the state's population died in the catastrophe. Two million people perished outright, and another three million were killed soon after by fires, disease, and starvation.

If the quake had occurred a year earlier, when the total population of California exceeded forty million, the death toll would have been much higher. But beginning in April of the preceding year, California, like the rest of the world, had been assaulted by one disaster after another. Plagues, famine, drought, civil wars, and disease had already decimated the population. Millions of people, including a quarter million Saints, had evacuated the state and sought refuge in safer lands to the east.

Ralph Taylor was a good man. He didn't consider himself an ideal Mormon, but he went to church regularly and fulfilled most of the assignments he was asked to do. But when the Prophet had called on the Saints to leave Babylon and come to Zion last July, he had found better things to do. After all, if he had abandoned his growing business in California, how would he support his family? Besides, if times were really going to get tough, a business selling food storage and survival gear should really become lucrative. Before long, he'd have enough money to buy his wife Lynette a new minivan, pay for those piano lessons, help his fellow man, and save for the future.

So when Lynette and the four children had pleaded with him to drop it all and move to the Rocky Mountains, he simply didn't hear them. Lynette had done everything possible to convince him, but when he continued to refuse, she had packed up early one morning when he was still asleep, piled the kids into her old jalopy, and set out for Utah. She figured that was the only way to save her children and wake her husband up.

The trouble is, Ralph never did see the light. Even though he had lost the food storage to wandering thieves, he had managed to save most of the survival equipment. The things which were selling the best were the seventy-two-hour kits and the water purification devices. He had made a fortune, but to make sure the business was safe, he had found it necessary to sleep in his shop on South Raymond Street in Pasadena with a high-powered rifle close to hand. It was a lonely life. Several times he had succeeded in contacting his wife with the help of a ham radio friend, and had tried to convince her to return to Pasadena. She had always refused and tearfully begged him to join her.

On Wednesday morning Ralph awoke early. He dressed and ate a can of chicken noddle soup for breakfast. At 7:30 he stepped outside his shop to get some air. He was surprised to see so many people and so much traffic at that hour. As he turned to go back in, he felt a violent lurch which knocked him against the jamb of the door and then to the concrete. He tried to rise, but the shaking was so vigorous that he could do nothing except sit on the concrete and hold on to the frame of the doorway. However, terror filled him when the wood of the frame splintered suddenly and the entire building began to collapse, threatening to crush him.

Lying almost flat on his stomach, he crawled frantically toward the street. Pieces of concrete and sections of roofing pounded his body and disintegrated on the sidewalk around him like bombs falling from the sky. He felt excruciating pain as the debris tore a bloody gash on the right side of his head. He had the strange sensation that his ear had been ripped away. Afraid of being buried alive, he ignored his pain and continued to crawl.

At that moment he heard a deafening roar which seemed to bear down on him from the north like some colossal freight train. He glanced up the street, and beheld the sidewalk and the entire street rise and fall like waves in a stormy sea. The lamp posts and trees shot into the air as if they had been fired from a great cannon. Every person on the street had been knocked to the ground, and vehicles of all sizes had been hurled against the crumbling buildings on the far side of what used to be a street. Above the roar of nature, he heard the screams and the wailing of the people around him. But he realized that there were many others who had been silenced suddenly under the crushing weight of collapsing buildings. In an instant, he saw what his life meant, felt his sins, and knew that he had been foolish not to listen to his beloved wife. He wondered if the shaking would ever stop.

After he had crawled almost half way across the street, he heard a great ripping sound, and his heart was filled with horror when he saw in the distance a fissure traveling down the center of the road and growing deeper and wider as it approached at high speed. There were a number of people lying on the road directly in the path of the moving cleft. When the street opened next to him, Ralph was sure he would fall into the crevice, and he pushed away from it with all his might. He succeeded in avoiding the disaster, but he knew that others had not. Fascinated, he glanced into the chasm, whose bottom was lost in the shadows. Seconds later, the sides of the fissure screamed as they clamped shut like the jaws of hell devouring their prey.

And then it was over. Ralph's heart raced wildly, and he struggled for breath. He was astonished to see that his world could be annihilated in less than a minute. Yet he was still alive! Near him and in the distance he heard the sound of crying, explosions, burning, ruptured mains, and the silence of death. He sat up painfully, but could not get to his feet.

"Help me, please!" a plaintive voice called not far away. He looked down the street and saw a woman on her knees. She was staring at a three-story apartment building which had been demolished. "Help me, please," she cried again and again.

Fifty people staggered up and down the street like zombies, trying to go somewhere, but having nowhere to go. Those who stumbled past the crying woman completely ignored her. As Ralph forced himself to his feet, searing pains shot up his back and his right leg. He must have several broken bones. He checked the right side of his head and was relieved to feel his ear still there, though it hurt terribly and was covered with blood. Hearing the woman again, he dragged himself toward her.

When she caught sight of him fifteen feet away, she cried out, "Help me, please! My baby! In that building!"

Ralph looked at the lower part of her legs and realized that both were broken. "Don't worry. I'll find him. Or is it a girl?"

"A little boy, five years old," the woman moaned.

Ralph climbed onto the rubble and searched for ten minutes, digging with his hands until they were raw and bloody. It seemed hopeless. He could displace some chunks of construction material, but others were impossible to move without heavy equipment. Then he noticed the woman pointing to the south side of the building where a twenty-foot section of the outer wall remained standing. As he dug in that area, he felt that the wall might fall and crush him at any minute. The woman watched him anxiously, but eventually crumpled to the ground unconscious. Ralph knew he had to continue in spite of his pain. Soon two men with shovels and a wrecking bar joined him, and they attacked the debris together.

After digging an hour under a huge slab of concrete, they finally managed to break into a dark narrow passage. Ralph thought he heard a faint cry. He strained to listen. There it was again!

"He's in there," he said to the other men. "Alive!" Joyously, he turned toward the street to tell the mother, but saw two paramedics carrying her away. Ralph guessed that they were taking her to Central Park, not far away.

"Let's get him out!" said one of Ralph's helpers as he began to enlarge the hole.

When the opening was large enough, Ralph slid under the slab and began to crawl through a long tight passageway. After he had crawled a short distance and made a partial turn, the tunnel became blacker than a moonless night. It reminded him of the night when, at ten years of age, he had disobeyed the signs and crawled seventy feet through a dark, constricted tunnel beneath Tweedy Boulevard in Los Angeles when the city was enlarging the street. Halfway through, the tunnel had become so tight that he couldn't move forward or back.

At that instant, he had had one terrible thought after another. Would he be stuck there until he starved to death or the workers filled in the tunnel? Would the tunnel collapse and crush him or bury him alive? Would he ever see his parents again? The panic had been so dreadful that he could scarcely breathe. But at last he had calmed himself enough to think. Then for a half hour he had wormed his way forward a fraction of an inch with every movement, until the tunnel began to widen. Five minutes later he had climbed out, filthy but free. As he had walked home, he had thought that it really wasn't such a big deal after all—but he'd never do it again!

Later, as an adult, he had reflected often on the many crazy, dangerous things he had done as a child, and was amazed that he was still alive.

Realizing now that the five-year-old child buried in the ruins must be experiencing the same fear that he had felt years ago, Ralph fought his way forward. Again and again he felt as though the walls around him were crushing his chest and he gasped for breath. After he had struggled along the tunnel for what seemed an hour, guided only by the tiny voice ahead, he finally saw the child's head. The rest of his body was completely buried in rubble.

Upon seeing his rescuer, the boy smiled and said, "I knew you'd come!"

Ralph could tell by his tear-stained face that he had been crying. To the left he saw a vertical pillar which had caught some of the falling debris and had made a pocket of air the size of a small closet. He figured that was the only thing which had prevented the child from being crushed or smothered to death.

It took an hour to remove the boy from his prison, and as he worked, he partially uncovered the arm of a corpse entombed to the right of the child. He checked the boy for injuries and was amazed that he found none. He told the child to follow him as he crawled backwards up the passageway. During this struggle up the tunnel, both of them coughed and choked constantly from the dust and lack of air. Often he had to pull the boy toward him In order to keep the child from thinking about the danger, he questioned him about his family and what he enjoyed doing. In this way, he discovered that the child and his mother had been living alone in the apartment.

A half hour later they emerged from the hole. Ralph breathed the air with joy and, limping badly, led the chattering boy slowly toward the park. Now he understood that his business and his fortune were nothing in comparison to his life, his family, and his beliefs. Feeling an overwhelming gratitude toward God, he began to think of ways to travel to Utah.

When the earthquake struck downtown Los Angeles, hundreds of tall buildings swayed a few seconds as if they were giant trees in a gale, and then collapsed in great heaps of rubble, like useless old buildings toppled systematically by countless charges of dynamite. Instantly thousands of tiny human beings disappeared under mountains of stone, brick, and concrete.

*****

The European media was in a frenzy of activity because today, Wednesday, April 25, the great rally of MOM, or Mothers Opposing Madness, was to take place. For weeks television broadcasts had reported that 500,000 mothers and others from every part of Switzerland would march on the House of Parliament in Berne to demand that national leaders outlaw guns of any kind in this peace-loving country.

Two months before the great march, four people had met in a room at the Bellevue Palace, Kochergasse 3-5, to plan the event. Three of them, two women and a man, were political activists from Paris and Berlin. The fourth person, who directed the meeting, was Martin Gannt, UGOT's Assistant Director of Media Relations. As soon as everyone had arrived, Martin invited them to sit around a table in the spacious kitchen. Nearby was a second table covered with bowls of fruit and bottles of wine.

"Well, people, thank you for coming," Martin said in English. "I know you by reputation and I've seen you on television. And, of course, I had a hand in choosing you for this assignment. But it is a pleasure to finally meet you in person." The three guests smiled and nodded. Martin knew that these people had been among of the most dedicated gun-control advocates in Europe for many years, and had been highly effective. "Do you know each other?"

"Not really," one of the women said.

"All right, let me make introductions." He pointed to the woman who had just spoken. "This is Marie Fayard. She comes from Tours, France, and is relatively new to our cause. I assure you that she's totally dedicated, shrewd, and full of boundless energy." Marie flushed at this praise. She was short and stout. The gray streaks in her hair suggested that she was in her late forties.

Martin nodded toward the second woman. "This is Ann Latimer. She's from Kingston, not far from London. I don't know if you realize it, but she played a major role in outlawing guns in New Zealand several years ago." The others looked at Ann enviously. She was a tall, slim blond of forty-three. In spite of her square jaw and thin lips, she was very attractive. Her forceful personality seemed to hold a strange attraction for most men. Martin admired her most for her confidence and skill in handling the media.

"And this is Friedrich Bauer, from Berlin. He has been an important force in getting much gun legislation passed in Europe." With a quick movement of his head, Friedrich threw his long blond hair out of his eyes, and nodded arrogantly. He was obviously proud of his handsome face, tall muscular body, and all-round macho-ness. Martin considered him to be one of the most ruthless and skillful planners in the gun-control movement.

Martin went on, "As I told you on the phone, Ann will lead our campaign here in Switzerland. I ask you, Marie and Friedrich, to help with planning and to assist Ann in any way you can." Marie and Friedrich indicated their acceptance. "Are you all parents?"

Friedrich and Marie shook their heads, but Ann beamed and proudly announced that she had a five-year-old boy. Martin laughed inside, knowing that, like many film queens and other professional women, Ann had taken a break in her career as a lobbyist to "experience" motherhood, as if it were just another life event that a woman should go through at least once to feel what it was like. He couldn't resist thinking that this attitude was not too different from what some people have when they order a strange new dish for the first time in an exotic restaurant.

"Wonderful, Ann!" Martin said. "Be sure to mention that fact if the media questions you."

"Yes, I will," Ann replied. "My son is the real reason I go through this labor and pain. I do it for him and all the other innocent children!"

"I knew your motives were noble," Martin said. He looked at Marie and Friedrich. "And how do you feel about our cause at this time?"

Marie said with passionate conviction, "Guns cause crime and violence. I believe that if they were illegal everywhere, the world would be a safer and happier place in which to live."

"I completely agree. And you, Friedrich?" Martin said.

"Well, I have to admit that I enjoy a good fight. I love to take the arguments of the gun people and prove them wrong. It was even more fun when the NRA existed. Sometimes you have to juggle the statistics a bit, but it's for a good cause."

"Yes," Martin said, "the means justifies the end."

"That's not to say I don't believe in our cause completely, you understand," Friedrich added.

"Of course you do. I'm pleased to see that each of you is still dedicated to our great cause." Martin sipped his wine. "Drink! As much as you want. It's on the house."

They poured glasses of wine and put grapes and apple slices on plates in front of them. Martin reached into his briefcase and removed materials. "Now, I should like to hear your ideas on how to handle the rally scheduled for April 25," he said. The others also removed notebooks and papers from their briefcases. "Ann, would you like to begin?"

"Yes, thank you. First of all, I think we should stick to the basic theme that MOM has always stressed, and avoid any other. We mothers are marching to save the lives of our children from gun violence and gun accidents."

"But there have been very few such accidents in Switzerland," Marie pointed out.

Ann replied, "True, but the public doesn't know that. If we declare openly that it has occurred, even frequently occurred, and repeat it over and over, the people will believe it sooner or later."

"Yes," Martin said. "People seldom take the time to investigate the facts. They usually don't have access to them. So if they hear something on television often enough, they'll believe it, even if it sounds ridiculous to begin with."

Friedrich laughed. "How true! Because of clever promotions and propaganda on TV, the public now accepts homosexuality and same-sex marriages as legitimate lifestyles."

Struggling to maintain his composure, Martin seethed inside. He was an avowed homosexual and was furious that this ignorant fool didn't know it. But he went on as if Friedrich had said nothing, "Even if some try to check the facts, they'll have to get their information from the authorities. And I can assure you that UGOT has consulted with the Swiss Government to make sure that the statistics any investigators find will verify that gun accidents have killed many Swiss children. It's a technique we learned from the defunct American bureaucracy.

"In any event, you are right to place the primary emphasis on the issue of saving children from the dangers of guns. Too many issues will confuse the public and weaken our position. Above all, the messages you convey must be full of emotional, heart-rending stories of personal tragedies. Make them up if you have to. You must convince people that they're against mothers and children if they don't outlaw guns. If you can, avoid statistics and logical arguments. They can only get us into trouble."

Ann noted, "We've had a problem in the past which has given us a lot of trouble, and it might occur again. Those who oppose gun control stress over and over that most violent crimes, such as murder, are committed by criminals, and that guns in the hands of decent citizens deter criminals. They conclude that guns save the lives of people, including children."

Martin smiled. "Well, if you can't avoid getting into such a debate, try to persuade people that the evidence proves most victims are murdered by individuals they know, such as relatives and acquaintances."

Marie countered, "But that doesn't square with the facts."

"It will if you get creative with language. If you define the word 'acquaintance' very broadly to include gang members killed by other gang members, drug pushers killed by junkies and other drug pushers, cabdrivers murdered by customers, prostitutes executed by clients, and so on, then it instantly becomes true that most victims are murdered by acquaintances or relatives."

"Tricky!" Friedrich exclaimed.

"Yes, you can do so much with vocabulary." Martin observed.

"I see," Marie said. "So if the government doesn't outlaw guns, these violent relatives and acquaintances—these 'friends'—will kill our children too?"

Martin replied, "Exactly! In that way we can work the argument around to support our primary theme of protecting children... All right, let's move on! Whom did you choose to symbolize the MOM march?"

Ann replied, "We found a wonderful woman! She's a tall, lovely brunette about forty-eight years old. The ideal mother! Two of her six children were playing with her husband's handguns and killed each other in a western-style gun battle. It really touches your heart when she tells her story."

"Wonderful! I want you to present her as the organizer and the soul of this march on Parliament. She's Swiss?"

"No, German."

Martin pondered a moment. "That probably won't matter. Her German will be quite different from that used by the Swiss, but if you get her a linguistic coach and have her memorize a prepared script, it should be fine."

Friedrich said, "We have also procured the services of two other women—Swiss this time—who will relate their tragic stories in German."

"Good! What about stories for the French and Italian populations of Switzerland?"

Marie replied, "One of my friends and I will tell our sad tales in French."

Martin laughed. "About the terrible loss of your children? I thought you said you were childless."

"That doesn't matter," Marie said glibly. "Like you said, the end justifies the means. So ridding Switzerland of guns justifies making up a story."

"I'm more pleased with that than if your story were actually true!" Martin replied.

"Thank you, Martin... But to continue, I found two Italian women who lost children. One child was shot by a robber, and another by her father."

"Seven testimonials! That should do it... Now, tell me about the people you're bringing in to support you."

Ann said, "We're advertising this march throughout Europe, encouraging people to sign a pledge that they'll come to Berne to participate. The response from both women and men has been excellent so far!"

"How many pledges?"

Ann checked her notes. "After five weeks, uh, we've received 90,000 pledges. I hope we'll get at least 130,000 people to show up by the time we're done."

"Tell the media that a half million mothers will be in the march."

"A half million? I doubt we'll ever—"

"I understand. But neither the media nor the public will know the difference. No one is going to walk around and count heads. Besides, 130,000 people gathered in one place can easily pass for a half million. We care about the effect, not the truth."

"I love it," Ann gushed. "I wish we had thought of that technique when we fought against guns in New Zealand." Marie and Friedrich looked impressed also.

Martin was proud of himself. "That's what I'm here for. To suggest the latest techniques... Okay now. Tell me about the opposition."

"Oh yes! Our loyal fanatical opposition. Well, let's see. With the generous budget UGOT provided, we were able to hire about six hundred people. We're already using them to gather the pledges, but at the rally they'll function in the normal way."

"I know how I would employ them, but how do you intend to do it?"

Ann extracted a planning sheet from her notebook and began to read. "Okay, we'll make sure they're in Berne two days before the march. We'll plant them in key places. We'll have them dress and act in ways which suggest to the public that they're fanatics. They'll carry provocative posters. They'll purposely incite violent arguments with our marchers."

"Please explain what you mean about planting them in key places," Martin said.

"I mean we'll put them in bunches of a hundred near the positions used by the media. In this way, when the television crews pan their cameras, viewers will either see my scary fanatics, or the peaceful citizens of Berne, or my well-behaved marchers."

"Excellent! That's exactly what I would have done. I suppose you'll also place several thousand gun-control advocates along the route to cheer the marchers."

"Standard procedure."

Martin was delighted. "I'm happy with the way you three are handling this. I'm sure UGOT will reward you appropriately if this march is a media success."

Next Martin pulled out a list of questions which covered the details of the operation. They spent the rest of the day, and the following day, going over their plans. When it was over, Martin flew back to London, pleased with the report he would give to Gerald Galloway. UGOT was very concerned about Switzerland. In a population of nearly thirteen million people there were an estimated twenty million guns. Since the country had no standing army, every male from twenty through forty-two was required to serve in the citizens' militia and to keep his ammunition and weapons, normally automatic assault rifles, at home. And when the men retired, the law allowed them to keep those weapons.

Also, the Swiss had numerous gun clubs, even for children. They felt that target practice was more healthy and enjoyable than sports like golf. Indeed, UGOT would find it impossible to control the Swiss unless it became illegal to possess fire arms in their country. Even that was no guarantee that a large segment of the population would not simply ignore the new laws. In any case, this rally was important because it might be the first major step in outlawing guns in Switzerland. Martin shivered to think of UGOT's armies trying to control a populace armed with small weapons. Five million crack-shot guerrillas in a country full of mountains! The lessons of Afghanistan and Somalia had proven that the world's greatest nations were powerless to defeat such determined citizens. No wonder Hitler had left the Swiss alone.

On April 25 the march on the capitol was a stunning success. The media reported that 500,000 demonstrators, most of them mothers, had gathered in the vicinity of Helvettaplatz in Berne by 8:00 a.m. The actual number was 120,000. The crusaders were very polite and well-behaved. At 8:30, these champions of children marched proudly in a line a mile long, tears streaking their faces, northward on Kirchenfeldbrüke Street. Soon they turned west on Kochergasse Street and headed for the House of Parliament. Their posters and banners proclaimed their deep concerns to the world: "Save Our Children," "My Child's Life Ended With A Bang," "Guns Kill people,"

"Stop The Slaughter Of The Innocents," "We Love Kids More Than Guns," "Cease Arming Criminals," "Gun Laws Work," "Loopholes Lead To Bullet Holes," "Mothers Outgun Morons." Ann Latimer didn't see that last one until too late.

And the "opposition" was combined. From the sidelines they hooted and stamped their feet. They strove to provoke shouting matches, or yelled insults at the marchers. They had their banners too: "Guns Don't Kill—Criminals Do," "Gun Laws Disarm The Good Guys," "Guns Deter Crime," "Only Governments Commit Genocide."

At first, the marchers ignored these fanatics and remained serene in the conviction that they were doing the work of God Himself. But then, as they followed the predetermined route, some marchers, seeing the disgusting slogans of their opponents and hearing the insults, could bear it no longer. They raced to the side of the road and ripped enemy signs to shreds. Others got their message across with furtive obscene gestures.

When the marchers finally reached the House of Parliament at noon, the seven mothers told their touching stories and moved the hearts of millions. As a result, a number of brave politicians stepped forward and announced that they would do anything in their power to stop the slaughter of those innocent children. The Swiss came by the thousands to see the festivities and hear the speeches, and millions of others saw it on television. But few had any clear idea as to what the fuss was all about.

Chapter 13

Steven and Mary were grateful that most of the sick were recovering from their disease by Tuesday evening. Steven consulted with the leaders of Pioneer One to see if the caravan should rest the next day. They declared as one that they wanted to continue the journey without delay, and that they were confident their people would support them in this decision. So on Wednesday they set out as usual at 9:00 a.m. and continued east on I-80. Steven had organized a troop of fifty armed men on horseback to search the countryside near the freeway ahead of Pioneer One, and he felt safer knowing they were out there.

As they rode their horses up and down the line of wagons, Steven and Paul noticed that the Saints seemed to be in good spirits in spite of the ordeals of the last few days. Many were weak and tired from the illness and from lack of sleep, but they smiled at the brothers and manifested new self-confidence. Steven knew, however, that a number of the travelers were still so weak that they were lying on beds in the wagons. Only those who had lost loved ones showed signs of despair and sadness. Steven's heart went out to them.

By 11:30 a.m. the sun and heat had become almost unbearable. If one stopped to examine the long line of travelers, it was not unusual to see people faint suddenly and collapse to the ground. A few suffered from hallucinations and hysteria. On the advice of several leaders, Steven ordered an early halt for lunch. The Saints sprawled out in any shady spot available, mostly in or under their wagons. Following the instructions of the leaders, they boiled the water they took from Heirner's Creek, which flowed north of the highway, before they consumed it. In the early afternoon, Ruther Johnston emerged from the northern mountains and rode up to Steven's wagon.

Steven heard the approaching animal, but before he could crawl out from under his wagon, his three children slid past and attacked Ruther as he descended from his mule.

"I'm so glad ta see ya, Ruther," Andrew said, hugging the old man.

Jennifer grabbed his arm. "I love you, Ruther."

"We sure feel safer when you're around," William declared.

Ruther hugged each of them in turn.

Suppressing a twinge of jealousy, Steven peeked out and said, "Ruther! It's you!"

"These pills of yours sure do the trick," he said to Steven. "Glad ya made me take a few along. Stomach up and started hurtin' 'bout ten last night. Popped a few of these little fellers and felt better by sunrise."

Steven scrambled from beneath the wagon and stood up. He was still weak, but getting stronger. Mary looked out from inside the wagon and, seeing who it was, climbed to the pavement.

"Glad to hear it," Steven said. "What did you do out there?"

"Hah! Checked their main camp. Seems them boys done took off as if their backsides were afire and hightailed it north. Must be near Bear Lake by this time. Don't figure you'll ever see 'em again. They beat it out of that camp so fast, they left lotsa valuables laying around. Have ta admit that I scooped up a few trinkets for my trouble."

Steven grinned. "Come and set—sit—for a while. Would you like some lunch? We still have food left."

"Don't mind if I do."

They watched him devour Mary's soup with great relish, smacking his lips noisily. When he had finished, he sighed deeply and looked at Steven. "Had time ta do some thinkin' up thar in the mountains."

"About what?"

"Religion... Got lots of things ta put ta ya, but now's not the time. I'm plain tuckered out! You got room under that contraption of yours for one more?"

Steven laughed and invited him to share their space. William hurried away to spread Ruther's good news. When Steven awoke at 2:30, he walked a few hundred yards down the highway and saw the exhaustion of the Saints. He had just decided to let them remain there for the rest of the day, when two colonels rode up.

"Why aren't we moving?" Jasper Potter asked. "It's past time."

"The people are beat. They need more time to recover from their sickness and fatigue."

Jasper grinned. "I don't think you're giving them enough credit, Steve. Have you asked them? I bet that if you give the command, they'll meet the challenge!"

Steven studied their faces, wondering if he was paying too much attention to his own fatigue. "All right. Tell them to move out."

The colonels laughed, turned their horses, and trotted away. Within ten minutes the caravan was on the move. It continued up the road laboriously, but steadily, until Steven stopped it at 5:30. When he saw the sign for Exit 180, he estimated with pride that the people had traveled seven to eight miles that day in spite of everything.

Shortly before dark, heavy black clouds began to swirl in from the northwestern sky, and soon the pioneers felt a light rain descend upon them. During the night, thunder boomed and lightning flashed in the mountains around them, and the children clung in fear to their parents. Since the rain fell continuously the following day, the Saints received hoped-for relief from the heat and made good time. Their temporary travel schedule was over, and they traveled ten hours. By the end of the day, Steven calculated that they had covered fifteen miles. He was surprised at this because they had lost a great deal of time crossing a number of gaping fissures in the road. Twice the wagon train had found it necessary to drive into the gully-strewn fields to go around chasms in the road which were to steep to handle.

The blizzard hit the next day, on Friday, April 28, at 10:00 a.m. Mary saw the storm coming from the north and wondered how bad it would be. Even though Steven had ridden away with Ruther, Douglas, and the bachelors to check on the wagon train, she was grateful that the three children were in the wagon with her. Within fifteen minutes, the wind-driven snow was so dense that she couldn't see the highway in front of her. She feared that at any moment the furious gale would blow her wagon over, or that she would drive the mules off the highway by accident and be lost in the whiteout. Now she realized one of the great disadvantages of being the lead wagon. She asked herself how on earth such a storm could occur as late as the end of April. Then she remembered that day years earlier, when a blizzard struck Provo on June 6. It had come with a vengeance, but had completely disappeared by 1:00 p.m., without leaving a trace of snow on the ground. Something told her, however, that this blizzard wasn't going to end quite so quickly.

On and on she drove in the blinding wind, determined not to stop. After all, what would Steven and the other pioneers think of her if she didn't have the strength to face this little trial? But where were the scouts who preceded the wagon train in order to assure the safety of the pioneers? Had they gotten lost in the storm? At first she could determine where the road was by the posts and rails along the side, but soon they disappeared from view under a shroud of snow. She had to depend on the instinct of the mules and on the slight curvature of the road which was barely perceptible ahead.

William insisted on sitting next to her on the wagon seat, and took the reins from her regularly when her frozen hands could hold them no longer. She admired the courage of this thirteen-year-old boy who reminded her so much of Steven. Jennifer and Andrew, wrapped in blankets, stayed directly behind her, close to the opening, and stared in awe at the stark whiteness.

Mary turned and shouted to Andrew, "Look out the back and see if the Cartwrights are following." As the boy went to check, she added, "And fasten the flap!"

A minute later Andrew returned. "They're not there. I don't see anyone."

Now Mary was starting to panic. Where were the others? Did they stop as soon as the storm began? What would happen if she drove the mules into a gigantic hole in the highway? No, that's not possible. Ruther had told her that the mules were very intelligent and could sense danger ahead, even when they couldn't see it. According to him, mules were much smarter than horses. Then Mary began to worry about the mules and the cow tied to the back of the wagon. Were they suffering out there?

"Andrew, is Lucretia still tied to the wagon?"

"Yes!"

Thank you, Father in Heaven, she thought. Then her mind turned to Steven. Where was he? She had no wristwatch and the blizzard prevented her from estimating the time from the position of the sun. But he must have been gone for hours. Had he ridden off the highway without realizing it and wandered into the wilderness alone? Maybe she would never see her husband again! Finally, Mary stopped the mules, figuring it had to be close to lunchtime. They would eat and remain where they were, waiting for the others.

Yelling above the howl of the blizzard, she told the children to move to the center of the wagon and climb under their blankets. The wagon shook violently, buffeted by the gale, and she feared that at any moment it might be blown over or torn to pieces. She expressed to God how grateful she was that it was heavily loaded. She waited fifteen minutes, watching through the rear canvass flap, but no other wagons appeared. Then, thinking of the animals again, she grabbed as many blankets as she could carry and climbed out the front of the wagon. Struggling against the wind, she moved up to the closest mule on the left and tried to cover it with a blanket, using her right hand only. But the wind struck the blanket and hurled it away to the south and out of sight.

Determined to help the animals, she set all the blankets on the ground except one, stepped upon the pile, and wrapped the mule's head with the blanket in her hands, tying its corners securely. In this way she succeeded in attaching four blankets to the heads of four mules. When the task was accomplished, she worked her way back to the wagon, leaning against the mules for support. She was astonished at how strong, patient, and immovable they seemed.

By the time she reached the wagon, she couldn't feel her hands or feet. In spite of her distress, she fought her way alongside the wagon until she reached Lucretia. She tried to cover the cow's head with the last blanket, but the animal swung her great head back and forth, mooing excitedly. At last, after ten minutes, she finished the job and climbed through the back of the wagon. When she reached the children, she was so exhausted and cold that she had to lie next to them for twenty minutes before her body would permit her to search for something to eat.

When they had eaten, Mary insisted that everyone lie back under the covers to sleep. She told the children that by the time they awoke, there was a good chance the other wagons would have overtaken them, or that Steven would have found them. The children fell asleep quickly, but it wasn't so easy for Mary. The howling of the wind, the shaking of the wagon, which slid sideways at times when it was struck by gusts of wind, and the mooing of the cow, kept her awake. But eventually her fatigue took over, and she drifted into sleep.

She awoke with a start and was struck by the complete silence outside. Peeking through the rear flap, she saw nothing but dim whiteness. And the cow. She realized at once that night was approaching, and the cold was biting. She glanced at the children and saw that they were still sound asleep. She gathered five blankets and clambered out of the wagon. Running as fast as she could through the foot of snow which covered the road, or what she believed was the road, she hurried to the animals and covered the backs of each with a blanket. Back in the wagon, she nestled against the children and waited.

The six riders watched the northern sky for several minutes. Finally, Ruther glanced at Steven and said, "Looks like a storm. Headin' this way."

"More rain?"

"Nope. Blizzard."

"Blizzard! In April?"

"Sure. I don't know why you're so shocked. We're livin' in the last days, ya know. It's blisterin' one day and freezin' the next."

Steven knew the old-timer was right. For months he had been amazed at the wild extremes in the weather. Still, this storm caught him by surprise, and he didn't know what to do. "What do you suggest, Ruther?"

"Find shelter quick or your people will be in trouble, especially them pullin' the little carts. I noticed an open spot 'bout a mile back when we first started checkin' the train. Lotsa cliffs and trees. All of ya ride ta the front with me, and I'll show ya the place. Then while the boys and I guide the wagons onto the campsite, you kin ride on ta the lead wagons and turn 'em back."

Steven shouted, "Okay, let's do it."

They took off at a trot, heading for the front of the company. But soon the storm hit with all its fury and began to blanket the region in snow. Steven was so blinded by the driving snow that he was forced to cover most of his face with his hat. He could barely see Ruther ahead or the others nearby. He was astonished that the old man could even stay on the road. By the time they reached the place where Ruther wanted to leave the freeway, the caravan had stopped. Alone, Steven rode ahead another mile, searching for his wagon, but saw nothing except bleakness. He hesitated a moment. Should he continue on to find Mary and the kids or help Ruther turn the wagons?

He decided that his family was his most important responsibility. As he trotted the mustang up the freeway, he peeked from beneath his hat so he could stay on the road. He went on for what seemed forever, and his fear grew. After ten minutes he pushed the horse into a gallop, and almost immediately the animal lost its footing on the slick surface. Both of them tumbled to the ground. Ignoring the pain of the fall, Steven jumped up and looked around, afraid that the mustang had broken a leg. But the horse was already standing, waiting for him. He remounted rapidly and continued his journey in the blinding snow. He felt a pang of guilt for abandoning the wagon train, but what could he do that Ruther and the others couldn't?

He moved up the freeway at a slow trot for two hours, but found nothing. He was frantic. He couldn't understand how they could have come this far. Is it possible he had missed the wagon? Had Mary left the freeway without realizing it? Were they lost somewhere in the wilderness, at the mercy of the storm or some unknown enemy? Before long, the wind died, and the sky began to darken. Soon it would be as black as a mountain cave out here. At last Steven decided to go back and search the sides of the highway as he returned to the wagon train. He prayed fervently that he would find some clue which would lead him to his family.

As he walked the mustang down the center of the road, he scrutinized the snowy fields until his eyes could bear it no longer. He closed them frequently to stop the burning, and then returned quickly to the exasperating search. A half hour later, he saw a black dot on the right some distance from the road. At first he dismissed it as nothing except a small tree standing above the white earth, but then he had the feeling he should check it out. He turned off the road, crossed the gully, and headed for the dark object. When he reached the spot, he dismounted and picked the thing up. It was one of his blankets!

Steven mounted the horse and walked away from the freeway at the same angle. He had the impression that beneath the snow there was a narrow trail. Fifteen minutes later, he rounded a knoll and saw his wagon two hundred yards ahead. He spurred the mustang forward. As soon as he reached the wagon, he climbed in and found Mary. "Wake up, sleepy head," he said softly, a wide grin transforming his face.

Mary's tired eyes opened slowly, but when she finally realized to whom the bleary face belonged, she popped up and threw her arms around her husband. "I knew you'd come," she said, tears welling in her eyes. "What took you so long?"

After hugging his excited children, who awoke with shouts of glee, he explained the whole thing, especially the part about finding the blanket. Next he removed the coverings from the animals and turned the wagon back toward the freeway. The cold was becoming more bitter than ever. After they had traveled west on the highway for some time, it became so dark that Steven had great difficulty telling where the road was. He was afraid they would miss the place where Ruther and the others had left the highway. But soon the figure of the mountain man appeared suddenly in the dark, only a few yards away. High atop his big mule, he was waiting for them beside the road. Steven pointed his flashlight in Ruther's direction and saw the old man grin and wave for them to follow.

Ruther guided them to the pioneer camp, a quarter of a mile from the highway. The location was excellent. On the north there was a long ridge, and on the south, extensive groves of trees. The pioneers had rolled their wagons five abreast into the space between the trees and the bluffs. They had unhitched their animals and sheltered them at the base of the ridge in under-cuts dug by erosion. The handcart people had pitched their tents between the wagons and the animals.

Steven brought his wagon into the line and, with the help of Ruther and the bachelors, unhitched the mules and took them to shelter. Afterwards, they pulled Steven's wagon up close against the others. Steven checked with them to see if any of the Saints had run into trouble, and was pleased to hear that the move to shelter had been a success. Finally, Ruther and the bachelors left for their wagon, and Steven joined his family. As soon as they had eaten the simple meal prepared by Jennifer and Andrew, Steven read to his family by the light of the lamp until he noticed that they had fallen asleep.

They ate breakfast around their campfire at 7:00 a.m. The night had been very cold, with temperatures not far from zero, and their bucket of water had frozen solid. Steven was grateful that Ruther had spotted this sheltered area from the highway. The old man had told him several times that as leader of a company he should learn to read the trail. If he could do that, he would know how to spot places which offered food and water, good campsites, and natural protection against attack. Steven felt guilty that he hadn't even noticed the trees and the line of bluffs as they passed them the day before. Years ago, he had read in many Louis L'Amour novels the same lessons which Ruther taught. But still he couldn't really see what he was looking at. While they ate, Mary told everyone what had happened, and how Steven had found them.

"That was right fortunate, you puttin' that blanket around the cow's head," Ruther commented. "Because if she hadn't throwed a fit and shaken it off, Steve here might never've found you... I'm not saying we wouldn't have found ya eventually, but it might have taken days... And I hate ta think of ya out thar alone with those kids in this bad weather, especially in these dangerous times."

Mary's face turned red in spite of the cold. "Yes, but if I hadn't covered the heads and eyes of the mules, they probably wouldn't have walked off the highway onto that turnoff in the first place!"

Steven didn't think it was really a turnoff. The main road had turned slightly to the right, and there just happened to be a gravel road which went straight ahead. The dip into the small road was hardly noticeable. "But, Mary, I'm not sure that made them lose their way," he declared. "Besides, you protected them from the storm."

"Yes, if it hadn't been for you, the mules might be dead now!" Elizabeth Cartwright said. Douglas and the bachelors bobbed their heads in agreement.

"Yes siree!" Ruther joined in. "Dead, or with a bad case of the flu in their eyes and nose. And I wouldn't be too sure they'd walk off the road because their eyes was covered. A mule's an uncanny smart beast, and he always seems ta know where he's a goin'."

"You're all trying to make me feel better," Mary insisted. "I know I was stupid."

Steven was proud of Mary's courage. "Mary, you did what had to be done. A good person never goes wrong by following her heart!"

That made Mary smile. "By the way, I'd sure like to know what happened to the advance scouts. I never did see them."

"I talked to a couple of them," Steven said. "It appears that they went right past you sometime during the storm."

After discussing the blizzard awhile longer, everyone left to do chores and to prepare for departure. The caravan set out at 8:00 a.m., but it took the entire day to travel eight miles on the snow-covered road. By 6:00 p.m. the sky had cleared, and the snow began to melt.

On Sunday, April 30, the pioneers insisted on traveling after their morning services, because they wanted to make up for lost time. The sun was bright, and the heat returned. At 11:00 a.m. they spotted a small wrecking yard on the left side of the freeway, seventeen miles from Evanston, Wyoming. The Moderns went wild. Even some of the Ancients were happy too, because they hoped to replace their wagons with better transport. Both groups swarmed the yard looking for the right vehicles.

Before long, they found eight conveyances which they could use: two vans, three family trailers, a U-haul trailer, a camper trailer, and something hard to describe. The lower half of this latter contraption appeared to be the undercarriage of a large trailer, with modern axles and wheels. The semicircular top of corrugated metal looked like a small Quonset hut. The vehicle sat high above the road and had a stovepipe protruding through the roof. The Ancients argued for an hour over who should possess it. By 3:00 p.m. the Ancients and Moderns, working together diligently, had prepared the eight "new" vehicles well enough that the teams of draft animals could pull them. They planned to finish their work when the company stopped for the day. The other pioneers learned patience as they waited for their fellow Saints to do this important work.

By Monday afternoon on May 1, the caravan reached Evanston. From his seat on the wagon, Steven saw the people coming from a half mile away. Hundreds of them, running, shouting, and waving their arms wildly. Some carried guns. He stopped the wagon abruptly, grabbed his rifle, and watched them intently as they approached. Five LDS advance scouts came galloping back to the caravan as fast as their horses could run. Ruther, Douglas, the bachelors, and fifteen others came up from behind. One held an Uzi. John Christopher had distributed a few of the weapons obtained from the bandits to certain individuals, but had secured most of them in a special trailer.

"Ya want I should dust their thunder a bit, Steve?" Ruther said nonchalantly, holding his Sharps ready.

"No, we don't know what their intentions are yet." Steven descended from the wagon.

Everyone watched the strangers carefully, growing more nervous by the minute. When the mob was three hundred yards away, they stopped abruptly. Steven figured that one of the leaders had given them a command. Maybe his next command would be for the townspeople to take cover and attack Pioneer One. Strung out along the highway, the Saints were in a vulnerable position. Fifty additional brothers and sisters came forward to see what was going on. Steven was shocked by what the crowd of strangers did next. They laid their weapons on the highway and came on slowly and cautiously.

"Hold your fire," Steven shouted. "I think it's okay."

When the throng was fifty feet away, they stopped again. A tall man stepped forward and walked up to the waiting pioneers. "Welcome!" he said grinning broadly. "We knew you were coming. One of the men here has a radio and heard you talking to Salt Lake... But what took you so long?"

"It's a long story," Steven replied with relief.

As soon as the greetings were done, the mob rushed forward and embraced the Saints with joy. Within fifteen minutes nearly two thousand people were milling on the freeway and the adjacent fields, hugging one another, weeping, and chattering happily. Then the multitude walked slowly toward the town. While the men exchanged jokes, the women walked arm in arm and shared experiences.

Even the townspeople who were not Mormons welcomed the pioneers openly. Because the countryside had been ravaged by famine and disease, and roving bands of lawless barbarians, nearly every inhabitant of this corner of Wyoming had perished. Only the people of Evanston had joined their hearts and resources and had survived. In spite of that, the population had been reduced from ten thousand to slightly more than a thousand, due to lack of food and diseases for which they had no medicines. Since there were so few decent people left in Uintah County, they were overjoyed to see the bedraggled Saints.

That night the pioneers left their wagons on the highway and joined the people of Evanston in a celebration near the center of town north of the highway. The town brass band played, and the people had a square dance. The townspeople contributed flour and sugar from their meager supplies, and the women made hundreds of small cupcakes. Later in the evening, they sat around dozens of campfires and swapped tales and experiences. Some of the town leaders invited Steven, Mary, and their friends to join them at their fire. Steven looked around in amazement at seeing so many jubilant people.

"They're really whooping it up, aren't they?" the town mayor said to Steven. "I haven't seen my people have this much fun in a long time."

Steven replied, "I can't believe it under the circumstances. They act as if they don't have a care in the world."

"It's hard to walk around being miserable all the time," Douglas Cartwright observed.

Elizabeth added, "Yes, even when things are the worst, people grasp desperately for any chance to express happiness."

"Reminds me of a friend I had a few years ago," Ruther said. "Got mauled so bad by a bear, thar was no way ta save him. Happened in the Uintahs." He pointed to the southeast. "The ole boy was in agony fer days, but all he could do was tell one joke after another. Right up ta the time he died."

"I believe that shows great courage," Mary said.

"That's how I figure it. He knew I was doin' my best fer him, and he didn't want ta get me worked up."

The conversation continued another hour, and then the mayor said, "I'm wondering if you folks can stay in town a few days. Maybe we could help each other solve some problems."

"I wish we could," Steven answered, "but we're already behind schedule. We have many things to do in Missouri before winter comes."

The mayor was LDS and understood Steven completely. "Yes, of course. But do you have medical people with you? The marauders killed or kidnapped our health care people, and we don't know how to deal with a lot of the problems we have."

"We'll do our best to help."

Steven sent the bachelors to round up the doctor and the nurses, and the mayor led them to the high school where the sickest people were cared for. They spent the rest of the evening and part of the night doing their best to help, but there was little they could do because of the lack of medical supplies. Grapefruit seed extract could have helped many of the patients, but Pioneer One had already exhausted its supply. While Steven helped Mary, the Cartwrights watched Steven's children.

Chapter 14

On Tuesday, May 2, the pioneers arose at 6:00 a.m. and pulled out of Evanston at 8:00. The townspeople, waving sadly, watched them go. Many citizens gave the travelers small gifts.

Two days later, an hour before the caravan halted for the day, one of the sisters screamed as she passed over a small creek below the freeway. Within fifteen minutes, half the females in the caravan had run off the freeway to the south, packing homemade soap, towels, and bundles of soiled clothes. Having stopped his wagon when he first heard the shrieks, Steven checked his map and saw that the stream was called Smith's Fork Creek. As the rest of the women and girls poured off the highway in a mad dash for the water, the men walked to the north side of the freeway and waited.

Since they had gone through this routine many times, the men knew better than to look off the south side of the road to make sure the bathers were okay. They especially had to keep their eyes on their young sons. It was very painful, but the men knew it was worth it, since the females would be much more pleasant to live with later. At times like this, some of the men also took advantage of the nearby water as soon as the women had finished. But often the other brethren, used to the sweat and grime, were so impatient to move on that those who were anxious to clean up had to forego the pleasure.

For the next two weeks the pioneers made good time, averaging more than fifteen miles a day. In many places the highway looked as though it had been hit with bombs, and some sections were completely washed away by immense floods. The Saints had to endure great heat during the day and freezing cold at night. A maddening hot wind buffeted them unremittingly. It dried their skin and parched their lips, covered their clothes with dust, and forced dirt and debris into every body orifice, especially their eyes. There was no way to escape it.

And yet, in spite of this misery, Steven had the impression that the Saints were grateful to face enemies they could understand. He was delighted to see that many who had been chubby at the beginning were now trimmer. Even those who still carried extra weight looked stronger and fitter.

The pioneers saw no human life on the trail until they reached Rock Springs after a week of travel from Evanston. As they had approached the town, they saw a dozen people watching them from a rise south of the highway. Steven and Mary studied them through the binoculars. Jennifer peeked around the canvas cover and, shielding her eyes against the blowing wind, strained to see.

"They look like homeless derelicts," Mary said sadly. "Their clothes are filthy rags, and some are holding out their hands... They probably need food and water. They're not even armed. Steven, can we—"

"Too dangerous. It might be a trap."

Mary continued to watch through the binoculars. "Oh no! I see a mother and a small child. Please, Steven."

Steven voice took on an edge. "There's probably an army hiding behind them!"

"Dad," Jennifer retorted, "didn't the Prophet say that if we show kindness to others on this trip, Father in Heaven will reward us the same way?"

Steven sighed, knowing he was outvoted and outargued by two kind-hearted females. He stopped the wagon and called for William, who was riding the mustang not far away. After pointing out the beggars to the boy, he instructed him to tell Paul to take supplies to the people, but to be careful. A few minutes later, Paul and several men left the wagon train and rode out to the derelicts. They talked for a short time. Steven was shocked when he saw that, instead of taking the supplies and leaving, the beggars followed Paul back to the caravan.

When the group reached Steven's wagon, Paul called out, "Steve, these people are Mormons! They want to go to Missouri with us."

Steven jumped from his wagon and went to greet the newcomers. He was upset that Paul had told the wanderers that they were traveling to Missouri. Mary watched him from the wagon. There were two middle-age men, two middle-age women, a young woman with a baby, a girl about eighteen, two boys around thirteen, and two younger girls. Eleven people in all.

"Welcome!" Steven said. "So you're LDS?"

"Some of us," said one of the older men. He was tall and skeletal, and his clothes were filthy and torn to shreds. The other vagabonds were in the same condition. It was clear that they were starving. The teenage girl's left arm was partly covered with a bloody bandage. "My name is Elmer Gleason." He nodded toward the people standing close to him. "This is my wife Luella, my daughter Erika, and my sons Jerry and Tommy." He pointed to the other man and his family. "That's my friend Luke Small, his wife Camille, and his two little girls Sophie and Clara. I don't know the young woman or her baby. We just ran into them a short time ago."

Her eyes glistening with tears, the young woman said, "I'm Kinsey Ritter. My baby's name is Emily. We live in Rock Springs. My husband was murdered three days ago by hoodlums."

Steven replied sadly, "I'm terribly sorry." Then he spoke more loudly to all the newcomers. "We offer you assistance and protection. You're more than welcome to travel east with us."

"For that we are grateful," Elmer Gleason declared. "Luke and I came from Chicago with our families. We've been traveling nearly seven months now, struggling to reach Utah. But I doubt we'd ever make it alone. Since my family and I are Mormons, we'd be thrilled to join you no matter where you're going. I know Luke and his family feel the same way." Luke nodded.

Steven was thunderstruck. Chicago seven months ago! "That's about the time—. You were in Chicago when the hydrogen bomb hit?"

"Fifteen miles east of Chicago. We survived the attack because we had the protection of my bomb shelter. A month later, we left for Utah. Luke and his family too. We've been traveling ever since."

"You're lucky to be alive," Steven declared. When Steven saw the expression on the faces of Elmer and Luella, he guessed that they knew why the wagon train was heading east. But this was not the time to discuss it. "Please go with my brother Paul and these other men. They'll make sure you have food, water, and accommodations. Unfortunately, we may have to separate some of you for a few days until we can make arrangements for you to have your own vehicles."

As the vagabonds left with Paul, Steven climbed into his wagon and sat next to Mary.

Mary leaned over and kissed him. "Thank you, sweetheart. You're a good man."

"You're the one who's good. The girl is hurt. Do you want to treat her?"

"Yes." Mary found her medical kit, climbed from the wagon, and started down the caravan.

That same evening, John gravely informed Steven that he was no longer able to contact Salt Lake City on the radio, because broadcasts were being jammed from some unknown source. For days afterward, Steven had difficulty shaking the feeling that they were completely isolated and abandoned.

Traveling during the following week was very difficult. After they left Rock Springs, they began the long trek across the Red Deseret, which extended a hundred and six miles. The terrain was monotonous, the sun blazing, and the hot dry wind battered them endlessly. Their only diversion was the hundreds of wild horses, which still roamed the countryside. Every day Steven and the bachelors led parties of men on horse hunts, because the caravan needed mounts and meat. The rugged animals led the inexperienced brethren on one merry chase after another, and it was only on their sixth attempt that they finally captured a number of horses.

Twenty-five miles east of Rock Springs, the sisters abruptly insisted that the caravan stop. A couple of them had sighted Bitter Creek two hundred yards to the south, and in minutes hundreds of sisters headed for water. Since the stream was not next to the freeway, Steven, Paul, and Douglas hurried to check things out before it was too late. As Steven approached the stream, he saw that its banks were twenty feet high and were littered with appliances, car parts, and every kind of trash. Fearing the water might be dangerous, he asked the sisters to wait until they found cleaner water. But several women informed him that the creek couldn't be as polluted as he said, because it had fish swimming in it. Steven turned and headed back to the caravan, knowing that their argument was better than his.

A week after leaving Rock Springs, they reached Creston Junction, approximately a hundred and eighty miles from Evanston. Since it was almost 7:00 p.m., Steven called a halt. Seeing no threat, he did not put the wagons into circles. The pioneers followed the usual schedule: feed the animals, supper, chores, and talk around the campfire. They were too exhausted to dance or sing. After his 8:30 meeting with the leaders, which lasted only fifteen minutes, Steven joined his family and friends around their campfire. Steven asked Paul about the vagabonds they had rescued and was pleased to learn that several pioneer families had "adopted" them.

There was a short period of embarrassing silence. Then Ruther declared with great emotion, "Well, folks, ain't it great out here in God's country? Plenty of room ta breathe. No pollution. No noise. No city lights. No walls ta close ya in. Delightful grub. And a beautiful, star-filled sky ta sleep under."

Mary fired back, "I've always hated camping. My father and my ex-husband always insisted on doing it the old-fashioned way. But even with modern equipment it's a pain. I'll never forget the miserable times I've had. The dirt and grime. Fires that won't start, or gas stoves which threaten to blow up in your face. Smoky, burned food. Irritating cleanups. Trash bags which rip open. Mosquitos, yellow jackets, ticks, and flies which relish your flesh and follow you around camp. The smelly bug repellent you have to use, or forget to bring. Stupid tents which take Einstein to erect. Tight sleeping bags and the hard, bumpy ground. Interminable, sleepless nights. The wild animals..."

Elizabeth piped up, "You forgot a few things. Abominable outhouses with their ghastly stench—you always wonder what's down there in that black pit under your exposed bottom. The frightening darkness. Supplies you forget or lose. Kids who insist on sleeping with you, and then crowd you or pee on you during the night. Snakes, lizards, and other crawly things. The times you sit in your tent all day while it rains. Tents that cave in the moment you finally doze off. Freezing lakes full of long slimy things..."

"Whew!" Ruther said. "Guess I opened a can of worms. Can I take back my words?"

Steven laughed. "Yes, it looks like you pushed the wrong button, Ruther!" Steven didn't admit that he agreed with the women.

"I guess I did."

"The women have a point," Douglas said. "I can think of a few delightful things myself. Chapped lips. Poison ivy and poison oak—stuck myself into some once when I had to go. Campfire smoke which follows you around no matter which way the wind is blowing. People who talk all night or play loud music... Yes, you really have to love the outdoors to appreciate camping."

"You surprise me, Doug," Paul said.

But Mary wasn't done. "The thing that amazes me is how bad my memory was. I used to dream about traveling to Missouri to help establish the New Jerusalem, the most wonderful city on earth where everyone would be righteous and perfectly happy. It would be the most marvelous experience of my life! But I completely forgot about camping. I didn't realize that traveling to Zion would be like going on the worst camping trip ever! One which would last for months, maybe longer. And without the modern equipment!"

Elizabeth backed her up, "Well, I'm not LDS, so I never dreamed about going to Zion, but somehow I imagined that this trip would really be fun. Now I understand how foolish I was. Still, in spite of the many trials, I'm honestly glad I came. I have learned to love you people so much! And I'm also learning to depend upon the Lord and trust Him in every way."

Tears welled in Mary's eyes and she hugged Elizabeth, who immediately started to cry. "Yes! I guess it's been worth the tribulations, regardless of my whining," Mary said.

Although Steven was touched by their display of affection, he couldn't resist making a joke. "When you think of it, this trip is a piece of cake in comparison to what the Israelites went through."

"What do you mean?" Mary asked suspiciously.

"Well, the Lord made them wander around in the wilderness for forty years. They didn't have modern equipment either. Apparently, God wanted to delay their entry into the Land of Promise until the rebellious died off and the others were chastened and sanctified, worthy to receive their inheritance."

"That's certainly encouraging!" Mary exclaimed.

With a glint in his eye, Ruther added, "Yep, and I understand the wilderness they were in would make this place look like the Garden of Eden. Much more bleak and deserty."

Mary laughed. "I'm not so sure their wilderness was quite that barren, Ruther. Besides, the Israelites got a lot more help than we're getting. All that manna, and springs flowing from rocks." Ruther's eyes opened wide, but his mouth stayed shut.

Douglas spoke up, "Well, I think you and Elizabeth are much better than manna and flowing springs."

Everyone laughed, especially Jennifer and the two women. After they chatted for a while about various things, Ruther finally said, "Ya know, I like you folks so much, I really wish ya had a better understandin' of the holy scriptures. If ya did, you'd probably be raptured some day like all us true believers."

Steven was amused at the way Ruther loved to bait them into religious conversations. "What do you mean?"

"Well, in the first place it seems ta me ya have the wrong idea of who Jesus is. And I figure ya don't understand what the scriptures say about how people get saved."

Steven said, "That's two different subjects, and we probably don't have enough time tonight to cover them both. So which would you like to discuss?"

"Shucks! Don't matter ta me. I suppose we could talk about how we get saved."

"How do we?" Paul asked.

"First, why don't ya tell me what you Mormons believe?"

Steven noticed that Douglas and Elizabeth seemed very interested in hearing the answer. After looking at Steven, who signaled the go-ahead, Paul said, "We believe that through the atonement of Christ, people are saved if they believe in Christ and obey His commandments."

Ruther replied, "But don't the scriptures say that man is saved by faith alone?" Once again Ruther pulled out his old Bible. He thumbed through the book, obviously enjoying himself. He had marked the passages with pieces of paper so he could find them quickly. "Here we go. In the Book of John it says, 'He that believeth on the Son hath everlasting life.' It don't say nothin' about good works." He flipped to the next passage. "And Paul in Romans says, 'Man is justified by faith without the deeds of the law.' And over here in Ephesians, Paul says we're saved by grace through faith, and not by works, lest any man should boast. Because of them scriptures, and lotsa others, I don't see how you Mormons are goin' ta be saved when ya depend so much on yer good works."

The three bachelors grabbed their own scriptures, which they had brought with them. They had been having so many religious discussions with Ruther that they had developed the habit of keeping their scriptures close at hand.

Elizabeth was visibly upset. A Methodist, she believed in the importance of Christian charity. "But Christians must do good works or they aren't followers of Christ."

Ruther replied, "Of course, we do good works, but they don't save us.

Only faith in Jesus saves. The works come automatically."

Steven looked at Paul and his companions, knowing it was only a matter of time before they let poor Ruther have it.

Jarrad spoke first. "Ruther, tell me what you think about Mark, chapter sixteen, verse sixteen."

Ruther turned to the passage and read, "He that believeth and is baptized shall be saved; but he that believeth not shall be damned."

"Doesn't that say you must believe and be baptized to be saved?"

"Yep."

"Isn't being baptized an action, a work?"

Ruther paused. "Uh, yes, but it sorta comes automatically. What about the times Paul the apostle says works aren't important?"

Paul answered, "If you read the passages in Romans and Ephesians in context, you can see that Paul is saying that the deeds or the works of the Law of Moses will not save people. Jewish converts to Christianity in ancient times were still set on practicing the rituals and performances of the Law of Moses, and Paul is correcting them. When he speaks of faith, he's talking about the gospel preached by Christ, which includes works greater than those of the Law."

"All right," Ruther said. "Tonight I'll read all the scriptures around the ones I quoted ta see if what you're sayin' is right."

Jarrad spoke up, "Ruther, I suggest you examine the writings of the other apostles on this subject too. For example, let's look at the second chapter of James." Ruther turned to the place. "Here the apostle is instructing true believers in Christ to do good works. In verse fourteen James asks if faith can save a man if he does not have works. Look especially at verses seventeen and eighteen. In verse seventeen James declares, 'Even so faith, if it hath not works, is dead, being alone.' So if faith does not include the works of Christ, it is dead, or in other words, it is not true faith."

"But young Paul here just said that the word 'work' refers to the Law of Moses," Ruther observed.

"The term has two meanings in these scriptures," Jarrad replied. "In this case, it refers to the works of the gospel, not the works of the Law."

Ruther answered, "I have ta admit that you boys make a good argument. Still, it seems ta me that you're saying Paul and James teach two different gospels."

"Why do you think that?" Paul said. "The faith Paul talks about includes works. Do you remember what he says about faith and charity in chapter thirteen of First Corinthians?"

Ruther recited grandly, "Though I speak with the tongues of men and of angels, and have not charity, I am become as sounding brass, or a tinkling cymbal."

"That's it! But in verse thirteen, which is the greatest between faith, hope, and charity?"

"Charity is the greatest."

"And charity is simply another word for good works."

Ruther wasn't about to give up easily. "Of course, ya have ta be charitable. But since ya believe in Christ, He takes yer life over, and He's the one who does the works, not you."

Steven had heard this strange argument many times before. "Are you saying that Christ controls your behavior, that you lose your free will? Does He move your mouth when you say kind things. Does He move your hands and legs when you help someone?"

"In a way, yes," Ruther replied.

"But then how can you merit the reward for good deeds when you don't even do them yourself?"

Ruther answered triumphantly, "Because you accepted Jesus and have faith in Him!"

Douglas said, "But Ruther, if that is true, why do the prophets and apostles, including Paul, constantly encourage their people—the true believers—to develop and display the Christian virtues if they don't have the power in themselves to do it?"

Suddenly Ruther was stymied, but he didn't want to admit he had no answer. "You folks are pretty good at ganging up on a poor, ignorant old man. If I had a couple of Southern Baptist ministers with me, we'd give ya a run fer yer money."

Everyone smiled, but no one replied. It was obvious that Ruther had run out of arguments.

But Ruther continued, "So it's right what I heard!"

"What did you hear?" Steven asked.

"You Mormons believe ya can earn salvation by yer own good works."

"Not really. We believe that it's a partnership between God and man. Christ does His part, and we do our part. However, I have to add that without Christ's atonement, no man could go to heaven no matter how righteous he was or how many good deeds he did. We can save ourselves, but only through the Lord."

Ruther replied, "That's very clever. But why in tarnation do ya have ta complicate things by havin' two kinds of salvation?"

Steven laughed inside at how Ruther's words made it sound that they had made up these doctrines to suit their own convenience.

Now Elizabeth's face showed confusion. "Two kinds of salvation?"

"Let me explain it to you, Liz," Mary said. "We believe that man fell because Adam transgressed God's law. The result was that all mankind would die and never be resurrected—unless God provided a remedy. We would remain spirit beings forever. As spirits we could never live with God, but would have to live with Satan in perdition forever. Obviously, if that happened, God would be unjust because people would receive a terrible punishment for a transgression they didn't commit."

"Yes, it would be unfair," Elizabeth observed.

"So God sent His Son to die for us, to pay the penalty. Because of that, we can be resurrected and saved from Satan. That's our first salvation."

"What's the second one?" Douglas asked anxiously.

Mary went on, "Well, just because people can be resurrected, it doesn't mean they're righteous. It doesn't mean they're worthy to live in heaven with God."

"Of course not," Elizabeth agreed.

"So to receive the second salvation, to live with God, they must obey the Gospel of Jesus Christ. However, as Steven said, even if people are righteous, they could not inherit heaven without the atonement of Christ. So the atonement has a double effect: it permits all mankind to be resurrected, and it allows the obedient to go to heaven."

Steven was pleased with Mary's simple summary of a doctrine which had many complexities to it.

"That's wonderful!" Elizabeth said. "It shows that God is both just and kind."

Even Ruther was impressed, but he wasn't about to admit it.

Elizabeth added teasingly, "Mary, I'm glad you placed the blame for the world's problems on a man."

Douglas looked at her in surprise. "What?"

"Mary said mankind fell because of a man—Adam."

"But Eve started it all," Douglas objected. "She talked Adam into eating the fruit."

Elizabeth poked her husband in the ribs playfully. "Well, he didn't have to listen, did he? What was he, some kind of robot?"

Later in their wagon, after the children had fallen asleep, Mary said, "I'm sorry I griped so much about camping. It was stupid for me to talk like that when I'm supposed to set a good example."

Steven rolled over and snuggled up to her. "You can't be a good example all the time. It isn't human." He was beginning to feel the fatigue of the day.

"I know, but I still feel guilty."

After a moment of silence, Mary asked, "Why do there have to be so many trials?"

"What did you expect?" Steven replied sleepily. "The Lord to swoop down and carry us to Missouri in the twinkling of an eye?"

"I don't mean that. I was thinking about the pioneers. Why do they have to fight so much, and complain, and talk about you behind your back? They're supposed to be Saints."

"They're talking about me again? What is it this time?"

Mary hesitated. "Not just you. They also gossip about me, Paul, John, and others."

"So what's the latest?"

"Paul told me that some are accusing you of abandoning the wagon train during the blizzard for personal reasons."

"Oh brother! I felt my family was in danger so I went after them. I left the company in good hands."

"I know. It's stupid. But that's the way gossip works. Both John and Paul think that you have an enemy or enemies in the company who are spreading these rumors because they're out to get you."

"Have they found out who it is?"

"Not yet, but they're trying hard."

"Good." After a moment of silence, Steven said, "As for the trials we're going through, I believe they're God's way of sanctifying the people. He can't establish Zion through the Saints until they are holy enough to do it. So He chastens them."

"We don't have to be perfect, I hope."

"No, not perfect, but a lot more righteous than we are now." He gave her a kiss. "Well, we need to get some sleep. It's another big day tomorrow."

They tossed and turned for a while. The heat made it difficult to sleep. Finally, Mary said, "I can't sleep."

"Me neither."

"It's probably the heat."

"Right."

"Also, I was thinking about Ruther."

"Oh?"

"Do you think we were mean to him tonight? We kind of ganged up on him."

"Heck no! Ruther loves it. He tried to shake us up on purpose."

"Do you really think so?"

"Yes."

"I'm glad. I really like him. I hope he stays with us all the way to Missouri. He risked his life for you, you know."

"I realize that."

Mary hesitated, then said, "You've been sort of depressed since the fight with the bandits."

"Who me? I always act this way."

"No, you don't... And I think I know the reason."

"You do?"

"Yes. You killed a man, and it's bothering you. You just don't want to admit it."

Steven swallowed hard. Suddenly, he felt very unhappy. "I suppose you're right. I've relived that scene many times during the night."

"You'll get over it in time."

"Maybe. But I'm afraid that some day I may have to do things which are even worse."

Chapter 15

The shining being appeared to Colton Aldridge more frequently now. Whenever he needed the faith and the power to perform a great miracle, he secluded himself in a dark room, poured out his heart, and soon received the visitation he so frequently desired.

And tonight was no exception. After Colton had spent no more than a few minutes on his knees, a dazzling burst of light penetrated the ceiling and filled the room with splendor. Then a god-like being descended slowly in a pillar of yellow flame. The glory of the magnificent entity infused his body with joy. The light was so bright that it forced Colton to shield his eyes with his hands. But soon the brilliance gradually contracted to the body of the visitor until Colton could bear his presence.

"Lord, thank you for answering my prayer," Colton declared humbly. He was grateful that god had found him worthy of transfiguration. Without that, he knew that he would have been consumed by the entity's glory. It seemed that even his lust for women did not render him impure, for he always received his Master's permission before he took the women unto him.

"Behold, I am the Son of the Most High," the being said. "And thy reward shall be great, my son, for thou hast been faithful in the commission which I gave thee in the land of China."

"Thank you, Lord." Colton was burning to ask the Master the question which had been torturing him for so long, but he dared not do it just yet. "But, Master, what do you want me to do here in Japan?"

"Gain control of the government."

"But how?"

"By warning Japanese leaders of a great disaster."

"How will that give me control?"

"They will not believe thy prediction. But when the disaster occurs, they will be struck by fear and give thee and thy friends more influence in this 'land of the gods.'"

"What catastrophe shall I predict?"

The personage revealed to Colton exactly what he must say and do. "Now, I perceive that thou desirest to know thy standing in my future Kingdom."

Colton was delighted that his god had read his thoughts. It did not occur to him that he himself had openly expressed to many what he believed his role would be. "Yes, Lord, thank you."

"Verily I say unto thee, thou art the one mighty and strong who shall set my house in order and steady the ark of God. But before that day cometh, thou must continue thy work among the nations, as I have instructed thee before."

At these words, the personage ascended and the light disappeared with him, leaving the room dark. Colton was ecstatic. He already believed he was above the rules followed by ordinary men because he lived at the highest level of gospel law. His Master had taught him those laws himself. But now he knew he was the one. The chosen servant of God. After he had reflected on his vision another hour, sitting alone in the dark, he finally arose, turned on the lights, and ordered a late night snack. Later while he was eating, he heard an abrupt knock. He went to the door and was surprised to see Lucienne Delisle.

"Colton, it's good to see you. The desk told me you were in room 613. May I come in?" She looked at the tray of food near the bed.

"Of course." Colton stood aside to let her pass.

Lucienne hurried to the tray and began eating his strawberry short-cake. "I hope you don't mind. I'm so hungry!"

"That's fine. I'm getting too fat anyhow... So what brings you to Nagasaki?"

Lucienne sat on Colton's bed. "Gerald sent me to see how you were doing."

"Yes, of course," Colton said with irritation, "But where are your people? In this hotel?"

"We have four rooms on the next floor down," Lucienne said, licking her fingers. "And yours?"

"They're all on this floor. I prefer my privacy, however, so I don't share a room with any of them."

"Do you have an appointment with the Prime Minister?" Lucienne asked.

"Tomorrow at ten," Colton said. "Gerald's operatives in the Japanese government made the arrangements."

"Any trouble?"

"Not at all. Ever since UGOT threatened to raise tariffs on Japanese manufactured goods sold in the West, the government and the Diet have been fairly cooperative."

Lucienne probed. "So what are you going to do tomorrow to make the government even more cooperative?"

Colton felt his irritation rise. Even though Lucienne was the director of UGOT's Ministry of Religion and Spiritual Welfare, he resented her interference. Why had Gerald chosen her to head the ministry instead of him? After all, he was the prophet. "Well, the Prime Minister and his leading cabinet members are either Shintoists or Buddhists. They adhere to the beliefs and rituals of those religions. But at the same time, they're pragmatic men of the world. My job will be to convince them that there is a power greater than that found in science or their religions."

Lucienne leaned forward, intrigued. "How are you going to do that?"

"You'll see tomorrow if you join us at the meeting."

"Tell me now."

Colton's voice hardened. "No. I've been instructed to tell no one."

"Your master again?" she said cynically.

"Yes."

Lucienne was disgusted. "You know, you're just like Gerald. He sees his bright angel often, but refuses to tell me what he learns. I don't know why it's such a big secret. It's my job to know. Besides, if you don't tell me what your boss said, I'll die of curiosity! What harm can it do?"

"I don't know the reasons, but I must obey."

Lucienne downed the last of the treat. "At least tell me what happened in China. I read your report, but it lacked the juicy details."

"There's really not much to tell. My 11:00 a.m. appointment was with the Chairman of the Military Commission of the Communist Party, the most powerful man in the country."

"You went to his office at the government building in Beijing?"

"Yes. As soon as I arrived, they brought me to him. He was surrounded by the six members of the standing committee of the Politburo. I had my interpreter with me."

"The Chairman is the man with AIDS?"

"In its final stages. I put my hands on his head and told him he would be cured by the power of God within two hours. The entire blessing took thirty seconds. Then I told them I would go for lunch and be back at 1:00 p.m. They looked at me like I was insane, but I also saw awe in those beady little eyes. When I returned, the old guy was gorging himself on some strange food, his energy had returned, and his cough had disappeared."

"So he was cured?"

"His doctor thought so. He checked him, and the sores were gone."

"That's incredible! What happened next?" Lucienne knew that Colton had already visited China several times, and had gained a reputation as a miracle worker. A miraculous healing like the latest would only confirm his powers in the minds of the Chinese and their leaders.

"I warned them that if they did not put a great army at UGOT's disposal some day, at the time the army was needed, I would curse all twenty members of the Politburo with a disease ten times more virulent and horrible than AIDS."

"Do you think they believed you?"

"Absolutely! You never saw such fear."

"You can actually do that?"

Colton straightened his body, and his eyes were full of conviction. "Absolutely! I can do anything."

Lucienne was very uneasy, but struggled not to show it. At that moment she realized that this man was too dangerous to have around. She and Gerald would have to eliminate him as soon as he had served his purpose.

The next day the guard ushered Colton and Lucienne into a temporary office used by Yoritomo Muratari, the Prime Minister of Japan. He and three cabinet ministers were touring the Nagasaki Prefecture to inspect the serious damage caused to the coast of the southern island of Kyushu by a series of tsunamis. The Japanese officials bowed deeply, and the visitors mimicked the bow. The translator provided by the Japanese government translated their words quickly at the end of each speech. After the preliminaries, the Prime Minister presented his point of view.

"We appreciate the advisors UGOT has sent us," Yoritomo said, "but we cannot give them more power in our government. We alone are in a position to make wise decisions for our country."

Colton replied, "You do not understand. We can supply you with valuable information which you cannot get from your leaders or your experts."

"What kind of information?"

"Successful products to manufacture. Where and how to build public works. How to solve problems of inflation, unemployment, health care for families. These are a few examples."

Yoritomo laughed. "But we have many sources of information to help us solve such problems. We've been doing it for decades."

Colton began to loose patience. "Do you know when earthquakes will hit your major cities? Do you know when your volcanoes will erupt? Do you know when the next famine will strike?"

In spite of their powerful cultural beliefs in the rituals of politeness, the four leaders grinned at each other and almost burst out laughing. Yoritomo said, "No one can predict those things. We have the most knowledgeable geophysical experts in the world, and even they cannot do it with certainty."

Knowing the immense value of surprise and a display of authority, Colton declared, "Mount Unzen will erupt today at 12:16 p.m. It will be the worst eruption in the history of that volcano, and many people will die. It is unlikely that you have enough time to evacuate the city of Shimabara."

Yoritomo smiled sardonically. "That's only two hours from now.

Besides, if Unzen were acting up, Kyushu University at Shimabara and The Committee for Prediction of Volcanic Eruptions in Tokyo would have informed me. I'm sorry, but it's impossible."

"Fly to Shimabara then and see for yourself. Since it's close to Nagasaki, you've plenty of time. Stand at the foot of the volcano if you dare."

Yoritomo was angry now. "I do not have time for this foolishness. We'll listen to your advisors when it suits us, but we will not give them more authority in the Japanese government. Good day, sir."

"You won't even warn the people of Shimabara?"

"No."

"In that case, their blood will be on your head." Colton took Lucienne by the arm, and they exited the office without another word. She said little on the way back to the hotel, but the moment she entered Colton's room, she turned on the television, made herself comfortable on a couch, and waited expectantly.

After Colton and Lucienne had left his office, Yoritomo promised the ministers that he would find any excuse possible to expel every UGOT representative from Japan as soon as possible. Then they returned to their maps of Kyushu to examine the flood zone, completely forgetting Colton's strange prediction.

At 12:16 Unzen erupted, throwing one cubic mile of material into the atmosphere. This was four times as much rock and dirt as had been ejected from Mount St. Helen's in 1980. The deadly pyroclastic flow buried Shimabara and killed more than fifteen thousand people. The volcanic ash in the atmosphere spread a distance of 450 miles within hours.

Yoritomo and his friends were not injured in the blast, but they heard it from twenty miles away. After watching the news reports on the eruption for a half hour, the Prime Minister telephoned Colton's hotel and asked to speak to the visitor from Europe in room 613.

As soon as he had finished talking to the Japanese Leader, Colton turned to Lucienne and said, "I think he'll listen to us from now on."

"Colton, that was the most astounding thing I have ever witnessed in my life!"

"Wonderful wasn't it? Well, what country do we visit next?"

*****

At noon André Renan left his perch overlooking the Rhine valley below and made his way down the rugged trail to the camp where Mireille and the children were hidden. Once again, he had nothing exciting to report.

Three weeks earlier, they had driven the minivan up a tortuous road to an isolated spot in the Vosges Mountains in northeastern France, a few miles west of Colmar. After hiding the van, they had hiked a few hundred yards farther into the forest and had built a makeshift shelter of branches, covering the floor with grass and leaves.

At 12:30 p.m. André reached the floor of the mountain valley and followed a deer trail to the shelter. Mireille and the four children were playing a game near the hideout when he arrived. The two younger children, a girl and a boy, belonged to their friends Pierre and Diane Laborde.

Mireille was always relieved to see her husband return. "See anything?" she asked.

"A few military trucks off to the west, but nothing coming our way."

"Did you eat your food?" André had left before breakfast to watch for signs of the enemy, and Mireille had insisted he take a small meal with him.

"Of course. It was delicious. Thank you. How are the kids?"

"Restless. They say they're sick of camping. It's understandable after nearly three weeks." Mireille handed him a cup of water and a sandwich. "I made this for lunch."

"You're an angel. Thank you."

After watching André eat for a while, Mireille said, "How much longer do you think we'll have to hide in these mountains?"

"I don't know. A few more days perhaps, and then we'll head for Strasbourg."

"But there's no guarantee it will be any different with the people there!" They had sought refuge several times with Mormon friends in eastern France, but when they had arrived at the arranged time, they had discovered that their friends had already fled from persecution.

"I know, but we have to try."

"And if the green coats or the police have also imprisoned our Strasbourg friends?"

"We'll just have to keep moving," André replied.

Mireille sighed. "What do you think happened to Diane and Pierre?"

"Don't worry. I'm sure they're safe." He noticed that the two Laborde children were listening to every word they spoke.

Mireille put her face into her hands and burst into tears. André moved to comfort her as best he could.

*****

The largest concentration camp in France was a few miles from Arras in the north. On the day that Diane and Pierre Laborde were brought to the camp, there were 3,028 men in one compound, and 7,164 women and children in another. The puppet government of France transported two truck-loads of people into the camp every day. The prisoners belonged to any religious or political group which UGOT saw as a threat. Among them were 986 Mormons.

As soon as the new prisoners arrived, they were lined up next to the trucks, issued drab gray uniforms, and cited the camp rules. And the list was long. It was made clear that anyone caught trying to escape, fraternizing with prisoners of the opposite sex or the guards, or breaking any other rule would be executed immediately. The camp commandant, Jules Pigalle, was proud of his sterling record. In the four months that the camp had been in operation, he had found it necessary to shoot only four men for trying to escape. He knew that UGOT hoped to redeem these lost souls, and so he gave strict orders that any guard caught abusing the prisoners beyond the camp guide-lines would also be shot.

Pierre had listened to the indoctrination every day from ten to noon in a barracks large enough to seat two hundred men. He understood that many other sessions were being held all over the camp at the same time. It was always the same thing. UGOT loved them and only wanted what was best for them and the world. Soon the planet would reap the benefits of having one mighty global government which would use the earth's resources for the benefit of all. No longer would the privileged exploit the masses. The new government would eliminate poverty, hunger, war, and disease. The only obligation the people had was to cooperate and obey. Most of all, they must not allow their religious and political beliefs to interfere with future world happiness. Pierre was especially angry when the speakers made subtle refer-ences to the great Semitic Plague which was supposed to be the prime mover of evil in the world.

While the teachers presented their lessons, Pierre sat there quietly, saying nothing. But his heart was full of fury. It was everything he could do to keep from standing and shouting that UGOT was nothing more than another Satan-inspired tyranny. Even though he said nothing during the sessions, he openly attacked UGOT when the prisoners were alone in their barracks at night. He did his best to expose the promises of UGOT as a hoax. He knew that most of his fellow inmates agreed with him, but he didn't realize that soon he would have to pay for his open opposition.

But Pierre's greatest suffering did not come from the indoctrination of UGOT or the harsh conditions of the camp. He was in constant fear concerning the welfare his wife Diane, imprisoned in the women's compound, and his two small children. He had no idea where the children were or even if they were still alive. Many times he considered taking the dangerous risk of escaping from the concentration camp in order to search for them.

*****

The Prophet sat before his counselors, nine members of the Quorum of the Twelve, and other church leaders in a small conference room not far from his office. It was 7:00 a.m. "Brethren, I called this second special meeting today to report on the Mexican problem. First, I want to review the information we have gathered. Then I will relate a communication I had with the Lord... The party we sent to investigate the reports concerning the possible danger from the south returned this morning and confirmed that an army is marching north. Our scouts risked their lives to bring us as much information as they could. Even at that, we do not have many details. Evidently, the army is called the Mexican Army of Liberation. They are nothing except renegades in government uniforms. This army has been forming for five months in the vicinity of the city of Morelia, west of Mexico City. Our latest report indicates that the main part of the army is now approaching the city of Chihuahua, 234 miles south of the U.S. border." The elderly Prophet paused. He was obviously exhausted and having difficulty concentrating. "Perhaps you brethren could help me by asking questions."

The junior apostle said, "President, do we know how many soldiers are in this so-called army?"

The Prophet turned to Elder Jason Widtsoe. "I'll ask Brother Widtsoe to answer that question. He's been working closely with me on the Mexican problem."

Jason replied, "Our scouts don't know for sure. The army seems to be approaching in different divisions by separate routes. The group which they believe to be the main one comprises about ten or fifteen thousand soldiers."

Samuel Law, the Prophet's second counselor asked, "Do we know why they're traveling north? How do we even know they intend to attack us?"

Jason answered, "The radio transmissions which our people intercepted gave us that indication. As for our scouts, they only succeeded in obtaining vague hints that such was the case."

"How long before we can expect them to reach our area?" Harris Craven asked. Harris was the senior apostle.

"No one knows for sure. It might be one month, maybe two."

The junior apostle observed, "But we have many church people living near the Mexican border."

"That's true," Jason agreed.

Another apostle said, "President, I understand that you sent out warnings to church leaders throughout the Rocky Mountains several weeks ago, after our last meeting. I was wondering if you were able to contact most of the stake presidents."

"Most, yes," Josiah said. "We contacted some by radio. To others we sent riders. However, because of difficult communications, it is not possible to update everyone continually. This is especially true now, because someone has been jamming our radio transmissions for the last eight days. We can't even reach Pioneer One."

The Presiding Bishop exclaimed, "Jamming on all frequencies?"

The Prophet waved toward Jason, who replied, "Yes. Whoever is doing this has some sophisticated jamming devices."

The bishop said, "So in effect, it could take weeks for us to contact the entire church in the Rocky Mountains."

"We might be able to do it in a week," Jason answered. "But there's also the problem of how old our reports are when we get them. Remember, brethren, we live in primitive conditions, especially since we no longer have radio communications."

The Prophet stood up and stretched. The joints of his back and knees cracked. "Sorry, brethren, I guess I'm getting old... But now I need to reveal what the Lord told me last night." The leaders sat forward in their chairs. Many of them considered Josiah to be a prophet as great as Moses and knew that the Lord spoke to him face to face. "He said that a multitude of wicked men from the south lusted after the blood of the Saints, and that his people must take action to protect their lives. He commanded me to send word today to warn the Saints."

There was a stunned silence. Finally, Bennion Hicks, the Prophet's first counselor, said solemnly, "So the threat against us is certain, not simply a possibility. What do we tell the Saints to do, President? Did the Lord provide any details? Should we form an army and move south to intercept the enemy?"

"The Lord didn't say. I prayed all night, but He gave me no further directions. However, I intend to continue praying in the hope that He will bless us with that information. At this point, we'll simply tell the Saints what He has revealed. It should be sufficient." The Prophet paused to collect his thoughts. "All right, let us turn to the problem of Pioneer Two. At our meeting on April 26, we decided to postpone the second wagon train because of the outlaws on I-80 and the threat of an attack from the south. Even though the mountain bandits seem to have withdrawn to the area of Bear Lake, there are other problems. At this time we cannot afford to send 5,000 people into the wilderness. First, we do not have the supplies. Second, we should keep our able-bodied men in Utah to meet the present crisis. As a result, I propose to cancel the second wagon train indefinitely. Do any of you disagree?"

The brethren accepted the Prophet's recommendation without question. Most had already come to the same conclusion since their last meeting.

Samuel Law inquired, "What about Pioneer One, President? Won't they be left completely without support?"

"No, the Lord will provide for them."

*****

Carlos Gutierrez, head of military operations for the LDS Maracay colony, and a number of other Venezuelan church leaders, had watched the troops of the National Guard arrive all morning. It was a frightening scene. Their fellow countrymen surrounding the settlement, preparing to use military might to destroy them because of their beliefs. But the Saints knew the real culprits were the men sent by UGOT, the arrogant politicians and the green coats, to infiltrate and control the government and the military.

At noon another Mormon lookout arrived from his post in the hills behind the gathering troops of the Guard. After speaking briefly to Carlos, he returned immediately to his post through one of the tunnels dug beneath the canal which surrounded the LDS community. Carlos motioned for the other leaders, who were standing nearby, to approach. Some were colony residents, but others were visiting from different parts of the country.

"The lookout brought me a report from Ángel Chávez, leader of the Mormon Militia, who estimates that government troops number about ten thousand now. One of our church members in the National Guard sent him a secret note saying that the Guard plans to begin shelling us at 1:00 p.m., an hour from now." The Mormon Militia, which now comprised four thousand soldiers, were concealed in the hills behind the National Guard.

A stake president, Brother Gomez, said, "It looks like they now have from twelve to fourteen pieces of artillery." Gomez, who lived in the colony, had been watching the Guard through binoculars.

A bishop, Jaime Martinez, said, "What are you going to do, Carlos?" Jaime was one of the church leaders who visited the settlement from time to time. Like many Mormons in Venezuela, he helped support the colony, but did not live in this part of the country.

"Nothing...for the moment. We must be sure that they strike first."

"Why haven't you given us more information about what the Guard is doing? How can we help if we don't know what is happening?" Jaime complained.

Carlos replied, "I'm sorry we haven't given you every detail. Even the church leaders here do not know exactly what my plans are. There have been many leaks—"

"Leaks!" exclaimed Pedro Cierva, another visiting bishop.

"Yes, perhaps from this settlement itself. There may be traitors among us, or members who can't keep their mouths shut. We couldn't take chances on the enemy learning how the compound is built or what our plans might be."

The leaders looked at each other with alarm. The very idea of traitors among the Saints was inconceivable.

"Can you tell us now how you plan to defend the settlement?" Ricardo Lerma inquired. Ricardo was a bishop in one of the colony's wards.

"I will only tell you that we have a surprise for the government troops."

The stake president, Brother Gomez, declared, "I know what's in your mind. You propose to shell them or drop bombs on them. But why wait? Let's do it now before they attack. By waiting you risk our lives!"

Carlos frowned. "We can't do that, President Gomez. We've been on the radio with the General Authorities—"

"You succeeded in contacting Salt Lake City?" Bishop Martinez asked.

"Yes. In spite of the jamming, we finally made contact with Elder Jason Widtsoe. Just for a few minutes late at night. We told him about our situation, and he made it clear that the Prophet did not want us to attack first."

"The Prophet is right!" Bishop Cierva exclaimed ironically. "We must not take the offensive, even if they slaughter us before we can move to defend ourselves."

Carlos caught the tone of the bishop's words. "Apparently, bishop, you've forgotten why we built all those bunkers and placed most of our homes underground." Normally a kind, patient man, his voice was now hard. "I suggest we get everyone into the shelters as soon as possible."

An hour later the barrage began. It shook the reinforced concrete bunker where Carlos had secured his wife and grandchildren twenty feet underground. Even though the assault forced the occupants of the shelter to place plugs in their ears and filled their eyes with dust, it caused no serious injuries. After fifteen minutes, the bombardment suddenly stopped.

Carlos heard distant explosions and what seemed to be the rat-a-tat of machine guns. He surmised that the Mormon Militia and their friends must be attacking the National Guard from the hills on the north. He knew also that hundreds of soldiers from the settlement were striking the enemy from the south after crawling out of the compound through the hidden tunnels. This coordinated effort had been carefully planned by Carlos himself weeks earlier. He desperately wanted to leave the bunker and join the fray, but he felt that a man of seventy would be of little use in such fierce fighting. After five hours the noise of the battle ceased, and there was a strange silence. Carlos grieved, knowing that many brave young men had perished that day.

"How did it go?" Carlos asked his young general after climbing out of the bunker at 6:30.

The general smiled proudly. "I believe we accomplished the goals you gave us. Stop them from firing on the settlement, and box them in. We could have wiped them out, but resisted doing so, as you directed."

"I'm grateful you know how to follow orders. We have many brothers in that government army."

"Yes, of course."

"How many men did you lose?" Carlos asked.

"So far the reports say eighteen."

Carlos was amazed that the number of casualties had been so low. "Well, we can be grateful for that." He looked at the chaos around him. "Of course, their artillery destroyed nearly every structure which we built above ground."

"It's a price we had to pay," the general observed. "So what do we do now?"

"We move to the second part of our plan, as soon as it gets dark."

By 10:00 p.m. all was quiet. An hour earlier, the Mormon Militia had withdrawn several miles into the hills so that they would not be seen as an immediate threat by the government camp. In the distance Carlos heard the whine of gears growing steadily louder, as a heavy truck made its way over the winding roads, and then started downward into the federal camp. Standing close to the fence which enclosed the LDS settlement, he listened intently, fearing that at any moment he would hear the sound of guns. But he heard only the muffled shouts of soldiers, and the low growl of the motor as the truck continued to the center of the enemy camp. So far, so good, he thought. Now, if only the natural inclinations of these men would take control of the situation.

A half hour later, unusual things began to happen in the distant enemy camp. Lights flashed in a dozen places, and one could hear the uproarious laughter of men and women and the joyous sounds of music and dancing. Carlos smiled to himself. His plan seemed to be working. The revelry continued until the early morning hours, when at last the enemy camp became still. With the help of his men, Carlos opened the main gate to the Maracay colony, lowered the long ramp, and walked to the National Guard camp. Four hundred armed men followed him, ready to fight at a moment's notice. As he approached the camp, Carlos saw soldiers lying everywhere, helter-skelter. They were clearly sleeping off a heavy drunk. A guardsman suddenly rolled out of an APC and hurried toward him, his face transformed by a wide grin.

"Well, it worked, Brother Gutierrez. Just as you expected."

"So these boys couldn't resist that strong brew we shipped in last night?" Carlos hoped that none of the drugged guardsmen turned out to be Mormons.

"Nope. They sucked it up until they dropped. Fifteen barrels of it, I think."

At that moment they were joined by other LDS guardsmen, soldiers of the Mormon Militia, and two dozen sisters in wild party dresses.

Carlos laughed. "You sisters sure don't dress like that in church! And what about the word of wisdom?" Even though he was sad that some had died in the battle, it could have been much worse. He was delighted that his stratagem had saved so many lives.

The first soldier grinned even more than before. "We only drank from the barrels marked with a red stripe, the ones full of Kool-Aid."

"Yuck! I despise the nasty stuff!" a relief society president said, her mouth ringed by a bright red stain.

Carlos replied, "Come here, all of you. I want to smell your breath—no, I'm just kidding. And what about the morals problem?"

A primary president scowled. "Hah! Some of these boys got pretty frisky at times. But we handled it fine. A lot more whiskey and a purse with a rock inside!"

"Brilliant!" Carlos exclaimed. "I should have thought of that myself. Did you disarm all these boys?"

"Certainly," the relief society president replied. "With the help of our fantastic LDS soldiers. We're very wise to the ways of the world, you know."

"That's what I'm afraid of," Carlos teased.

*****

The assassin's bullet almost killed David Omert. An inch or two to the left and it would have exploded his head. Fortunately, a woman passed by, just before the gunman pulled the trigger, and spoiled his aim. The bullet struck the tip of David's left ear, and the attacker quickly disappeared in the crowd.

"Do the police have any clues as to who the shooter was?" Menachem Hazony asked. Menachem was David's uncle and the current Minister of Defense of the State of Israel. By his brilliant planning and bold operations, he had saved his country from destruction in the last war with the Arabs.

David held the towel against his ear to stop the flow of blood. "No, no one saw anything."

Chaim Yehoshua said, "They suspect it was an Arab nationalist or a Jewish extremist."

The doctor entered the hospital room, removed the towel, and examined David's ear. "It's not serious. I'll have a nurse dress the wound." A moment later a nurse arrived with a bandage and some antiseptic and began to treat the injury.

Menachem said, "He could have belonged to a dozen different factions, all of them violent. There are so many groups in Israel today who think that violence is the only solution to their problems."

Chaim said, "The worst are the Palestinians. Do you know how the average Palestinian kid is raised?"

"Yes," David replied. "He's taught to hate and destroy his enemies from the time he's a baby."

Menachem said, "Is that right? I didn't know they were that extreme. I'm ashamed to admit that I've never known any Palestinians personally. I do my best to stay away from them. Since I've been Minister of Defense, they've threatened my life a hundred times and opposed everything I've tried to do."

"You should see how they train their children," Chaim said. "They teach their boys and girls to attack physically anyone they see as their enemy. They praise them when they win a fight and ridicule them when they lose."

"That's incredible!" Menachem declared. He looked at David. "Well, have you decided how you're going to handle Israel's problems when you become Prime Minister in a few days?"

"I'm not certain that Likud will capture the majority of seats in this election," David said.

"I believe it's a done deal," Menachem replied.

Chaim said, "I agree with your uncle, David. It's a certainty that Likud will win and that it will choose you as Prime Minister. Then you can reinstate Menachem as Minister of Defense, name me as Chief Advisor, make permanent friends of the Arabs, solve the Palestinian problem, and create a united Israel for the first time in history."

"Chaim, you should be a stand-up comedian. As if it were that easy. The truth is, I don't have any cures—instant or otherwise. The leaders of Likud only informed me three weeks ago that they wanted me to take the position."

Chaim replied, "True, but you've been analyzing the problems for years... At any rate, the extremists made a mistake in assassinating Abraham Samet."

"Yes, indeed," Menachem said. "David's a much better choice for the Likud than Abraham Samet... Of course, nephew, your greatest problem will be how to reconcile the Israelis with the Palestinians and the other Arabs, and still maintain the freedom and security of the State of Israel. Knowing that you will be Prime Minister, I'm reassured that Israel will not surrender the Golan Heights to Syria simply because they make offers of peace. If you did, Syria would control our sources of water to the Sea of Galilee and the Jordan River."

David said, "I'm well aware of your feelings concerning the Golan Heights, uncle. I assure you that I agree with you completely."

Menachem smiled. "But have you thought about what you'll do to draw Israel together? We've forty political parties who can't agree on anything, seven terrorist groups, regular suicide bombings and assassinations, thousands of teenagers toting guns in broad daylight, religious intolerance, a growing crime rate, open displays of hatred on the streets, and a ring of implacable enemies who watch for every opportunity to annihilate us."

Chaim said, "You forgot that UGOT is promoting every kind of propaganda against us, and the fact that we no longer have the support of the former United States. And what about the cultural differences among the Jews themselves? On the one hand, we have the westernized yuppies who spend their time in fancy restaurants and expensive resorts, don't believe in any God, and whose only concern is how much their investments will bring in. On the other hand, there are the religious Jews, who wear strange clothes and hair styles, and believe the slightest deviance from traditional ways is a direct offense against the God of Israel Himself."

"Yes, the problems seem insurmountable," David muttered sadly.

Chaim went on, "It does seem that way. But if you're not voted out in the next election, which is usually the case, and if you're not assassinated—"

At that moment Chaim saw Menachem glaring at him and his mouth snapped shut.

David laughed at his friend. He knew that Chaim often acted like a comedian, and many leaders did not take him seriously, but there was no one David trusted more to give him honest, insightful suggestions. "Listen, both of you, I've dreamed of ways to solve these problems, but as yet I've no certain answers."

Menachem softened, clearly sensitive to the position his nephew was in. He put his hand on David's shoulder and said, "It's a great burden to place on one so young."

Chaim could not resist one more statement. "No problem. With our help, David will solve every difficulty in no time at all."

Chapter 16

On Wednesday, May 17, Pioneer One began their final schedule. It meant arising at 5:00 a.m., hitting the road by 6:30, and stopping at 7:30 p.m. Knowing that they would travel twelve hours a day from then on, under normal circumstances, Steven hoped to make much better time. He figured that the caravan was at least a week behind schedule. Even though there were many up-and-down grades, the overall climb was fairly gradual. The people who took bicycles enjoyed themselves going down, but worked up a terrible sweat going up. From checking his maps, Steven saw that the elevation at Creston Junction was only about four hundred feet higher than it was at Rock Springs, eighty-four miles back.

By 8:00 a.m. a cover of clouds filled the sky, blocking the hot sun. From time to time it drizzled, making travel cool and pleasant in comparison with the heat of past weeks. The greatest difficulty was that the caravan had to leave the highway every ten to fifteen miles to bypass sections which were demolished by floods or explosives.

After riding up and down the caravan to check on his people, Steven dismounted, tied the mustang to his wagon, and came forward to walk where he could see Mary. He looked at her often, puckered as much as possible, and threw her kiss after kiss. At first her eyes danced, then rolled, and finally refused to look his way. His three children and the six Cartwright kids alternated between trudging beside him, chattering incessantly, and running around the wagon playing games and screaming so loud that he heard their voices echo from the nearby bluffs. He was delighted that his legs no longer hurt and that he felt stronger and more fit. He knew that many others in the wagon train had the same feelings.

At about 10:30 Ruther rode up to the wagon. After tying his mule next to the mustang, he caught up with Steven. "Makin' good time?"

"Yes. We just passed Junction 196. That means we traveled more than nine miles in four hours."

"Not bad. Think we'll make twenty-seven miles by day's end?"

"I doubt it. The people get tired after 3:00 p.m. I'd be pleased if we made twenty-two or twenty-three miles."

"Well, the weather's right fer it."

They walked a hundred yards without speaking. Then Ruther said,

"Hope I didn't upset you folks arguing about religion and sech last night."

"Heavens no! I loved it. It wasn't an argument, but a friendly conversation."

"I see'd one or two people frownin' and I figured they was annoyed at me fer questionin' things."

"I didn't notice. Besides, who cares? It never fails that when some people hear others discussing a serious gospel subject, or any subject for that matter, the first thing they say is 'contention is of the devil.' You can be talking in the kindest, calmest way possible, and still they cry 'argument!'"

"I wonder why that is," Ruther replied.

"There are dozens of reasons, no doubt. I suppose it depends on the person."

"Maybe so," Ruther mused. After a moment, he went on, "Ya don't think much of us Baptists, do ya?"

Steven dodged the Cartwrights' five-year-old boy, who came charging by, pretending he was Geronimo. "What? I love the Baptists. They're wonderful people."

"But ya think we're lost on a trail headin' nowheres."

"Oh no! I just think some Baptists are intolerant of the beliefs of others."

"What do ya mean?"

"Well, last January, I read Floyd McElveen's book called God's Word, Final, Infallible, and Forever. Floyd's a conservative Baptist."

"Yep, I've read it. He spends a lot of time attackin' you Mormons.

"That's right. At first he claims he loves the Mormons. He only wants to bring them to God. But in most of the book, he misrepresents what we believe—actually he doesn't understand what we believe. And he uses arguments produced by Mormon apostates. At the same time, he ignores all the evidence which Mormon writers have given to show the falsehood of the apostate arguments."

"Yep. I admit that Floyd gets purdy ornery sometimes."

"He sure does. And he constantly shifts from one argument to another."

"What do ya mean?"

"He constantly makes the point that God's word is perfect and true and unchanging."

"Ya disagree with that?"

"No. Mormons agree on that point. But again and again, Floyd moves subtly from talking about the perfection of God's word, which is easy to accept, to the perfection of the Bible, which is impossible to prove. We agree that God's word is infallible and complete, but that's not the same as saying the Bible is infallible and complete."

Ruther looked perplexed. "Why not?"

"Mainly because the Bible is not the only word of God. We accept as the word of God many scriptures which are not in the Bible."

Ruther replied, "I heard about that. Ya also have yer Mormon Bible."

"Yes, and other scriptures."

"So ya think I do the same thing as Floyd?"

"No, I haven't seen you do that. But you seem to interpret the Bible like Floyd does. Many Baptists do the same."

"What do ya mean?"

"Well, they maintain that the readings of the Bible are perfect and should be respected. But when they explain scripture, they make personal interpretations of some verses and ignore others."

"Ya mean when we pick the passages on faith and ignore the ones on works?"

"That's one example out of many. That's why we get so many different perfect interpretations from the Baptists we meet."

"I like the way you think, Steve," Ruther said. "I'm not sayin' I go along with ya, but I like the way ya think. Do ya have a copy of that thar Mormon Bible? I've read the regular Bible ten times, and it might be relaxin' ta read somethin' a bit different. I'm not sayin' you're pursuadin' me ta become no Mormon, but I'd like ta see what yer book preaches."

"I'll get you one when we stop for lunch."

By the time they stopped at 12:30 for lunch and rest, the pioneers had traveled twelve miles beyond Creston Junction, and Steven was very pleased. The light rain which had fallen during the morning had become little more than a pleasant mist carried on a gentle breeze. While Mary and Jennifer made lunch, Steven decided to explore the country north of the freeway. With his rifle slung across his back, he followed a draw for a quarter mile until he was out of sight of the wagon train. A few minutes later, he came to the top of a ridge and saw a small valley a hundred yards ahead. There was a tiny stream flowing through the valley, and this side of the stream, a stand of trees. He hiked down to the trees and sat on a boulder in the shade. He was impressed by how pleasant the place was and how completely isolated from the rest of the world. For a moment he forgot his filthy, sweaty clothes, which had not been washed or changed in a week.

After resting for a while, he arose to return, but was startled by a noise behind him. He whirled around and was shocked to see a man standing twenty feet away, smiling agreeably. He appeared to be about twenty-seven years old and six feet tall. He had light brown hair and piercing blue eyes. His strikingly handsome face showed no blemish, and communicated candor and innocence. His body was average in build, but his movements suggested great physical strength. Steven was surprised at the man's clothes. He wore Levi's, hiking boots, and a multicolored sport shirt. He had no hat to shade his eyes from the rays of the sun. But the shocking thing to Steven was that his visitor seemed to have just stepped out of a fashionable spa in clean new clothes for a pleasant stroll in the hills.

"Good afternoon," the stranger said in a friendly voice.

"Good afternoon," Steven replied.

"Out for a walk?"

"Yes, and you?" Steven wanted to ask him why he was so clean.

"Yes, it's a good day for it. Rather isolated here, isn't it?"

"It sure is."

The man raised his hand to shade his eyes from the sun, which suddenly appeared from behind a cloud. "Do you belong to that wagon train on the highway?"

"I'm the leader," Steven said with a touch of pride. He saw the glimmer of a smile return to the stranger's face.

"I see. I should have guessed. You do have the appearance of a man of authority. But it seems strange to see such a large group of people traveling in this dangerous, forbidding land. May I ask where you're going?"

Steven hesitated, not wanting to reveal anything to a stranger. "We're heading east."

The man grinned. "I see that."

Steven couldn't resist any longer. "May I ask you a question?"

"Of course."

"What are you doing out here? Where do you live? Why aren't you carrying a weapon? Why are your clothes so clean?"

The man continued to smile maddeningly and did not look at his clothes. "That's four questions."

Steven was embarrassed by his overwhelming curiosity. "I'm sorry. It's just—"

"There's a small community about a mile from here." He pointed to the north. "On the other side of that ridge. It's a trading post, so to speak. We used to live in Rawlins, the town twelve miles east of here. However, when that town was occupied by bandits, we left to seek refuge at our cabin."

"Who is *we*?"

"A few trusted friends and I."

Steven said, "Do you have any supplies to spare?"

"I'm afraid not. Only enough for our needs. So why are you going to Mi— east." The stranger frowned.

The man had slipped, and Steven knew it. How could this man possibly know they were heading for Missouri? His instincts told him to disclose as little as possible. "We're seeking a land where we can be safe and happy."

"But you're moving away from the only safe place in the entire conti nent. Utah and the surrounding region are the only areas where you can find food, shelter, and safety."

"How do you know that?"

The irritating smile continued. "We hear radio reports. I have learned that after you pass Laramie, this freeway no longer exists. The land all the way across eastern Wyoming and Nebraska has been scorched by armies strug- gling to destroy each other. There is not a tree or blade of grass left. The lakes and rivers have either dried up or been poisoned. The same is true in Iowa and Missouri. To travel east is certain death. Death from famine, drought, pollution, or roving gangs of maniacs who survive only by destroying the innocent. I cannot tell you what to do, but I say that if you love your wife, your children, and your people, you will turn around and go back."

Steven's mind was seized by a terrible fear, and he struggled hard to control himself. "Thank you for your advice. I didn't realize how bad things were. The reports we have must be mistaken. I'll present your information and suggestions to the other leaders of the wagon train."

"You really have no choice," the stranger said. "You are the one who is responsible. Their lives are in your hands."

"I'm sure you're right."

"Yes, of course," the man said calmly. "Well, I have other things to do now. Good day and good luck." At that, he strolled eastward down the valley near the stream until he disappeared from sight.

Steven's heart was pounding wildly. He had never felt such fear. Somehow he knew that the stranger had sensed his terror and had relished it. Steven wasted no time. He climbed the next ridge, the one on the north. From the crest he searched the wide basin below for some time with a small pair of binoculars. Then he hiked back down the hill toward the wagon train.

Several hundred yards from the pioneer column, he thought he saw a movement on a descending ridge to his right. Could it be the same young man? Was he spying on Pioneer One for some reason? Steven decided to check. Turning right out of the draw, he labored up the slope. He surmounted the ridge and descended into another gully. There was no one in sight. He continued downward until the shallow gully emptied onto the flatter land not far from the highway. A short time later he saw a woman standing in the shade of a nearby cliff. It was Anastasia. As he drew near, she spun around, and he saw tears streaming from her eyes.

"Anastasia! Do you need help?"

She quickly wiped the tears from her eyes and said, "Steven! It's you... No, it's nothing."

"What's the matter? Can I help?"

At those words, she threw herself into his arms, sobbing. As he felt her face wet against his neck, his eyes darted around to see if anyone was watching.

After a minute of weeping, she couldn't keep her secret. "He doesn't want me!"

"Who doesn't want you?"

"Pierce Hudson!"

"Oh."

"He told me he loved another woman!"

"Who?"

"Rachel Crell. He wants her because she's younger and more beautiful than me."

Steven remembered that Rachel was the third bachelorette traveling with Anastasia and Andrea Warren. It was difficult for him not to laugh. Anastasia was always so melodramatic. He couldn't imagine any woman in the caravan being more beautiful than she. If Pierce chose another woman over Anastasia, he certainly had better reasons than those Anastasia imagined.

"Anastasia, that's not possible. You're one of the most beautiful women in our caravan." He tried to free himself from her embrace, but she held on stubbornly. "Anastasia, please let me go. Someone might see and get the wrong idea."

In a flash she stood on tiptoe, kissed him squarely on the mouth, and released him abruptly. "You're so sweet. It's too bad you're married."

In spite of the theatrics, Steven sensed that deep down she really was hurt that Pierce had picked someone else. He decided to console her as much as he could. "There are at least six or seven young men in the wagon train who would give anything to marry you. All you have to do is show some interest. Besides, if Pierce chose another woman, why should that upset you so much? It's good for you to know now how he really feels. I can't think of anything worse than ending up married to someone who doesn't truly love you." Steven felt stupid. Every possible consolation he could think of rolled from his lips, without much thought. Some counselor he was!

"You simply don't understand how a woman feels in a situation like this. I'd rather die than think of another man. No, I'll never find anyone as wonderful as Pierce... But thank you for caring, Steven." After crying awhile longer, she dried her tears and said, "What young men?"

Steven rattled off the name of every available man he could think of, including Paul's. After listening to him intently, Anastasia declared with spite, "Well! I might have to marry every one of them to end up with one decent man!" At those words, she stomped away toward the caravan.

During the six hours of travel in the afternoon the caravan covered a record ten miles, for a total of twenty-two miles that day in spite of the grade upward. They pulled off the highway at 7:30 just past the continental divide and drew the wagons into three separate circles. They were only two miles from Rawlins. During the evening, as he went about his regular routine, Steven couldn't stop thinking about his unusual encounter with the stranger in the hills. During the leaders' meeting at 8:00, he considered mentioning it, but finally decided against it.

Besides, the leaders could talk about nothing except the dangers their families might be facing in Utah. They became even more anxious when John dropped the bombshell that the batteries he had saved for use in the radio were now depleted.

Steven decided to discuss the stranger with Mary later. He wondered if Rawlins was really inhabited by bandits as the unusual man had said. To be safe, he asked John to double the guards for the night watches.

That night, when their family was alone, Steven and Mary read to the children by the light of a lamp. Because of the increased hours of travel, the kids were extremely tired and fell asleep fifteen minutes later. After putting out the lamp and snuggling up to Mary as usual, Steven related the story of the stranger.

"That's weird!" Mary exclaimed. "Who do you think he was?"

"I'm not sure. At first I had no reason to doubt what he said. He seemed like a good man, a very special man. But then he said things which didn't ring true. And by the time he left, I was scared half to death."

"I know who he was."

Steven laughed. "How could you? You weren't even there."

"No, but from what you said he said and did, it's perfectly clear."

"It is?"

"Yes."

"Okay, Miss Smarty-pants, who was he?"

"Satan."

"You're kidding!"

"No, I'm serious."

"What makes you think that?"

"A lot of things," Mary said firmly. "He appeared out of nowhere, looking clean and fresh as a daisy, and carrying no weapon. He was young, good-looking, and had light brown hair. He knew we were heading to Missouri. He lied about there being a lodge on the other side of the ridge. He contradicted the revelations of the Prophet by trying to get you to turn back after his frightful description of the dangers ahead. He inspired terrible fear in your heart. And finally, he strolled off into nowhere as if he were heading for the mall."

"Don't you think your imagination is getting the best of you? Do you think Satan would be dumb enough to make a verbal slip which showed he knew we were going to Missouri?"

"How could a regular person, a genuine stranger, know where we were going?"

"Good question," Steven answered. "But why didn't I experience some cosmic evil force oppressing me like Joseph Smith felt in the Sacred Grove when Satan was there?"

"I don't know. Maybe he handles different people in different ways," Mary said simply.

Steven thought about that a moment. "Okay...but what do his looks and hair have to do with it?"

"That's an easy question to answer. In the first place, Joseph Smith said Satan has sandy-colored hair. Also, we know he's an ageless spirit and used to be the Son of the Morning and the Bearer of Light. These things suggest to me that he's good-looking and in the prime of youth."

"But, Mary, wouldn't his great wickedness make him look very ugly?"

"He's ugly inside, but not outside. That's one of the reasons why he can deceive people and appear as an angel of light. It's related to the idea that Satan often tells people the truth to get them to accept a lie."

"Where do you get that from? Satan appearing as an angel of light?"

"Steven! You've heard that before. Joseph Smith said it, and it's in Second Corinthians."

"But in the Book of Moses, when Satan appeared, Moses said he could distinguish Satan from God because Satan had no glory. That suggests to me that he didn't appear as an angel of light. How do you explain that?"

"Well, as I said before, he appears to people in different ways," Mary said. "Sometimes he appears in glory, and at other times he doesn't... Wait! I have an idea. Maybe he can appear to an unrighteous man as an angel of light because he has more power to deceive him. But he can't do it when he comes to a righteous man, like Moses, who can see through his deceptions."

"So where does that put me?"

"What do you mean?"

Steven gave a mischievous smile. "Well, my visitor, the man you think is Satan, appeared to me looking something between glorious and ordinary. So what does that say about me?"

Mary poked him in the ribs. "You sure can be silly sometimes. I was only making a few personal observations, not reciting orthodox doctrine. Actually, you must be a real threat to Satan for him to try to influence you that way."

"You'd better believe it!" Steven giggled and began to wrestle with Mary until she let out a loud squeal. "Whew! That was fun! Now, to get back to Satan. If I really believe it was Satan, I'd be scared to death right now. But the truth is—and I hate to admit it—I'm impressed by your idea that the stranger might have been old Lucifer. It never occurred to me."

"You need to pay better attention, young man. As the leader of this wagon train, you should develop the spirit of discernment."

"Why should I? I've got you."

Mary poked him a few more times, and he answered by tickling her until she couldn't stand it. After they rested for a while, Steven said seriously, "You know, the problem of light and glory gets even more confusing when you think about deity appearing to mortals."

"What do you mean?"

"Well, sometimes God appears to people in glory and they must be transfigured by the Holy Ghost to avoid being consumed. That happened to Moses on the mountain. But when the resurrected Lord appeared to the two disciples on the road to Emmaus in the Book of Luke, they didn't recognize Him or realize He was a divine being. There's no evidence that they were transformed. And when God appeared to the murderer Cain and questioned him about Abel, there was no way such a wicked man could have been protected from God's glory by the Spirit."

"So how do you explain it?"

Steven laughed. "I explain it by saying there are a lot of things I don't know how to explain. Maybe He just withholds his glory when there's a good reason. In any case, it tells me how kind and loving He really is."

"Why do you say that?"

Steven sighed and put his arm around Mary's waist. "Well...I used to ask myself why God didn't simply reveal Himself. Then I could ask all the questions I wanted and get it over with."

"But we have to live by faith."

"That's essential, of course, but there's another reason too."

"Which is?" Mary replied sleepily.

"If He appeared when we wanted Him to, we would probably be consumed by the fiery heat of His celestial body. That's why we must first be holy enough to receive the Holy Ghost, who transforms us so we can endure the Lord's presence. On the other hand, God may also use the technique of restraining His glory."

"It's funny to hear you describe it as a technique... But why do you say 'us'? What makes you think the Lord will ever appear to us in this life?"

"Mary! You know the answer to that."

"I do... Yes, of course... But I'm so...too sleepy to think. Remind me."

"The prophecies say He will visit the Saints at New Jerusalem and Adam-ondi-Ahman. There's a chance we'll be there."

Mary's eyes popped open in the dark. "Oh great! Now I know what I'll dream about all night."

The next day Pioneer One reached Rawlins by noon. At the head of a group of twenty men, Steven rode into town. They found a small community of five hundred survivors, who were very friendly and grateful to see them. They had a small amount of extra flour, salt, and sugar, and asked the brethren if they wanted to trade. When Steven offered them some of the guns and ammunition recovered from the bandits, the townspeople accepted immediately. They too had trouble with roving outlaws and would soon be without the means to protect themselves. They threw the supplies into two wagons, and the entire community followed the Mormon party to the wagon train.

As soon as they reached Pioneer One, the townspeople expressed amazement that so many people would dare to travel such a great distance from their homes. After unloading the supplies, John and the bachelors put fifteen automatic rifles and a thousand rounds of ammunition into the wagons. Then the townspeople and the pioneers fellowshipped with one another during the lunch break. Seeing the kindness of these people, Steven realized that the stranger in the hills had lied when he had claimed that Rawlins was infested with bandits. Maybe Mary was right about him being Satan, Steven thought.

Two hours later, the Saints hugged and kissed their new friends and said farewell. They exchanged mementos they really didn't need, and the pioneers gave the citizens copies of the Book of Mormon. The townspeople accepted the gifts with tears, especially the books, for their enemies had burned their reading material in a huge bonfire several months before while the people were running for their lives in the wilderness. Two non-Mormon families joined the wagon train in vehicles the Moderns had found for them in the local wrecking yard.

That night the Saints halted at Exit 221, having covered twenty-two miles under the protection of a sky full of clouds. The next two days they trekked another forty miles. On the second day they stopped at Exit 260, not far from Elk Mountain. After such strenuous travel, the pioneers were grateful that the next day was Sunday, a day of needed rest. Steven had heard that sometimes the wind could gust to more than eighty miles an hour on I-80 near Elk Mountain, but today, thankfully, the breeze was just gentle enough to cool the travelers down.

On Sunday morning one of the sisters awoke to find her fifty-year-old husband lying dead next to her. Dr. Price examined the body, but could discover no specific cause for the death. After a quick burial ceremony, the Saints held their meetings as usual. Even though there was sadness in the camp, they were becoming accustomed to death, and so in the afternoon they spent their time reading, playing games, singing, and talking. The leaders had difficulty controlling the children who wanted to run off into the fascinating countryside to explore. As always, a ring of guards kept watch over the encampment. By late afternoon, Steven began to notice that Mary seemed sullen and avoided looking at him.

When he finally saw her alone, preparing the evening meal, he sat beside her and said, "What's the matter? Are you mad at me?"

"What do you care?" She arose abruptly and stormed away.

He looked after her, having no idea what the problem was. Selena, his ex-wife, had often run away exactly like that when she was upset with him. It was usually something he should have done or said, but hadn't. Once, Selena had styled her hair in a new fashion, and he had not noticed—after all, hair is hair! But he should have noticed—somehow! And once he had bought her a fancy electric can opener for her birthday, but he shouldn't have—for some reason—because she was very upset. To this day he still didn't know why she had been so mad.

And that business about repairs. All Selena had to do was mention— one time in an offhand way—that she wanted him to fix something, and before long he was in deep trouble. Usually it was some trivial thing she wanted done, which he genuinely planned to do some day—just to make her happy, not because he thought the darn thing needed fixing. And anyhow, why did she ask him in the first place when she knew he was a complete klutz who had difficulty screwing in a light bulb? The result was, well, he simply forgot. Then the expected happened: he paid a heavy price for his little oversight for weeks afterwards!

And women could be so emotional. One minute you thought they hated you and regretted marrying such a jerk, and the next minute they were bawling their heads off because you didn't kiss them good night. Steven sincerely doubted that there was any man on earth who could truly understand a woman.

Steven was lost in these "profound" thoughts when Andrea and Paul appeared. After they had spent several minutes talking about very little, Paul said, "What's up, Steve? Why so sad?"

"Oh, Mary's mad at me. And I have no idea why."

"I can tell you why," Paul replied quickly.

Steven looked at his brother hopefully. "Why?"

Paul grinned and his eyes flicked to Andrea. "She's a woman. They don't need a reason."

Andrea punched him. "You little baboon. You'd give anything if one of the unmarried women around here would take you seriously." She looked at Steven. "I can tell you the real reason Mary's upset. That's why I'm here. Can I reveal the secret in front of this character?"

"Paul? Certainly. I trust him."

"Well, the grapevine has it that you were seen hugging and kissing Anastasia out in the boonies."

"What?"

"Not that I believe a word of it, mind you. But that's the gossip. It seems that someone started telling the juicy little story around camp a few days ago, and it got to Mary this morning."

"Have you heard this gossip too, Paul?"

"Yeah, I heard a few things, but I laughed it off."

Steven said, "Tell me everything people are saying."

Andrea began, "Okay. It seems that someone saw you and Anastasia leave camp together several days ago around noon. You spent some time holding hands and talking intimately, and ended up hugging and kissing passionately. The conclusion is that you've been having an affair with Anastasia."

Steven was outraged. "Not one word is true! How can Mary believe it? Actually, I don't remember ever being alone with Anastasia, except five minutes last Wednesday." Steven told them the story of his encounter with the weeping Anastasia.

"Have you told this to Mary?" Andrea asked.

"No. I didn't know there was a problem. But now, I doubt she'd listen to anything I had to say after the way she acted a few minutes ago."

"I'm going to solve this issue right now," Andrea said firmly. "Which way did she go?" Steven indicated the direction. "Stay here. I'll be back in a little while."

Paul said, "I'll help you find her."

"No. Stay here with Steve. This is a job for Superwoman. You'll only get in the way." Andrea stomped away, a determined look in her eye.

"Whew!" Paul said. "You don't want to mess with Andrea when she gets like that."

"Yes, she's quite a woman. Too bad some guy hasn't recognized it yet. What do you think she's going to do?"

Paul sat next to Steven. "I have no idea, but I intend to wait here and find out."

They spent the next forty minutes discussing the inscrutable nature of women. After deciding that they probably wouldn't uncover any profound truths, they saw Mary and Andrea approaching. Steven was shocked to see that both were smiling.

As soon as she reached Steven, Mary kissed him on the mouth and said, "I'm sorry. I love you."

Steven's eyes went to Andrea. "So what did you do?"

"I made Mary come with me to find Anastasia. It didn't take long. All I had to do was locate the nearest batch of available males, and there she was doing her thing. It's a good thing polyandry isn't legal. I told her we needed to talk. She said she was busy. I said that if she didn't come with us, I'd tell every eligible bachelor in the caravan what she said about them late at night in our wagon. She followed us immediately to a spot a little way from camp."

Paul said, "This is great! I can't wait to tell Jarrad and Leonard."

"This you will keep a secret!" Andrea said imperiously. Paul shut up. Andrea continued, "I related every bit of the gossip to Anastasia. She denied everything. I gave her the worst evil eye I could muster and asked her if she didn't have something she wanted to get off her conscience. She hemmed and hawed a minute, but finally admitted that she was the one who had hugged and kissed Steven that day, in spite of the fact that he had tried to escape. I told her that if she even so much as fluttered an eye at him in the future, I'd personally make her life a living you know what during the rest of this trip. After that, Mary and I left her standing there looking like she'd just lost her last bag of makeup."

Mary said sadly, "Steven, I'm sorry I didn't trust you. I should have known you wouldn't cheat on me."

Steven hugged her and said, "It's probably my fault. I know Anastasia is a flirt, and I shouldn't have tried to console her when nobody else was around. Hopefully, I've learned my lesson."

"You'll just have to be extra careful during this trip," Paul said. "Like me." When they did not laugh as he expected, Paul went on in a more serious vein, "The gossip seems unusually bad and it spreads like wild fire. Jarrad and Leonard believe that there are people traveling with us who are doing their best to discredit Steven, John, and me."

"I agree with you," Andrea said. "I've heard rumors that John is making up the story that a foreign army is threatening Utah. He's supposedly doing it so the pioneers will depend more on the Christopher brothers. Also, I've heard that Paul is a wild, unstable womanizer."

"Womanizer!" Paul exclaimed. "I don't even have one woman."

"You do now, my friend," Andrea quipped. "It appears that everyone knows who they are except you. I'm surprised people aren't saying I'm one of your girlfriends."

Paul replied, "Yeah, why aren't they? Is that so impossible?"

"Definitely. I don't believe in robbing cradles."

"Okay, you two," Steven said. "That's enough. We have a serious problem here. Paul, have you uncovered any further evidence as to who is circulating the rumors?"

"We're following some very good clues. It's only a matter of time before we find the guilty party."

"Okay, let me know when you get something substantial."

Chapter 17

During the following week the weather remained mild along I-80, and the sun was partially blocked by cloud cover. The temperature never rose above seventy-nine degrees, even during the hottest part of the day. The combination of a fairly decent road, good weather, beautiful scenery, and relatively few problems infused the pioneers with energy and enthusiasm. One could often hear them laughing and singing as they marched along. In the evening they square-danced, had miniconcerts, and played group games. In five days Pioneer One covered a hundred and twenty-one miles, moving between two great mountain ranges of the Medicine Bow National Forest, past the cities of Laramie and Cheyenne, and down onto the western edge of the semiarid high plains of eastern Wyoming.

The pioneers were surprised when they saw no inhabitants whatsoever during the entire week. Along the freeway they spied bears, elks, deer, prong-horns, moose, squirrels, hawks, and other animals, but no people. It was as if the pioneers were the only human beings left on the face of the earth. While they were traveling over the Laramie Plains heading for Laramie, Steven decided to dispatch scouts to investigate every town and city on the highway, before the caravan reached them. Soon his men came back with terrible reports.

Every community was a scene of horror. It appeared as though some great army had swept through the region, killing every person and burning every structure. After examining the evidence, Ruther and the leaders of the caravan surmised that the citizens of the area had fought bloody civil wars in order to survive, either between local factions or with government forces.

In the following days, the light rains and the cloud cover disappeared, and the temperatures soared. In spite of the fact that the highway was in good condition and was descending rapidly through eastern Wyoming and western Nebraska, the pioneers suffered greatly from the hot winds and the blazing sun. It was everything they could do to place one foot in front of the other as they trudged along slowly, bodies aching and bathed in sweat, clothes heavy with dirt. It was easier for the cyclists. They could frequently move at a fairly good pace, expending little energy, with a soft breeze in their faces.

Steven asked a number of pioneers if they wanted to shorten the travel time, for a few days, to make things easier, but they smiled and refused.

Steven suspected that some didn't want to be seen as weak, but he was sure that most wanted to please God and were searching within themselves to discover what they were made of. Steven had to admire them. Like their leader, the pioneers still had many weaknesses, but they were growing in strength, courage, and faith.

Because of this doggedness, Pioneer One averaged more than nineteen miles a day for two weeks, covering a total of two hundred and twenty-nine miles. As they passed some communities, including Kimball, Sidney, Ogallala, and North Platte, the pioneers found friendly remnants of people doing their best to survive the difficult times. They lived in primitive conditions, without public services, television, medical facilities, or modern industries.

In spite of that, they gave the Saints small quantities of food, helped them repair wagons, and added to their stock. They contributed a number of modern vehicles for the travelers to convert into "covered wagons." The pioneers paid for some of these things, but most they had to accept as gifts of kindness. At times the local residents allowed them to work for what they obtained. In contrast to the situation in Utah and Wyoming, the pioneers found an abundance of safe water, for now their route paralleled the north bank of the Platte River.

After resting on Sunday, June 11, they set out the next day at the usual time. By 10:00 a.m. a mass of dark clouds formed in the northwestern sky and the atmosphere became more turbulent. By the time they stopped to rest and eat lunch, after covering eleven miles, the storm hit them. Thunder rumbled in the distance, and lightning cracked all around them, illuminating the black sky with jagged streaks of light. As the pioneers ran for cover, the children screamed and clung to their parents.

The most violent part of the thunderstorm was over in forty-five minutes. All that remained was a moderate breeze and a continual downpour of drenching rain. At 1:30 p.m. the caravan started again. Steven, Ruther, and the bachelors walked a hundred yards ahead of the lead wagon, searching for barriers or breaks in the highway. Steven could barely see his scouts a half mile farther on. They were on both sides of the road, about two hundred yards out, watching for possible enemies. As they passed various landmarks, Steven tried to keep track of where the wagon train was on his map in spite of the wind and rain. He was pleased to see that they were still making good time. They would travel twenty miles by the end of the day.

All at once Paul stopped short and said, "Look! The highway!"

Steven looked up from the map and checked the road. Two hundred yards ahead he saw that the highway ended abruptly. He stared into the distance as far as he could see, almost a mile, and saw no trace of the road. "What happened, Ruther?" Steven asked frantically.

"Don't rightly know. But it appears ta me that a flood or somethin' just swept this entire road south. Probably inta the Platte River. It ain't more than a half mile from here."

They walked to the end of the highway and looked down. Not only the surface, but the entire roadbed had disappeared to a depth of seven feet. They saw nothing but a gigantic pit of mud which resembled the surrounding prairie. The wind began to howl and swept the rain in biting sheets against their bodies. A minute later Mary pulled up behind them and stopped.

"What do you suggest, Ruther?" Steven called.

"Well, it's up ta you. We can stay here on the highway and wait the storm out, or we can roll down the side and plod through the mud."

"How much time do you think we'll lose if we wait it out?"

Ruther grabbed his hat as a gust of wind nearly carried it away. Then he peered at Steven from beneath the brim dripping with water. "Cain't rightly tell," he yelled. "This here storm could go on fer another day or it could last two weeks. After that, ya might want ta wait until the mud dries a bit."

"How long?" Steven replied, getting more and more frustrated.

"Three or four days longer if the sun's nice and hot. It's hard ta tell."

"But what would you do?"

"Well, let's see now. If I was alone, I'd set here a month before I'd wallow in that muck. But, on the other hand, if I was you, I'd dive right in, considerin' all your responsibilities."

Steven turned to his brother and said in a loud voice, "Paul, would you climb down there and see how deep that mud is?"

"No problemo, chief," Paul shouted as he hurried to the side of the highway. Leonard and Jarrad followed him. Without hesitating, all three waded in and sank a foot into the mire. Tugging his feet out of the mud so he could turn toward Steven, Paul called up the bank, "Not deep at all. I walked on streets worse than this every day when I was in Atikokan." Paul had served part of his mission in Atikokan, Ontario, Canada, and loved to tease that it took a real man to preach the gospel in the Canadian bush country.

Steven knew he had to make a quick decision. If they waited, it would put them even further behind schedule and increase the danger that they would run short of provisions. But if they went into the mud, they might get bogged down and not be able to move at all. They might even lose wagons or endanger the lives of people and animals. He was still pondering the problem when the bachelors returned.

"I think we should keep going," Paul declared. "It'll be slow, but at least we'll make headway."

Steven wished John and the colonels were there. He glanced at Mary and saw her confident smile. The children were there beside her in the wagon.

"All right! We'll do it. I've a hunch the highway begins again in a mile or two."

He waved Mary forward and pointed to the place where Paul had left the road to test the terrain. Mary's eyes bulged in surprise and fear, but she followed his directions. While Ruther and the bachelors remained on the side of the road to encourage the other wagons, Steven sloshed into the mud, showing Mary where to go. To his amazement, his legs slid into the sticky guck half way to the knee! After dragging himself along a hundred feet, he turned and watched as the big mules entered the mud.

At first they seemed to have trouble with their footing, but soon plodded after him without too much slipping or sliding. When the big wheels rolled into the mire, the wagon sank downward a foot and a half, hesitated an instant, as if unwilling to touch the mud, and then rolled onward. Mary and Steven grinned at each other and continued to battle their way eastward. Ten minutes later Ruther joined Steven to help him maintain a straight course.

Steven was wrong. After six hours of fighting their way through the mud, and traversing only two miles, there was still no freeway. The rain was coming down harder than before. The vehicles with modern tires had a particularly difficult time of it. In order to keep these "wagons" rolling, the Saints used any means possible: men on horseback with ropes, extra teams, and any individual who could stay on her feet and push.

At 7:30 p.m. the caravan simply halted in its tracks. The exhausted pioneers did their best to feed the animals, fix a makeshift meal, and comfort one another in their wagons. Many were so tired that they crawled into bed immediately to sleep away the forbidding night. The clothes and the bodies of those who had pushed were covered with a thick layer of mud. Only their eyes peeked through the muck to reveal that they were human beings. Even those who had driven or ridden on horseback were soaked and covered with splotches of mud.

"Mary, can you light the lamp?" Steven said. "I have to find the pail. The animals need grain and fresh water. William, please milk Lucretia." The boy groaned, but did as he was asked.

It took an hour for Steven to feed and water the animals. When he climbed back into the wagon, Mary had completed the job of straining the milk which William had brought in. The cow had given two gallons in the evening milking. They took very good care of their thousand-pound holstein, and she still gave them three to four gallons of warm milk a day in spite of the constant walking. Douglas Cartwright appeared with sandwiches and took a gallon and a half of the milk, enough for the eight people in his family, Ruther, the bachelors, and another large family. Mary kept a half gallon, which was plenty for her family.

"William says Lucretia is fine," Mary observed.

"Must be," Steven replied. "She ate half a bucket of oats and sucked up two pails of water."

"Do you think the mud and rain will injure her?" Mary said, worried.

"Heck no! That cow is like the Rock of Gibraltar. She acts as if she loves this weather."

"And Jimbow?" Jimbow was Steven's mustang. Jennifer had chosen his name when they had first acquired him.

"He's fine."

"And the mules?"

"Tired and filthy, but perfectly fit."

Mary always went through this routine at night whenever there was a touch of cold, wind, or rain. "Won't they get sick standing all night in that mud?"

"Stop worrying. They'll be fine!"

Steven spent the next half hour trying to answer a dozen questions concerning the storm and the dangers they might be in.

Andrew was the most concerned. "Dad, how do we know that we didn't walk right into that Platte River in the dark without knowing it?"

"Because the deep water and powerful current would have swept us away a long time ago."

"That doesn't prove we're safe," William observed. "We could still get drowned. This rain might make the river overflow its banks and flood this whole area. It could hit us any minute. We might be sitting ducks."

"That's highly unlikely," Steven replied. He didn't like the sudden fear William's words aroused in his mind.

"How do you know for sure, Steven?" Mary said.

"Mary! You too? You'll frighten the kids."

Jennifer said, "We're already scared to death, Dad."

"Okay. I'll get out of the wagon and explore the whole area to see what's going on."

Mary cried, "You will not!"

"All right, we'll say a prayer and ask Father in Heaven to protect us."

Andrew corrected, "To protect the whole wagon train."

"Of course."

Steven said a sincere prayer, and soon his mind was filled with peace and confidence. From the looks on their faces, he could tell that his family felt better. "We'll be okay. Now let's get some sleep."

On Tuesday morning the rain had ceased, but the mud was thick and wet. And the highway was still nowhere in sight. They sloshed through the muck all day and succeeded in covering no more than four miles. Steven had just taken the reins from Mary and had resigned himself to spending a second night parked in the mud, when he heard a shout. He looked ahead and saw Ruther a quarter of a mile away on his mule. The old man waved him forward and pointed southeast. Steven became excited. Ruther must have found the highway. They traversed the distance as fast as they could, and soon saw the highway not far away. Never had they beheld such a welcome sight!

The column rolled slowly onto the freeway and stopped for the night, strung out a half mile. Even though they were exhausted and covered with mud, they danced, sang, and rejoiced. Then they joined together in small groups and gave thanks to God for His kindness. Steven was more convinced than ever that the Lord Himself was with them.

During the early hours of the morning on Wednesday, June 14, the third baby of the expedition was born, but died two hours later. Instead of burying the infant in the mud, they decided to wait until they could find dry land somewhere up the trail. The next day they found a beautiful spot on a bluff topped by a single lone tree. Steven himself performed the burial ceremony, while the young couple gazed sadly at the grave of their first child.

In the eight days following the death of the baby, the caravan traveled a hundred and forty-two miles, averaging slightly more than twenty miles a day. Steven knew that the country should be more populated now, but the Saints met only a few forlorn stragglers, who were delighted to see them and anxious to trade.

Since there was very little firewood available in their trek across Nebraska, the pioneers often had to do without a campfire in the evening. At every halt they searched the surrounding lands for small branches or dried dung chips left by passing animals. Once in a while they got lucky and rejoiced, but usually they found scarcely enough to cook a meal. Before, they had found an abundance of edible wild plants, but now the plants were becoming rarer as they continued east.

On Thursday, June 22, they had covered almost three miles when Steven stopped his wagon abruptly and pushed the brake forward. Not far ahead, at Exit 366, a large group of armed men blocked the eastbound lanes of the freeway. There were at least a hundred of them.

"Who are they, Steve?" Mary said.

"That's what I'd like to know."

"What do they want?"

"I don't know that either."

As Steven climbed from his wagon, ten pioneers, including Ruther, Douglas, Jarrad, and Paul, arrived. Ruther began to study the sinister band through his binoculars.

"What do you think, Ruther?" Steven asked.

"Seen this type before. Motorcycle gangs. Leather jackets, Levi's,

Harleys. Pretty wild bunch. Spend most of their time carousin' and all. I'd guess they been havin' a big powwow of all the gangs in these here parts. Probably in Blue River Park southeast of here. Probably tryin' ta figure out how ta get oil and gas fer all those big bikes."

"What bikes?" Jarrad asked.

"The ones ya don't see 'cause they cain't ride 'em."

Steven was fascinated. "How do you know so much, Ruther?"

"Heck, I ain't always lived in the mountains. Fact is, I was borned in a little town 'bout fifteen miles north of this spot. But I couldn't stand all these flat prairies, so I left for the Rockies when I was nineteen."

"I'm certainly glad you did," Steven said. "But what do you think they want?"

"Anything they can get."

"What do you suggest we do?"

"Don't give them nothin'. Stand up to 'em boldly and tell 'em ya don't kowtow to no riffraff like them. Tell 'em ya got five hundred sharpshooters ta back ya up."

Steven was flabbergasted. "But won't that infuriate them and provoke them to violence."

"Hah! I love the genteel way ya say things, Steve! Heck no. Them boys is cowards deep down, and they'll be afraid of ya, sure as shootin'."

Paul said, "Look! One is heading this way."

"Their leader, I'd say. Go out ta meet him, Steve, and remember what I said. He ain't nothin' but a coward. We'll stay back here ta keep ya covered."

Steven walked slowly toward the approaching man. Soon, however, he no longer looked like a regular man, but some great hairy monster from a child's nightmare. Steven wanted to pull his rifle from his shoulder and hold it ready in front of him, but was concerned how the gorilla might respond. By the time the beast was forty feet away, Steven was positive he was at least seven feet tall and weighed three hundred pounds!

Remember that this guy's nothing but a coward, he thought. When he was seven feet away from the creature, Steven looked up at him and said firmly, "Good morning. Nice day, isn't it?" He regretted the words the instant they issued from his mouth. What a ridiculous way to show the guy you wouldn't put up with any of his guff!

"Do you want to live, man?" the giant said matter-of-factly.

"Of course. What kind of question is that?"

"We own this road, and no one uses it and lives. Unless they pay."

"Pay what?"

"Whatever we want. In your case, we'll take twenty young females, forty horses, a ton of food, and all the gas and oil in your camp."

Steven had the urge to jump on the monster and tear him to pieces, even if he was killed in the process. But he controlled his anger and, remembering Ruther's words, quickly pointed his rifle at the Thing before he could react. "I'll give you and your boys ten minutes to hightail it out of these parts. I've got five hundred sharpshooters in this group here, and there's a thousand more coming fast a few miles back."

"You're bluffing."

"You think so? We came clear from Utah over the worst country you can believe. We've met bigger and tougher gangs than yours, and we're still alive and well. We chased those suckers a hundred miles across the wilderness and wiped every one out. Haven't you heard how violent Mormons can be? We're going to Missouri and we don't intend to let a few punks like you stop us. Remember: ten minutes!"

With those words, Steven whirled around and walked back to the wagons without looking back. It seemed to take forever to cover the distance. Any second he expected to feel a bullet crash through his back and smash him to the ground. The hair stood up on his neck, and he trembled with fear. It was everything he could do to steady himself, to keep going and not turn around. Then, at long last, he reached his men and turned to look back. The giant had already returned to his buddies, and they were gazing at the wagon train. Steven supposed they were discussing whether to attack or leave.

"Ya done a good job," Ruther pronounced. He had watched the whole thing through his binoculars and had given the others a play by play description of facial expressions and body gestures. "What did ya say?"

Steven looked at his watch, making the movement as obvious as possible in the hope that the enemy would think he was timing them. "I said exactly what you told me to. Of course, I embellished a little here and there."

Ruther guffawed. "Somehow I knowed ya would. You're a master at highfalutin and persnickety talk."

Five minutes later the motorcycle gangs packed up abruptly and left the freeway. Ruther sat on the seat of Steven's wagon and watched them for ten minutes. Then he scrambled down and shouted with glee, "They is hightailin' it out of here as fast as their bowed legs can go! I never see'd sech speed."

"Which way is they a goin', partner?" Paul asked.

"Back ta that recreation area, it appears." He walked up to Steven and gave him a great bear hug. "I'm right proud of ya, son. Ya done good—for a little Mormon boy. I expect we can mosey on down the trail now as happy as a pig in a poke."

At that moment Steven realized fully that Ruther was one of the best gifts that God had given to Pioneer One.

Chapter 18

The Mexican Liberation Army of 101,000 soldiers reached the outskirts of El Paso, Texas on Thursday, June 15, at 11:15 a.m. Their leader was the mighty warrior Fidel García. Although some El Pasoans had warned the city that a fierce invader was approaching, most of the citizens scoffed at such foolishness. They had mocked even more when 2,000 radicals had left the city on May 24, loaded with survival equipment, and had fled into the Potrillo Mountains forty miles to the west.

But on that fateful morning when 216,000 citizens finally realized that a great army was upon them, they ran for their lives. The enemy quickly tracked them down and slaughtered them without mercy. After plundering the city, the invaders moved northward, butchering everyone they found in their path.

To the west, a greater army of 355,000 renegades would soon attack Tucson, Arizona. The ultimate goal of both invading forces was to ravage the great Mormon Kingdom to the north.

*****

George Chester stood at the speaker's stand waiting for the 2,168 Saints in the auditorium to quiet down. He prayed that this meeting, which he had announced just yesterday, would give stake leaders ideas on how they might deal with the threat of a Mexican invasion force. President Chester had also invited representatives from four other stakes.

Church leaders in this southern Utah community had not heard from the General Authorities for two weeks and were frantic. And since the towns in this part of the state were isolated, and without modern communications, George could only guess that other Mormon communities faced the same problems as his. He hoped that similar meetings were taking place all over southern Utah.

In this meeting George especially desired to discuss the Prophet's recent communication with members of the stake. The message declared that a great wicked army from the south desired to destroy the Saints, and that they must act to protect themselves. The situation was especially frightening since the community had recently received unconfirmed reports that a foreign army was attacking southern Arizona with unbelievable ferocity.

According to these reports, the only resistance which the invader had met came from a few isolated groups of Navaho and Hopi Indians, who had boldly fired on the renegades from hiding places. However, in one attack five thousand Indians had succeeded in wiping out a small Mexican detachment. The Indians had captured some heavy weapons, including thirty-one infantry mortars and two wagon-loads of mortar shells.

The Stake President raised his right hand to hush the noisy audience. After reviewing the information he had, he asked the members to raise their hands if they desired to ask questions or make comments. The recreation hall was hot and stifling. Since there was no electric power, the air-conditioning did not work. However, the matter at hand was so urgent that no one seemed to notice the heat.

Daniel Conway, sitting near the front, raised his hand. He was a tiny man of eighty who was known for his kindness and his love of learning. He had the habit of cleaning his glasses every fifteen minutes and rubbing his hand over his butch haircut. After the President recognized the old man, a deacon brought him a mike, and Daniel declared, "Frankly, I don't even know why we're here to discuss the situation. To me the problem is a simple one. A powerful enemy is coming to wipe us out. So we need to gather guns and supplies and form our own army. If we stand together, the enemy can't destroy us."

Arthur Cotton struggled to his feet. He was five feet nine and sixty-two years of age. He enjoyed refuting anyone who seemed to disagree with popular opinion. Arthur had been a top executive with WHC, Western Health Care, earning a half million dollars a year. Now he did handyman work to support his family.

Without waiting to be recognized, Arthur exclaimed, "I think we should show wisdom in this matter. We don't have enough facts to make a wise decision. We don't even know that the supposed threat is directed at us. And if there is an army approaching, we don't know how large it is. I've heard rumors that this so-called Mexican Liberation Army includes no more than nine or ten thousand men, and is hundreds of miles away. If that's the case, we have plenty of time to decide what to do."

Louis Graham jumped to his feet. "I've heard the same thing. Besides, the army isn't even coming to Utah, but to Colorado. So I want to know why we're getting frantic. There's absolutely no danger at all." Louis was short, forty-nine years old, balding, always smiling, and very popular. He had been an investment banker in California before the banking system collapsed nine months ago, but now he eked out his living making shoes at home.

President Chester, who remained standing at the podium, looked at

Louis and asked, "So what advice do you have for us, Brother Graham?"

"I suggest we set up a fact-finding committee to ascertain the truth of the matter. We don't want to act foolishly."

Arthur, still standing, said, "I agree. We can't act judiciously without the facts."

It was clear from the reaction of the audience that many agreed with Arthur Cotton and Louis Graham. President Chester made notes in his spiral-bound notebook. "All right. We have two suggestions. Gather an army to defend ourselves, and establish a fact-finding committee." He scanned the audience and chose one of the twenty hands raised high in the air. "Sister, uh, Sister Moran."

Joan Moran was six feet tall, very intelligent, with coal-black hair. At fifty she was still strikingly beautiful. In a loud, clear voice, she said, "I don't think we should do anything until the Prophet tells us to. We're supposed to follow the Prophet." A large portion of the assembly nodded their heads in approval at Joan's words.

Daniel Conway stood again. "But the Prophet has told us what to do. He told us that we're in grave danger and should act to protect our lives."

"But we need more details," Joan replied. "We don't know the exact nature of this grave danger. We don't know when the danger will arrive. And we don't know how to act to protect ourselves. Do we hide in the mountains? Do we arm ourselves? Do we try to negotiate with the supposed enemy? Do we wait for an army from Salt Lake City to come and protect us? Don't you see? We need more information. So I say wait until the Prophet gives us further direction."

At the stand President Chester mumbled as he wrote, "Wait—for—the—Prophet."

Ivan Tompkins rose and declared, "But the Lord tells us in the scriptures that He won't command his children in all things. We must do many good works of our own accord. That's one of the ways He tests us." Ivan was forty-two, six feet four inches tall, intelligent, muscular. Before the economic crash, he had been a photocopier repairman, but now he worked a twenty-acre farm.

At the stand George Chester muttered, "Figure—it—out—for—ourselves."

Owen Bancroft got to his feet. "I agree with Daniel Conway here. The Prophet has given us general instructions from the Lord. Now all we need to do is to ask God to fill in the details that Sister Moran is worried about. If our local leaders go to the Lord in prayer, as they've a right to do, the Holy Ghost will guide them to all truth." Owen used to be a teacher at the local high school. Although somewhat of a pedant, he was honest and sincere.

181

President Chester murmured, "Ask—God—for—details."

Gloria Ford waved her hand vigorously as she rose to her feet. "Well! I advise the stake presidency to think first about our lives and the virtue of the women. Most of us have no idea how to use firearms and wouldn't stand a chance against trained soldiers. So I think we should gather up our kids and our belongings and head for the hills. The enemy can't hurt what he can't find." Gloria was outspoken, friendly, talkative, and loved her creature comforts, but was always willing to share with those in need. She helped her family survive by knitting blankets.

President Chester scribbled, "Head—for—the—hills."

Dallan Cook asked to be recognized. He was a young elder who had recently married a local girl. "I would like to say that I disagree with what this brother said." He pointed to Arthur Cotton. "We don't need to study the facts to see if we're in danger. We don't need to waste time doing research on what action to take. In my opinion, the Prophet has told us what to do. Brother Conway here is right. We must gather our own army to defend our homes." This opinion was also backed by a sizeable segment of the audience.

George Chester whispered as he wrote, "We—know—what—to—do."

Dorothy Morgan, a frail, gray-haired woman who seldom talked in public, raised her hand. The President called her name. "Since we're isolated from the Prophet and the other General Authorities, I think we must turn to our local leaders. President Chester, what do you advise us to do?"

"Frankly, we don't know what to do. That's one of the reasons we're having this meeting. As a precaution, the local stakes have already gathered three thousand soldiers. We'd like to increase that to ten thousand, but we don't know what the other stakes of the church are doing. They may follow different courses. I can assure you, however, that we'll present this matter to the Lord again as soon as this meeting is over."

After they discussed the issues another hour, President Chester concluded the meeting. Later that day he and the heads of several other stakes met in prayer. By the end of this session they had decided to increase the size of their forces so they might be ready in the event of an attack. Within seven days nine stakes assembled a total of seven thousand troops. George Chester had heard rumors that stakes throughout southern Utah were doing the same thing, but he couldn't confirm them.

At 7:00 a.m. on Thursday, June 22, Elder Jason Widtsoe knocked on the door of Georges' home. "Good morning. Do you know me?"

George was aghast. "You're Elder Widtsoe! Of the Quorum of the Twelve. Please come in." George showed the apostle into his living room and invited him to take a seat.

Jason got right to the point. "Please excuse my abruptness, but we need to conduct our business quickly. The Prophet placed me and Elder Keith Bartlett in charge of all Mormon forces. I'm sure you know that our people may be invaded by a renegade army from Mexico. How many men have you gathered to support our defense?"

"About seven thousand."

"Great. Are they ready to fight?"

"Definitely."

"The Prophet said you'd be ready. Apparently, the Saints in this region consulted with the Lord, and He gave them all the same answer—organize their forces. And it's a good thing too. We've been doing our best to contact the stakes in southern Utah to organize them in time, but haven't been able to reach them. And when we finally did, they had already prepared. Just like your stake. If they had waited, we might be at the enemy's mercy. From the figures coming in now, I estimate that we have several hundred thousand soldiers in southern Utah at this time. I expect them to reach their assigned posts in two or three days. In addition, we have approximately 200,000 soldiers gathering in northern Utah, but we're not sure when they can reach this area." Jason grinned. "I call our forces the Mormon Legion..."

"I'm grateful that we have so many men."

"Not only men. We also have about forty thousand female volunteers, and we're grateful to get them."

"Isn't that dangerous? The invaders are vile men."

"It might be, but we have no choice."

"You mentioned that our southern armies have been assigned posts. Where are they being stationed?"

Elder Widtsoe replied, "At five major roads into Utah, and near a few large cities. One of our big problems is, we don't have good information on precisely where the enemy is... Now let me give you your instructions and assignments quickly. Then I ask you to send men to the stakes I will indicate to give them the facts they need."

After the two men discussed other details, Elder Widtsoe cautioned President Chester to tell his soldiers to bring as much food and supplies as they could comfortably carry. He also explained how his stake would partici-pate in maintaining lines of supply for the Mormon Legion.

"When do you want us to leave for our posts?"

"Today, if possible."

*****

After the guards brought Pierre Laborde into the room without windows, they tied him to one of the ceiling beams by two thick ropes. As he

183

stood in the center of the room with his arms pulled above his head, the ropes bit into his wrists. The glaring lights from several incandescent bulbs without shades stabbed his eyes. Having strung Pierre up, the guards sat on five chairs placed on one side of the room and waited. Two men and a woman, dressed in prison garb, occupied chairs on the other side. Pierre recognized the men as inmates in his barracks. *Lousy spies*, Pierre thought.

A half hour later, the French commandant of the Arras encampment, Jules Pigalle, and another man entered the room. Jules faced his prisoner, while the second man pulled several items from a briefcase and put them on a table eight feet away. Pierre looked at the instruments and knew what his captors had in mind. He was grateful that Diane and his children were not there to see.

The commandant spoke to Pierre in French. "Monsieur Laborde, my people tell me that you openly attack our lessons on responsible citizenship. In other words, they say that you corrupt other guests in your barracks by your refusal to be reasonable."

Pierre cursed his foolishness. Two weeks earlier he had realized that the enemy must have spies among the prisoners, and that he had been exposing himself and others to danger by openly opposing the indoctrination of UGOT. At that moment, he had changed his methods and had pretended that he was being converted. But now he feared that he had acted too late. "No, I agree with the information your instructors present."

"That's not what I understand. Listen, I'm a busy man. I have no time to waste on you. You'll renounce your religion now or you'll be tortured." He nodded toward the man who had accompanied him. "My friend here is a master at getting people to do what he wants. He knows how to tear, dig, and cut just enough to make you scream and still keep you alive for days or even weeks."

"Please believe me. I'm not your enemy."

Jules slapped him viciously. "All right then, prove what you say. Renounce Jesus Christ and the Mormon church before these witnesses, or I'll let my friend start his work."

"I renounce Jesus Christ and the Mormon church before these witnesses."

"You will say that Jesus Christ was a fake and that your church is a false religion."

Again Pierre repeated his words exactly.

Jules turned to his friend and said, "How do we know this man is sincere?"

The torturer held up a long sharp knife. "Let me cut him up a little to verify his sincerity."

The commandant laughed. "What do you expect him to say? That he was lying to us?"

One of the prisoners sitting against the wall said fearfully, "Sir, may I speak?"

"Yes. What is it?"

"This man tells the truth. I saw him change..."

"Go on!"

"Well, he did show signs that he was beginning to accept our political and spiritual lessons. And I know these Mormons. They're complete fanatics. They would never renounce their beliefs, even if tortured. Because of that, I believe this man is sincere."

Jules looked at the second prisoner. "Do you verify this?"

"Yes, sir, he did change."

The commandant turned to Pierre. "So you've had a change of heart?"

"Yes, sir."

Jules scowled. "Remember your wife. She's in my power. If I find you're lying, she will die with you."

Pierre fought to control the great panic which filled his soul. "I understand."

"Good. You're a lucky man. I accept what you and these men say—at least for now. When you return to your barracks, I expect you to encourage the other residents to support UGOT. If you do this diligently, you'll save your life and that of your wife." He motioned to one of the guards. "Cut him down and take him back to his barracks."

An hour later Pierre's prison buddy, Claude Morel, sat next to Pierre. "What happened? I was afraid—"

"Not much." He related the entire story.

Claude was shocked. "You denied your religion? I never dreamed you'd do such a thing."

"What purpose would it serve if I had refused to do it? They would have tortured me to death. And who would benefit from my testimony and my courage? The animals in that room? They are so full of evil that they would have concluded I was nothing except a raving fanatic. It would not have converted any of them. Besides, it's easy for a person to think he'll be strong—no matter what—until he's faced with the ultimate choice."

"What about the prisoners in the room—the spies? They'll tell the whole camp what you did. It'll make all the Mormons here look like hypocrites."

"I know what I'm doing."

"Meaning?"

"I can't say."

There was a minute of silence as the two men stared into each other's eyes.

"Listen, Pierre, I'm not condemning you!" Claude said at last. "I might have done the same thing. You don't owe honesty to tyrants who use brute force."

"I prefer you don't repeat what I've told you. Maybe the spies won't tell the other prisoners what I did. It could blow their cover."

"Okay. Mum's the word. But won't the guards spread the story?"

"It's a possibility. We can't do anything about that. But if they do, the prisoners may decide, hopefully, that the guards are lying."

*****

Martin Gannt, UGOT's Assistant Director of Media Relations, was in a bind. Gerald Galloway had ordered him to do more to discredit established religions in the world media. The Supreme Leader wanted something big and he wanted it now. Martin cursed Gerald for forgetting so soon Martin's key role in the brilliant success of MOM in Switzerland.

Then one night Martin ran into his friend Jules Pigalle at a party in Paris. After drinking half the night, the media man poured out his heart. Jules offered a reasonable solution.

"Get some people to renounce their religion on TV," Jules suggested. "Telecast it to the world. You'll touch a half billion people that way."

Martin laughed. "And you think people would believe that kind of stuff. It's pretty obvious that such disavowals are a fake. Everybody will simply wonder how much the government tortured them to get them to say it."

"Not everybody. It depends on how you handle it. I'm sure you can convince hundreds of millions of viewers that the repudiations are genuine. Especially if you make it a regular feature. When the viewers see all those people denying their beliefs, one after the other, they'll buy it eventually. Repeat anything bold enough and long enough on international TV, and the people will believe it."

"You don't think much of the intelligence of the general public, do you?"

"No, the masses are, for the most part, stupid robots... You should at least try the repudiation method. At our camp near Arras we've used the normal lessons of indoctrination to control troublesome people for about a half year. But last month we received instructions from UGOT's Ministry of Dissident Control to experiment with as many techniques as we can to persuade dissenters to conform to the goals of the government. They want us to become more creative and effective. So recently we've tried using repudiations, both real and faked, to undermine the religious and political ideals of our residents. It's too early to ascertain the final results, but it seems to be working."

Martin said, "I don't know. It might work on international TV."

"It couldn't hurt to try. Even if it's only a partial success, at least the Twelve would get the impression you're trying hard to satisfy them."

"Yes, but it might backfire, in which case I might as well jump off the Eiffel Tower."

Jules finished his whiskey and began searching for a cigarette. "At any rate, you'll have to do something soon. Our masters aren't very patient... You know, I do what UGOT tells me but I'm still not clear as to its goals. What's Gerald Galloway's purpose in controlling and discrediting established religions? Is he simply against religion in general or is it part of his general plan to make UGOT the only world government?"

Martin offered Jules a cigarette. Jules took one, which Martin lit with his Bic. "In the final analysis, I suppose Galloway wants to promote UGOT. However, no one knows for sure what Galloway thinks. He's a man of mystery. I've heard he despises all traditional religions. On the other hand, there are rumors that he wants to establish his own world religion. That's why he has that crazy prophet of his running all over the world, visiting both the great and the small."

Jules laughed sarcastically. "Yes, I've heard of him. What a freak!" Suddenly, Jules grabbed Martin's forearm. "Listen, I may have the perfect man for you to start your TV series with. He's a Mormon, I think. A few days ago we had him in our little torture room, but before my specialist got started, he disavowed everything he's believed all his life. I've had secret informants watching him carefully, before and since, and he appears to be sincere."

"Hah! Why take a chance? I could use one of our own people. Someone who's a good actor."

Jules replied enthusiastically, "Why use an actor when you can have the real thing? And my man already has the reputation of being a dedicated Mormon and an opponent of UGOT. His face has been on TV a number of times. His recantation would really mean something. Also, the guy oozes candor and sincerity. He'd be very convincing on a special TV segment."

"What's his name?" Martin asked.

"Pierre something. I don't know for sure. However, I do remember what my spies say."

"Spies?"

"Yes, they live in his barracks."

Martin sighed. "What do they say?"

"He's always praying for his wife and children. The wife lives in my camp. They are another reason why we can depend on his cooperation!"

Martin smiled at Jules' emotion. "Well, my friend, let me think about it a day or two. You're returning to Arras tomorrow?"

"You mean today. The clock on that wall says five, and I must leave at eight. If the booze doesn't knock me out before then." They both laughed.

Martin said, "You can send this man to me here, if I decide to use him? Very quickly, I mean."

"You'll have him within six hours. I'll transport him myself."

Two days later, Martin telephoned Jules and asked him to send the man who had abjured his beliefs. Using the authority of his office as UGOT's Assistant Director of Media Relations, he convinced Planète and a dozen other major networks to preempt all programming in order to televise the religious abjuration of a man named Pierre Laborde during prime time the following evening. The segment, which would last fifteen minutes, including renunciation and commentary, would be seen by more than a half billion people. And if things went well, it would be repeated a dozen times within a week.

Chapter 19

By the end of the day Steven was overjoyed. In spite of the delay caused by the motorcycle gangs, and a few gaps in the highway, the pioneers had covered a record twenty-five and a half miles. He gave credit to the gradual descent of the road, the cloud cover, and the pleasant breeze, which made traveling easier. Mary teased him about being all smiles because of his triumph over the hoodlums. After supper Pierce Hudson and Rachel Crell appeared and asked him to marry them. They wanted him to perform the ceremony as soon as they reached Independence, Missouri.

Since they were only five miles from the great city of Lincoln, Steven was very concerned about what the pioneers would find there. After supper he told Mary he wanted to ask God what they should expect, and walked to a secluded spot several hundred yards from the encampment. When he returned, he called a special meeting of the wagon train leaders. He also invited Ruther.

"Brethren, we need to change our route. I want to remain on I-80 and head northeast, instead of traveling southeast on Nebraska Highway 2, as we planned."

Seth Crowell, one of the colonels, exclaimed, "But that's out of the way! We'll lose time!"

John Christopher said, "What's the reason, Steve? That route has to be forty miles farther."

"And we'll have to go through Omaha!" Seth said angrily. "That could be dangerous!"

Paul spoke up, "Calm down. I'm sure Steve has a good reason."

Seth replied, "I'm sure! I've heard he has good reasons for a lot of things."

John looked at Seth coldly. "What do you mean by that?"

"I mean he probably wants to lead us to another place instead of Missouri!"

"That's ridiculous," Paul said. "You shouldn't listen to idle gossip, Seth."

Seeing John's growing anger, Steven said quickly, "I prayed about what we should do, and the Lord told me to take the new route."

Kent Booth, another colonel, seemed upset also. "But why? It doesn't make sense."

"The Lord said that we would be in great danger if we followed Highway 2."

Jim Burnham, a third colonel, said, "I see no reason to argue. Steve's our leader, and if he says the Lord directed him to take another route, that's good enough for me." Jim was a small, compact man of forty who always supported Steven without question.

Seth Crowell replied, "I think we should discuss it for a while. Maybe vote on it."

"Listen, boys," Ruther said, "I ain't got no say in this group, but it seems ta me that ya'd better follow your leader. Don't ya believe God called him ta lead ya?"

The fourth colonel, Jasper Potter, said nothing.

Jim said, "Ruther's right. Besides, we don't make decisions by voting, unless Steven requests it."

"All right," Seth said. "I have no choice except to go along. Still, I don't see why the Lord couldn't tell us what the danger might be."

After discussing the new route for an hour, the meeting broke up, and the men returned to their families. That night Steven told Mary about the answer the Lord had given, and about how the leaders received it. She probed him for every detail possible. He explained that he had heard the same voice as before and knew it was from God. Even though the Lord had not given him details, he was determined to obey anyhow.

The next day they arose at the usual time, watered their animals once again in the creek which flowed near the highway, and allowed them to graze on its banks. Steven had not noticed the evening before, but today he saw that the stream had very little water in it. By 6:35 a.m. they were on the road. As they traveled, the surrounding countryside became gradually drier. When they had traveled an hour, Paul hurried up to Steven.

"I have something important to tell you," Paul said, dismounting from his horse.

"What?"

"I've heard talk that there's a mutiny in the works." Paul led his horse by the reins as he walked beside Steven.

Steven's interest was piqued. "What do you mean?"

"It seems that some people refuse to continue on I-80. They plan to follow Nebraska Highway 2, according to the original plan."

"I was afraid of that," Steven said sadly. "How many people?"

"I'm not sure. Most of the pioneers, I think."

"Where did you get this information?"

"Seth Crowell. He said the colonels consulted with their people and found that they plan to reject your idea of staying on I-80."

"When did this happen?" Steven said.

"Last night and this morning."

Maintaining his stride, Steven said with conviction, "Paul, I want you to go to Seth and tell him that if the Saints take Highway 2, they will endanger their lives and their property."

"You know this for a fact?"

"Yes."

"Okay. I'll make sure they get the message." Paul jumped on his horse and sped down the line of wagons.

Steven looked to his right at Mary sitting on the wagon seat. She had overheard most of his conversation with Paul and had a worried look on her face. By 9:00 a.m. they approached the suburbs of Lincoln. The scene which gradually unfolded before them was beyond anything they could have imagined. Desolation was everywhere. The pioneers stared in disbelief, trudging along slowly as if in a nightmare. Some great conflagration had consumed every structure and every living thing. Instead of moving closer to investigate, they continued on, dread oppressing every heart.

When they reached Exit 397, Steven, still walking, guided the wagon train northeast, continuing on I-80. He couldn't bring himself to look back, afraid of what he might see. Then he heard a shout from the second wagon. He slowed his pace until Douglas Cartwright overtook him.

Douglas leaned out from his wagon and said, "Some of the wagons aren't following us." Elizabeth, who was sitting next to her husband, was peeking back around the right side of the wagon.

Steven called, "I know, I know. Follow me." He picked up his pace until he reached the front of his wagon. He was grateful to know that some of the people would not abandon him. A mile later, after they had almost passed Capitol Beach Lake, he couldn't take it any longer. He motioned to Mary to keep going, walked to the right side of the road, and looked back. He had expected that all of the company, except his friends and family, would forsake him. But he received a pleasant surprise when he saw that approximately one-third of the caravan were following on I-80. Still, it was sad to witness so many others going the other way.

After another quarter of a mile, Steven decided to call a halt. Since Oak Creek was not far away, it was a good place to water and graze the animals. He waited for the others to pull up. Within ten minutes a noisy swarm of people surrounded him. Mary and Steven's children were at the front of the crowd. Near them he saw familiar faces: Paul and John; Douglas and Elizabeth Cartwright; the two bachelors, Leonard and Jarrad; Ruther, holding his Sharps rifle; Pierce Hudson and Rachel Crell; the "rebellious" captain, Frank Hamilton; Elmer Gleason and Luke Small, the vagabonds from

Chicago; Wesley Duke, supporting his injured ankle on crutches; Wesley's friend Judd Hawk; Byron Mills, the scriptorian; Jasper Potter and Jim Burnham, two of his colonels. The families of some of these people stood with them.

Jim Burnham raised his hand high, and the horde grew quiet. "Steve, I assume you know about the others."

"Yes, Jim, thanks."

"Well, we want you to know that we are with you."

The crowd cheered. Mary beamed, her eyes full of tears. Steven was deeply moved and couldn't speak. Soon the mob quieted down and waited for him to respond.

"Is there anything we can do?" Jim went on.

Steven said, "No, we can't force them to do anything. They have their agency, you know. Do you know who is leading them?"

"Yes. Seth Crowell and Quentin Price," Jim replied.

Steven was taken back. "Dr. Price?"

"Yes," John said loudly. "It seems that he's the ringleader."

"Why do you say that?" Steven demanded.

"From what Paul told me last night."

Paul jumped in to explain, "Well, in the last few days Jarrad, Leonard, and I learned from solid sources that Dr. Price is the one who started and fed the gossip attacking us as leaders. He tried to spread lying rumors to every person he treated."

"But why would he do it?" Mary asked.

"Beats me," Paul replied. No one else offered the answer either.

"I suppose we'll have to ask him," Steven said.

"But when?" Douglas Cartwright asked. "It could be weeks before we see him and the others again."

Steven smiled. "No, we'll see them in a few days."

Jarrad Babcock, the bachelor, seemed confused. "But how? I thought we were heading northeast."

Steven explained, "We'll rest here a few hours. I want our animals to get all the water and forage they can take, because those things will be more scarce later. Then we'll turn and follow the others."

Jim Burnham inquired, "Do you mind sharing the reasons with us, Steve?"

Steven answered, "Last night in our meeting I didn't tell you everything the Lord said. He commanded me not to. But now I can tell you more. He also told me that there would be a mutiny, that most of the company would take the wrong route, and that they would go through a great trial. He explained that the purpose of this tribulation was to try his Saints and chasten them so that they might learn obedience by the things which they suffer. They must learn to become a Zion people."

John hesitated. "I'm not sure I understand why you want to follow them if it's the wrong route, and they're facing a disaster?"

"I don't know, John. The Lord told me to do it, but didn't say why. However, we must obey His will."

They waited until 2:00 p.m. and set out again. By the time they halted for the evening on Highway 2, they had covered a total of fifteen and a half miles for the day and were still in the southern suburbs of Lincoln. Since they were anxious to leave this scene of devastation, they found it difficult to camp so close to the city. All day they had searched the road ahead, but did not catch sight of the brothers and sisters who had left them.

*****

Martin Gannt was worried. Because the renunciation segment had been put together so rapidly, the Program Director of Planète, Louis Lagrange, had not had time to order it videotaped beforehand. It was already 6:30 p.m., and the piece was scheduled to air at 7:30 p.m.

Martin looked at Louis sitting behind his desk in the spacious office. "What if this man tries to be a hero?" he asked in near-perfect French.

Jules Pigalle, commandant of the Arras concentration camp, spoke before Louis could respond, "It won't happen. Trust me. I assure you that Pierre Laborde will do what we say. He wants to live." Jules sat in an armchair next to Martin.

Louis Lagrange smiled with overweening self-confidence. "Yes, I'm sure we have nothing to fear in telecasting your piece live, Martin. I'll be in the control room myself. I've explained the problem to my technical director, Anatole Léger, a very good man. He and I will be watching the master monitor. One slip on the part of your man, and Anatole touches a button and cuts instantly to commercial."

"If there's a mistake, Gerald Galloway will make us all pay dearly!" Martin warned.

Jules replied, "There won't be any slipups. I warned Monsieur Laborde that if he gets cute, we'll kill him on the spot. And later his wife and children."

"So you'll have some of your men in the studio?" Martin asked.

"Four guards. I've instructed two of them to blast the prisoner at my command."

Martin felt better. "Sounds like you both have things under control... Now then, Louis, tell me what you think of my abjuration text?"

Louis picked up a paper from his desk. "Let me read it again. 'I, Pierre Laborde, have been a member of the Church of Jesus Christ of Latter-day Saints, or the Mormon church, all my life. I was taught in my youth that Jesus Christ is the Son of God, and that only through Him and His gospel can a person reach God's heaven. However, as a mature adult, I have completely reevaluated the beliefs of my youth, and I can now say, in complete freedom of conscience, that everything I have believed for so long is an absolute lie.' That's very good, Martin. And you had to write it so quickly. I have one question, however."

"Which is?"

"I thought this was supposed to be a casual conversation between my commentators and Monsieur Laborde. Don't you want to avoid the appearance of a rigid speech, given under constraint?"

"I do, I do. However, since the piece will last fifteen minutes, your interviewers will have plenty of time to ask friendly questions about Pierre's life and family. But near the end, I want Pierre to look at your TelePrompTer and give this speech word for word. It can be read slowly in about thirty-eight seconds. That way, there will be no mistake as to the message communicated to your viewers. After that, your newscasters can follow up with a few more friendly remarks, and the thing will be done. Viewers will believe Pierre is just another guest, and won't have a clue that he's a prisoner."

"That'll work," Jules remarked. "I'm sure of it."

"Okay, it's your show!" Louis said.

Fifty minutes later the special piece was only a few minutes from being telecast. Anatole Léger slumped in his seat before the row of television monitors in control room one. His shift had already started, but still his head was swimming. He cursed himself for drinking so much Vodka and getting so little sleep. But what a party it had been! He drank more coffee to clear his head. Hopefully, he'd feel better by the time control room two turned direction of the following segments over to them. He tried to focus on his control board, which was directly in front of him. It was made up of a confusing number of lights, buttons, and levers. Sometimes it seemed as if the whole mess became one big blur.

Anatole looked to his left and saw that the audio engineer, Pascal, was back from his break, looking as fresh as ever. Man, how he hated teetotalers like Pascal! It just wasn't natural. Then Louis Lagrange, the Program Director, entered the room and sat close by. Anatole drained his cup quickly and poured another, hoping the caffeine would straighten him up. If the director saw his condition, he'd be suspended again and he couldn't afford that! He looked at the line monitor and saw a man and a woman take seats on the stage. The interviewers! It was almost time.

Martin Gannt took a seat in the audience area next to Jules. He watched the television crew finish their preparations for the broadcast. Two men operated the broadcast cameras. A technician was adjusting the boom microphone. A woman stood ready next to the TelePrompTer, which would present a line-by-line view of Pierre's statement. All Pierre had to do was read what was printed on that roll of paper. A technical director with a head microphone in front of his mouth stood to the left on an extension of the stage. There were several other people seated in the audience area. Martin guessed that they were either employees of Planète or reporters.

Two interviewers appeared on the stage and sat in armchairs behind a low table which held three glasses and a pitcher of ice water. The entire background was a simulated view of the city of Paris. A minute later four green coats escorted Pierre Laborde onto the stage from the left. After Pierre took his seat, the guards separated, two in each of the wings. The sight of their semiautomatic pistols in a television studio was shocking to Martin. The technical director hurried forward from the left and placed a lavalier microphone around Pierre's neck. He rushed back to his post and called out a countdown for all to hear.

The first seven minutes of the interview went very well. The interviewers asked Pierre cordial questions about his work and family. He answered in an honest, straightforward manner. Martin was impressed by Pierre's sincerity and soon began to relax and enjoy the piece. He had heard that Gerald Galloway and other members of the Supreme Council were watching this landmark telecast, and he rejoiced at how pleased they would be. Pleased with him for thinking of the idea and pulling it off! Finally, the crucial moment arrived as Pierre announced that he wanted to make a statement. In spite of his efforts to relax, Martin's throat constricted involuntarily.

In the control room Louis Lagrange watched intently as the camera zoomed in to Pierre's face. He knew that if this man dared to show any signs of rebellion, he could cut him off the instant he made a move. Then Pierre began to read his statement from the TelePrompTer, and Louis could hear him clearly.

"I, Pierre Laborde, have been a member of the Church of Jesus Christ of Latter-day Saints, or the Mormon church, all my life. I was taught in my youth that Jesus Christ is the Son of God, and that only through Him and His gospel can a person reach God's heaven. However, as a mature adult, I have completely reevaluated the beliefs of my youth, and I can now say, in complete freedom of conscience, that everything I have believed for so long is the absolute truth. I bear my—"

Louis screamed at Anatole Léger. "Cut to commercial!"

"—testimony that Jesus Christ—"

"Cut!" Louis shouted again.

Anatole shook his head trying to clear his brain. "Huh? We should—"

"—is the divine Son of God, and that—"

"Cut!" Louis bellowed.

Anatole reached for the cut button, but had trouble finding it. "Okay...I'll cut."

"—the Church of Jesus Christ of Latter-day Saints is the—"

"Cut!" Louis hollered, charging toward Anatole's console.

"Can't find it," Anatole muttered as he pushed the wrong button.

"—only true Church on the earth."

At last Anatole found the right button and cut to a taped commercial. Through the intercom attached to his collar, Louis shouted, "We're in commercials!"

Every person in the studio was stunned, and for a moment no one said or did anything. But when the technical director heard Louis Lagrange's words on the intercom, he announced, "We're in commercials!"

Jules jumped to his feet and made a sign to the two green coats. They rushed forward instantly, raised their pistols, and shot rounds into Pierre's body. Pierre fell to the floor like a broken puppet, his head and chest gushing blood. Spellbound, Martin gazed at the terrible scene, realizing that in Pierre's death he also beheld his own destruction. Suddenly, he felt someone tug on his arm.

"It was my drunken technician who allowed this to happen," Louis Lagrange declared frantically. "He didn't cut him off in time." Martin gazed at him numbly, unable to speak. "And that stupid statement you wrote! All the fanatic had to do was change the last word or two."

"We're dead men," Martin finally mumbled.

The next day a female prisoner entered one of the women's barracks in Arras and approached Diane Laborde grimly. After she whispered something in Diane's ear, she turned quickly and left the building. Diane dropped to her cot and looked around at the other prisoners, as if seeking help. Seeing nothing except pity and vacant stares, she put her head into her lap and sobbed bitterly.

*****

On Saturday, June 24, Steven started the company as usual. Now they found the going much more difficult. The rolling hills surrounding them seemed more and more like a desert, and the vegetation which covered the loamy soil was sparse. They were alarmed to see that the Beal Slough had only a trickle of water running in it. At 7:30 p.m. they stopped for the night on the highway just north of the town of Unadilla. Fortunately, there was still some water in the Little Nemaha River, which ran close to the town, and its banks offered nourishment to their livestock.

Alone, Steven rode east for some distance to locate the advance group. He saw wagons miles ahead near a turn in the highway. With a heavy heart he returned to his people. That night all the pioneers gathered and kneeled as one, offering a prayer for themselves and their fellow Saints ahead. Many could not contain their tears, for a feeling of gloom and despair weighed upon them. After supper the usual friends and family gathered around Steven's campfire to discuss the events of the day.

"Tomorrow is Sunday, Steve. What are we going to do?" Paul asked.

"We'll keep traveling. I'm sure the others will continue on, and I don't want them to get too far ahead. Besides, we must get out of this region as quickly as possible. Do you agree, Ruther?"

A twig protruding from the corner of his mouth, Ruther replied, "Well, I'm not sure why ya want ta stay so close ta those who rebel against ya, but I agree with that part about gettin' out of this country."

"Why are you so concerned with keeping up with them?" Douglas asked.

Steven coughed from the smoke which seemed to track him around the circle. The memory of what Douglas had said about campfire smoke flashed through his mind uninvited. "I don't know for sure, to tell you the truth. But I don't feel complete without them, for some reason."

Ruther said, "Can I ask ya all a question that's been buggin' me?"

"Of course," Steven answered.

"Look, I don't want ta get yer dander up or nothin', but I cain't figure out why those people out there—the ones who left us—like ta call theirselves Saints when they don't act particularly saint-like a lot of the time. You know, spreadin' evil gossip about some pretty nifty fellers like Steve here, complainin' all the time, criticizin' people who don't part their hair the way they does, and then rebellin' like they done. Ta tell ya the truth, I don't get it. I always thought a saint was a pure, holy person, like Joan of Arc, who could do miracles and things like that there."

Steven replied, "We don't use the word saint precisely that way, Ruther. To us a saint is a member of Christ's church. It refers more to what we hope to be, not necessarily what we are. As for why we act the way we do, all I can say is that we need to learn to be more obedient to the Lord. That's why God put every person on the earth. But I've never heard a Mormon claim to be perfect. If you think back on everything that has happened on this trip, you'll have to admit that the people in this company, in spite of their faults, have put up with a lot and done some very courageous things."

Ruther pondered a moment, then said, "Yeah, I have ta give ya that."

The next day it was very windy. As they traveled along, Steven's company began to overtake stray wagons, whose owners were purposely moving slower than normal. When he overtook them, they sheepishly apologized for their rebellion. They explained that after praying about the problem over and over, the Spirit told them that they had made a mistake. Steven accepted their repentance with an open heart, and invited them to rejoin his group. At 11:30 a.m. Paul appeared and told him that it looked as though nearly half the company was with them.

"Do you want me to take down the names of those who are with us?" Paul asked.

"Why?"

Paul blushed. "Well, to keep track of the people who aren't trustworthy."

"Forget it, Paul, we're not running an Inquisition here."

"Okay, okay. It was just a thought."

Steven hugged his brother. "Thanks for your diligence, but I think we'd better avoid that kind of stuff."

At noon the highway turned abruptly to the northeast. Steven noted from the map that after they continued in this direction about two miles, the highway headed directly east again. He estimated that the other company was only seven or eight miles ahead. It was difficult to read the map because the wind had picked up even more. Next to him rode Paul, Douglas, and Ruther. William drove their wagon not far behind.

"Look!" Douglas said. "What is that?" He pointed to the northwest.

Steven looked in that direction and beheld a great storm moving toward them. However, the dark front had a yellowish tinge and seemed to be surprisingly close to the ground. The wind was becoming stronger, and the gusts which whipped them pushed the horses toward the right side of the highway. "Looks like a storm," he shouted. "Heading this way."

"It's a storm, all right," Ruther called, holding on to his wide hat. "A dust storm! We'd better take cover fast."

"How? Where?" Steven yelled.

"Roll yer wagons into the gully on the right side of the road, and git down!"

The four riders waved the front wagons toward the ditch, and the caravan began to roll off the road immediately. Even though the pioneers did not know exactly what the danger was, they reacted instinctively, dropping as low as possible in the depression and protecting themselves and their children behind or under anything they could find. Many of the animals turned their backs to the wind, while others dropped to the ground. Steven and Paul forced their horses to the ground at the bottom of the gully, and then rushed to Steven's wagon. After they had made sure Mary and the children were safe inside with their heads covered, they climbed the embankment to check the storm. Ruther stayed with Steven's family.

By this time the clouds of dust had filled the entire horizon and loomed thousands of feet above them, darkening the sky. The rotating waves were almost black near the earth, but as the border of the clouds turned upward in gigantic swirling lobes, they grew lighter and more yellowish brown. It looked like a tornado six thousand feet wide and fifteen miles long, lying on its side against the earth and rolling toward them. Steven was so fascinated by the unusual sight that he stared at it without seeking cover.

Paul pulled him toward the gully just as the main bank of clouds hit them. The wind drove the fine particles of dust into their noses, ears, eyes, and down their throats. Coughing and choking they stumbled down the embankment and climbed into the wagon. While Steven and Paul struggled to breathe, Steven's children peered at them from under their blankets.

The storm lasted twenty minutes. As soon as it was over, everyone scrambled from the wagon coughing and shaking billows of dust from their clothes. Steven couldn't resist laughing when he saw all those walking shadows of dust, with clear round eyes peeking out. He noticed that Lucretia stood there as unconcerned and immovable as ever, mooing softly. But she was utterly filthy! When he saw the thick layer of fine brown powder and debris which covered every object in sight, Steven estimated that it would take weeks before things were back to normal.

"Well, it appears like we done lucked out," Ruther declared solemnly.

"Lucked out! You must be kidding." Steven replied.

"Nope! We only got the edge of that storm. I'm a fearin' for yer friends up yonder." He nodded eastward. "They got the brunt of it."

"Can dust storms kill people?" Paul asked.

"You betcha. The bad ones kin cause lung damage, loss of eyesight, and all kinds of other problems. And lots of property damage."

"Would that be considered a bad storm?" Steven inquired.

"Durn worst one I ever see'd."

The pioneers spent the next hour shoveling debris from their wagons, caring for the animals, and cleaning themselves and their possessions. They could have spent the rest of the day performing these tasks, but since Steven was anxious to overtake the forward company, they left as soon as possible. Because of what Ruther had said, everyone feared what they would find.

As the wagons traveled east, they had to maneuver constantly around mounds of dust. In many places the storm had filled the gully north of the highway, and the dust had buried the side rails and spilled partly across the road. Many signs were partially buried or their posts ripped from the ground. Finally, at 4:30 p.m. the travelers saw people and wagons. It soon became clear that the dust storm had struck the advance company with such fury that it had blown most of the people, livestock, carts, wagons, and converted vehicles completely off the highway into the fields south of the freeway.

The scene was unreal. There were hundreds of people in the field, strung out for a mile, as far away from the road as a quarter of a mile. Some were struggling to upright vehicles. Others walked up and down looking for family members or possessions, stopping frequently to cough. Many were occupied nursing injured people or animals. A few sat alone, too dazed to know what was going on. None seemed to notice that the other half of Pioneer One had arrived.

Steven stopped his caravan, and hundreds of people poured into the fields to help. Steven approached one of the brothers who had followed Seth Crowell and Quentin Price. With the help of his wife and children, the man was repairing a wagon wheel.

He looked up from his work and said, "Good to see you, Brother Christopher. I had no right to expect it, but somehow I knew you'd come."

Steven held back his tears. How grateful he was for those words! "When did the storm hit you?"

"About four hours ago. Around noon."

"From the looks of things, it seems as though it just struck."

The man put down his hammer and stood. "Well, most of us were knocked out, or buried in mounds of dust, or simply too beat up to do much of anything until a short time ago. Except to make sure our kids were okay."

"It doesn't look like you folks took cover."

"No, we didn't know what to. No direction or guidance of any kind. I guess most of us thought it was nothing except another rain storm. We all waited for it to come, right in the middle of the highway."

Steven decided to ask the question which was bothering him most. "Any casualties?"

"I heard that at least seventeen people were killed. Quite a few animals too. Nearly everyone ended up with cuts, bruises, broken bones, or breathing problems. As you can see, there was a lot of damage to wagons. One thing for sure, we made a big mistake following Quentin Price."

Steven wondered if this man had the answer. "Do you know why Quentin did it?"

"I have a pretty good idea. Once, while he treated me for a cut, he complained about the leaders of Pioneer One, and said that the Prophet should have chosen him to lead instead of you."

"You're sure that's what he said?"

"Absolutely certain."

Steven shook his head sadly, "Thanks, Clint. I didn't know... Well, I need to check things out. See you later."

"Steve, before you go. I want to tell you how sorry I am. You were right all along. What we did was wrong, and I suppose we got what we deserved. From now on my family and I are with you no matter what."

"I appreciate that."

A few minutes later Steven learned that Dr. Quentin Price and his wife Rose were two of the people killed by the storm. They left three young children. In spite of Quentin's betrayal, Steven regretted losing him, for he had given valuable medical service to the Saints. In order to recover from the disaster, Pioneer One stayed in this spot, nine miles west of the Iowa border, for the rest of Sunday and the next two days. Those who were strong and well helped the weak and injured to the best of their ability. They buried the dead, repaired vehicles and equipment, and shared one another's burdens in every way possible.

Chapter 20

The pioneers trudged along more slowly now. The dryness, the heat, the mounds of dust, the mutilated road, the injuries, the supplies ruined by dirt, the scarcity of food, the depleted livestock, and the damaged vehicles all combined to make their lives much more difficult. And yet they scarcely seemed to notice the pain, for every heart rejoiced and gave thanks to God. More than ever before they were one—made one through trial and suffering! Steven was delighted to see their obvious increase in kindness, friendliness, gentleness, patience, and love. He felt the same growth in himself and in his family.

The pioneers covered less than fifteen miles a day in the following days. Many became so weak from a lack of food that they fainted and were laid in their wagons. Shortly after they crossed the Iowa border, they turned south on I-29 and headed for Independence, Missouri. There was devastation everywhere and no sign of life. When they reached St. Joseph, fifty-four miles north of Kansas City, on Tuesday, July 4, they stopped for rest. Eighty-one days had elapsed since they had left Provo, Utah. Because the Saints complained of flu and other ailments, Steven decided to stay near St. Joseph for two or three days to let them regain their strength. He figured that the gruesome scenes they were witnessing might be the real cause of their malaise. He asked the caravan leaders to encourage the pioneers to read prophecies about the New Jerusalem in order to restore their spirits.

Steven was surprised when many Saints came to him on Thursday, pleading to continue the journey. He grinned at their enthusiasm and ordered the company to march. Even on Sunday, July 9, after early morning services, the pioneers insisted on traveling, at least part of the day. Shortly after noon on that day, they stopped near Exit 6, a few miles northwest of Kansas City, Missouri. They had covered 143 miles from the place of the dust storm. In contrast to the bleakness of the rest of the country, this was a pleasant spot, for they could see Lake Waukomis a half mile to the east and three other lakes a little farther away to the west and southwest.

*****

The Mexican Liberation Army crossed the southern border into Utah on Saturday, July 1. Their general, Fidel García, boasted that he would invade

Salt Lake City within four weeks and conquer the entire Mormon Kingdom in two months.

The eastern division of Fidel's army, numbering 100,000 soldiers, entered Utah on Highway 191. This was the division which had plundered El Paso, Texas.

The route of the second army, made up of 352,000 troops, was more complicated. After attacking Tucson, this division had traveled north and pillaged Phoenix. At that point the division had separated into two units. The smaller detachment of 92,000 renegades had driven north and entered Utah on Highway 89, heading for Kanab. The larger contingent of 260,000 men had traveled northwest on Highway 93, anxious to raid Las Vegas. After pillaging that great city, it had rushed toward St. George on I-15.

In this three-pronged attack, Fidel García hoped to catch his victims by surprise. His troops possessed automatic rifles, .50 caliber machine guns, infantry mortars, hand grenades, and twenty light howitzers.

The leaders of the Mormon Legion were astounded when they learned the size of the enemy armies. They concluded that someone, possibly church members, had falsified the reports which had been sent north. It seemed that some people would do anything to save their lives and their possessions. The defenders were also surprised to hear that the Mexican army possessed twenty-five armored personnel carriers, sixty ten-ton trucks, and seventy-one jeeps. Later reports revealed that the enemy had been stockpiling war materiel, including gasoline and oil, for nearly a year, and had obtained a great deal of supplies from the cities and towns which they had pillaged.

The three enemy divisions struck with such savagery and suddenness that the defenders could not contain them. On the day the fighting began, the total force of the Mormon Legion near the southern borders of the state was 302,000 dedicated men and women. The problem was, they were not all in the right place. Another 199,000 volunteers from the north were racing southward as rapidly as possible, but were still three hundred miles from the battle fronts.

The Mormon fighters were well organized, had excellent leadership, and adequate lines of supply. However, they did not possess the military training of the enemy and lacked heavy weapons. Most of all, because of bad communications, betrayal, and inaccurate intelligence reports, they had little knowledge of enemy plans or movements. As a result, they had spread their forces too thin, trying to cover five roads along the southern border and a few of the larger cities.

After three days of fierce fighting the enemy had reached Cedar City via I-15, Panguitch on Highway 89, and Blanding on Highway 191. In spite of the fact that the invaders had superior numbers and fire power, they lost 17,000 men in this push, while the defenders lost 8,000. As time passed, the Mormons learned to organize a multitude of small patrols, whose job was to ambush the invaders from the hills, woods, and ditches adjacent to the main highways. This hit-and-run technique resulted in many enemy casualties, but could not stop their advance.

As the Mexican renegades proceeded north, they longed to ravage the countryside and kill every person they could find. But they went wild with rage when they found very few people to murder. The farms and towns they attacked had already been abandoned. The weaker victims had escaped to the safety of the mountains, while the stronger warriors had hidden themselves nearby, waiting for the chance to ambush enemy patrols.

The Prophet had personally chosen Elder Jason Widtsoe and Elder Keith Bartlett, another apostle, to lead the Mormon Legion in its defense against the foreign invader. They had military experience, youth, boldness, and a special link to the Holy Ghost. In the town of Beaver the two apostles sat at a table in a private home with ten Mormon generals.

"Do we have radio contact with any of our troops yet, brethren?" Jason asked.

One of the generals said, "My radio man has been able to get a few reports late at night on certain frequencies from various locations in the southeast corner of the state." This general commanded twenty thousand troops in the area of Hanksville in south central Utah.

"Well, that's an improvement!" Keith exclaimed.

"It sure is!" Jason said. "I wonder why the renegades seem less capable of jamming us now?"

The general stationed in Escalante replied, "Maybe it's because they're getting neglectful. Or overconfident."

"You may be right," Jason said. "In any event, what do the transmissions say?"

The Hanksville general replied, "All our troops in that part of the state have gotten the message that the enemy's eastern army is still pushing north on Highway 191."

"All of them?" Jason asked.

"Yes, about 100,000 troops."

Keith came in, "Are they handling the tactical defense the way we directed?"

"Pretty much. They're redeploying as fast as possible to head the Mexican army off from the north. I sent my army east under the command of three colonels."

Jason said, "Apparently, some of our express riders got through to them, because they seem to understand that our goal is to stop the enemy before they reach Moab, if possible... But what do you mean, general, when you say *pretty much?*"

"It seems that some of our people insist on attacking from the rear."

Jason saw Keith's consternation. "What do you think, Keith?"

"Well, it's all right if they strike from the rear, as long as they don't get trapped. It's too bad they don't have more fire power than rifles and pistols. They'll sting and taunt the enemy, make his life more difficult, but they won't stop his advance. However, I prefer to position the bulk of our forces to the north of the invaders. That way, we can impede their advance by blocking the highway with large objects, poisoning the water supplies, and burning the forage. Also, we have a better chance for devising ambushes and traps."

"I agree," Jason said. "We seem to get better results that way."

Keith said, "Okay, what about our other troops in southern Utah? Have they all received our messages about redeployment?"

The Escalante general said, "All the transmissions we've tried to send and receive have been jammed. However, several express riders have brought me reports that our troops in south central Utah are also moving to intercept the enemy army moving north on Highway 89."

Another general, who had been stationed at Cedar City, remarked, "We've gotten similar reports from our contingents in the southwestern part of the state."

"That's good news, brethren," Jason said. "I've been very worried about this, because of our lack of good communications. If it wasn't for our express riders, I don't know what we'd do." As part of their conduct of the war, Jason and Keith had set up a pony express service to transfer messages as quickly as possible between armies and command posts.

"They're sure as good as the old pony express," the Escalante general said. "Some of our boys travel seventy-five miles a day."

*****

The decent citizens of Kansas City and vicinity had lived in Wyandotte County Lake Park for fifty-six days, surviving as best they could, while small gangs of thugs tried their best to destroy them by guerilla tactics. Then toward the middle of June the gangs finally got the idea of joining forces. At 2:00 a.m. on June 15, more than twelve hundred hoodlums attacked the park in force. The defenders, now numbering nearly five hundred people, including women and children, were ready for them. After two days of fierce fighting, the defenders saw they were losing. The odds against them were simply too great.

In the dark of night on Friday, June 16, the families made their escape during a lull in the gunfire, carrying all the supplies they could. With as little noise as possible, they sneaked around the north edge of Wyandotte Lake, turned north on I-435, and crossed the Missouri River. Many of the women had to quiet their little ones by holding their hands over their mouths.

Anthony Luce, one of the leaders of the refugees, heard nothing but eery silence from the enemy until they had traveled about five miles. Then, as they turned onto River Road heading east toward the town of Parkville, he heard a burst of angry shouting and gunfire south of the great river. The hoodlums had finally realized that their victims had fled. Anthony rejoiced because he believed that it was too late for the enemy to stop them. He urged his people to hurry because they had another three miles to go before they reached Riss Lake.

Several days earlier, the leaders of the Wyandotte Community had heard that there was another well-established colony in the region of the three lakes, which were named Riss, Weatherby, and Waukomis. One of Anthony's scouts, while searching for supplies, had stumbled onto the other group and had returned with the report that the Riss Community was grateful to know they existed. The new colony already included more than a thousand people. If the Wyandotte people could reach them, their combined fighting force would total five hundred men. Also, Anthony figured that, if necessary, they could muster a supplementary force of women and teenagers.

The fugitives were overjoyed when they saw volunteers from the Riss Community coming to meet them at 1:30 a.m. Anthony figured that the newcomers had heard the gunfire and had decided to investigate. The two groups joined forces and hurried on together. Behind them from the west they heard the wild shouts of their pursuers. Fortunately, they reached the main settlement near the lake before the gangs overtook them and attacked.

For eighteen days, from June 17 through July 4, the war continued, with neither side gaining a decisive advantage. Anthony Luce counted forty-seven of their people killed, including a few women and children. There were at least a hundred individuals who had received wounds. As for the enemy, Anthony estimated that they had lost from eighty to ninety combatants.

The citizens of the new Riss Community spent part of their days burying the dead, including hoodlums whose bodies had been left to rot in the sun by their friends. Jared Luce, Anthony's son, recognized one of the enemy dead as Silas Kitch, the gang leader who had nearly succeeded in murdering his family as they were escaping from Kansas City six weeks earlier.

Then on Wednesday, July 5, Anthony, Jared, and other refugee leaders climbed a low hill and saw a new army tramp out of Tiffany Springs Park four miles to the northwest. As Anthony studied them through his binoculars, he was surprised to see that the ragtag army of about five hundred men had a small fleet of jeeps and pickup trucks. He saw no heavy weapons, but he did catch sight of what looked like submachine guns.

"Saved by the cavalry!" Jared hollered, as he reached for his father's binoculars. "Now the gangs won't have a chance!"

"What do you think, Lee?" Anthony asked. Lee Bates was one of the leaders of the Riss Community.

Lee gazed at the newcomers with suspicion. "We'll see."

They continued to watch as the small army continued south on I-435. At the junction of I-435 and Highway 45 the army stopped, and a pickup truck turned east on the smaller road and rolled toward them. The citizen leaders descended the hill and walked toward the road. Two miles farther along the road seventy Riss defenders also watched the approaching truck from hidden coverts. A few minutes later the truck stopped forty yards away, and a uniformed man got out, followed by an aide. Neither carried a weapon. The soldier smiled as he walked up to them casually.

"You are the leaders of this community?"

Anthony replied, "Yes."

"We've been watching you and your friends a couple of days now."

"Our friends?"

"Just an expression. I'm referring to that rabble spread out along the Missouri south of your camp. Why are they attacking you?"

"They're savages who love to kill, that's all," Lee responded.

"I see. Well, we must put an end to it. I'm general Norman O'Neill, commander of the Missouri Patriots Militia." Anthony recognized the organization as a paramilitary army. "We're the only force in western Missouri which holds the anarchists in check. They're nothing but filthy @*/&^%#. People like them, and the government, are the cause of the destruction of this great country... Do you want to be free of them?"

Anthony shivered to hear the usual derogatory terms referring to Jews, Mexicans, blacks, and homosexuals. "Certainly," he said.

"Okay. Follow my plan, and we'll wipe them out today. Take all the men and boys you have, or anyone who can carry a weapon, and go around Riss Lake until you reach a position on the enemy's east flank. In the meantime, we'll move in from the west. Then at noon we'll hit them at the same time with all we've got. Don't worry. We have some heavy fire power. I guarantee you that they won't last more than an hour or two."

"All right, we'll do it!" Anthony said happily.

"Yes, it's a great plan," Lee Bates agreed.

"Good! I like men of decision." The general checked his watch. "You have three hours to deploy your men. This afternoon we'll celebrate their destruction with some good old Missouri whiskey." He wheeled around, stomped to his vehicle, pushed his aide inside, and drove away. Anthony and the others started back to their encampment.

"Wow! What a leader!" Jared exclaimed. "That guy isn't afraid of anyone. With his plan, it'll be a piece of cake to defeat the anarchists."

"I don't trust him," Lee stated.

"Me neither," Anthony said.

"The guy's dangerous," a third leader observed.

Jared eyed them in disbelief. "But his plan—"

"Stupidest thing I ever heard," Lee noted.

"Great for him, disastrous for us," Anthony added.

Jared remarked, "You're not going to follow it?"

"Of course not," the third leader indicated. "It's an obvious trick. He wants us to leave our families defenseless, and then move in to enslave them or murder them."

"Kill the kids and capture the women," Lee declared.

"I trust him," Jared insisted.

Anthony put his arm around his son's shoulders. "Jared, that would be as dumb as trusting the thugs who tried to get us to drop our guns in Kansas City. These guys are the same type of creatures."

"But I thought the militias stood for everything decent and American."

"No. Some militias are good, but others are no more than renegades. Didn't you hear the ignorant words he used to show his hate for other races and people having moral problems?"

"Yeah, it was disgusting," Jared replied.

Anthony, Jared, Lee, and four other leaders watched the militia all morning from a knoll not far from Riss Lake. Instead of moving to the anarchists' west flank near the Missouri, one-fourth of the "citizens" army moved in that direction, while the rest headed directly for the town of Weatherby, located at the south tip of Weatherby Lake. From this place, four hundred militiamen would pose a deadly threat to an unprotected community. What the enemy didn't know, however, is that Anthony and Lee had posted hundreds of fighters in front of the four hundred militiamen. At 11:00 a.m., two hours after their interview with the "general," they witnessed their "supposed ally" and three other men traipse into the camp of the anarchists.

"The general certainly must think we're stupid," Lee remarked. "In broad daylight he surrounds us with his army, and then visits the anarchist camp in time for tea."

"Well, they're convinced that we're all on the eastern front patiently waiting for them to start the action," Anthony observed.

"I can't believe I was stupid enough to believe that fake general," Jared said with disgust.

"Don't sweat it," Lee said. "We all make mistakes."

Jared delivered a high karate kick. "I'd like to get my feet on that guy.

What do you think they're doing down there?"

Anthony replied, "No doubt explaining their plan to the terrorists."

Lee added, "Yes, and making plans on how to wipe us out and share the spoils."

At noon the action began. The northern contingent of the militia attacked with naive confidence in their power to make short work of any defenders who might still be guarding the refugee camp. But as soon as they came within range of the defenders' rifles, they suffered a devastating shock when twenty-three of them perished in the first volley.

On the southern front a thousand anarchists and a hundred and twenty six militiamen swept eastward in a huge wave, screaming like wild animals. They seemed to be mimicking an Apache war party attacking a hated enemy. It wasn't until they had pushed the "enemy" all the way to the freeway, three miles away, that they realized there was no enemy there.

By 2:00 p.m. the thugs and militarists finally understood that General Norman O'Neill's subterfuge had failed. So, more furious than before, they attacked the family encampment once again. Since the militia had joined forces with the anarchists, their army numbered about fifteen hundred men. However, even though they had superior forces and had surrounded the exiles, they could not gain a victory.

The battles raged on for days. Then around noon on July 7, there was a break in the fighting. The community leaders gathered quickly for a council and had to accept the fact that their defeat was only hours away. Two of them suggested they try to negotiate with the enemy, but most insisted that it would be better to fight to the last man. For the first time since they had begun their struggle with the barbarians, the leaders sent a message to all their people, asking them to plead with God that He might spare them. At 1:00 p.m. the leaders heard a rapid burst of gunfire. It sounded as if another great battle had begun south of the colony. Figuring that the lull was over, Anthony and Lee sent Jared up a tall tree to check things out.

"Indians!" Jared shouted down excitedly, pointing to the southeast.

"What did he say?" Lee asked.

"I think he said Indians," Anthony replied.

They waited as Jared climbed down. He hung from the lowest branch a moment, and then dropped to the ground.

"What did you say?" Lee inquired.

"I said Indians."

Lee was shocked. "Indians! I can't believe it. How many are there?"

"About five or six hundred."

"Are you sure? I didn't know there were that many left in the entire country."

"What are they doing?" Anthony asked anxiously.

"Attacking the enemy."

The Indian attack was such a surprise to the anarchists and militarists in the south that their army of fifteen hundred men fled to the west and did not stop until they had reached I-435, four miles from their original position. Before long, the militarists in the north also gave up their offensive and joined their comrades to revise their strategy. Late in the afternoon, the leaders of the Riss Community, which now included the Wyandotte Colony, saw a small group of Indians walking up the trail to their headquarters. All of them were clothed in the traditional dress of their ancestors. The community heads hurried to meet them.

"Welcome!" said Austin Meyer, one of the leaders.

The tribal chief stepped forward. "Thank you. My name is Vernon Freeman. I'm commander of the Northern Cherokee Nation. Looks as if we got here in the nick of time."

"Yes, you did," Anthony said. "We're grateful to you!"

Lee Bates asked, "Why would you risk yourselves for us?"

Vernon chuckled. "It's no risk really. People like these thugs have been persecuting our people for years, even before the government fell. Just two months ago a band of these same anarchists killed sixty-two of our people in a night raid near Clinton, Missouri. We've been tracking them ever since."

The colony leaders invited the chiefs to eat with them, and they all gathered in a secure grove not far away. Although supplies were short, the settlers shared what they had. During the meal, the men discussed strategy. Not far away, Jared leaned against a tree, listening intently. Lee posed an important question to the chief. "So you don't think the bad guys will give it up?"

"Never. They can't afford to. Rape, murder, and pillage is the way they survive."

"Then we have a serious dilemma," Anthony observed. "Since more of them arrive every day, their chances of cutting our access to supplies and overcoming us are increasing."

Austin Meyer said vehemently, "The only solution I see is to attack them in force. Wipe them out!"

"A very dangerous proposition," Lee noted.

The chief put his plate down, rubbed his belly, and sighed with grand satisfaction. The other tribal leaders grinned at their leader's antics. None had received a decent meal in weeks. "You won't have to do that," Vernon said.

"Why?" Austin asked.

"Because, we have five thousand warriors heading this way. They'll take care of our enemies in short order."

"Five thousand warriors!" Anthony cried.

"Maybe more. All Cheyenne braves," Vernon said as he picked his teeth.

"Are you sure?" Austin said.

Vernon looked insulted. "You bet I'm sure, man!"

"When will they arrive?" Lee asked.

"In about two weeks. They have to come from northeastern Oklahoma. All we need to do is hold out until then."

Chapter 21

By Sunday, July 9, the three divisions of the Mexican Liberation Army had pushed nearly two hundred miles into Utah. The division following Highway 191 reached Price by 11:00 a.m. Sunday and immediately pillaged the city. The force on Highway 89, after sweeping through Sanpete County, proceeded down the canyon on 89 toward Spanish Fork. As for the largest army on I-15, it reached the area of Santaquin by noon.

The defenders had fought valiantly, but had only succeeded in delaying the progress of the enemy. Many times they had mounted attacks, but the superior numbers and firepower of the invaders had always prevailed. The relief army of the Mormon Legion, which had been recruited from the cities of northern Utah, comprising almost 200,000 fighters, hurried down I-15, but were just leaving Salt Lake City on the morning of July 9. Jason Widtsoe and Keith Bartlett, leaders of the Mormon Legion, anxiously awaited their arrival, but they had serious doubts that the relief army would be any more effective against the enemy than their other troops. Also, Jason and Keith, now headquartered in Provo, had recently received reports on two strange mysteries.

After assembling his military leaders in a hotel in Provo, Jason remarked, "This report says the renegade army on Highway 89 stopped, but it doesn't give the reason. Why would the enemy do that?"

Keith answered, "I'm not sure. Maybe they're waiting for their eastern army, the one coming from Price, to join them."

General Bruce Wilkins noted, "I hope so. That would give us two or three extra days." Bruce had commanded a division of the Mormon Legion near Escalante.

"But why would they do that?" Jason asked. "Surely they know that by waiting, they give us more time to get our forces down from Salt Lake."

Another general, Arthur Conway, noted, "Perhaps they don't know that. Their communications aren't any better than ours. Also, it's possible that they believe our northern army is already in Provo. We've been circulating false reports for days concerning the whereabouts of our troops."

Jason said, "Whatever the reason, I hope they don't get the idea of attacking Provo and Orem before we're ready."

The other leaders expressed the same hope.

Keith was anxious to bring up the second mysterious report. "What about this communiqué regarding Indians?"

Jason had read the report also. "We don't know how accurate it is."

General Conway was perplexed. "Maybe you should fill the rest of us in, brethren."

Jason replied, "Yes, of course. Recently we received a report that bands of Indians are harassing the renegade armies."

"What Indians?" General Wilkins asked, surprised.

"No one knows," Jason replied.

"How many Indians?" Conway said.

"A great number, it seems."

*****

Wearily Steven looked at his watch. It was almost 1:30 p.m. and time to start the wagons again. *I'm getting to hate that schedule!* Steven thought as he tried to force his body to move. Finally, he gathered strength enough to glance around. Mary and the kids were still sound asleep. It would be cruel to disturb them, wouldn't it? His head plopped back onto the pillow. He had barely dozed another few minutes, when he felt William tug his arm.

"What's that, Dad?" William yelled.

Half asleep, Steven muttered, "Well, it's the Fourth of July, isn't it? Or pretty close. Oh no...it's the ninth."

"Dad! I'm serious. Listen. In a second you'll hear it again."

Steven rolled up laboriously onto one elbow. "Yeah, I'm listening." Just then he heard a volley of shots echoing over the rolling hills. He squirmed from beneath the wagon and stumbled to the west side of the highway. William and Andrew followed him. As he studied the area, he heard more shots. It sounded like a war. "William, run to Paul. Have him send word down the train to all the leaders. We need to talk!"

After William scooted away, Mary and Jennifer rushed up. "What is it, Steve?" Mary asked fearfully. "Are we in danger?"

"I don't know. There's a lot of gunfire, but I can't see anyone. Too many obstructions."

"It sounds as if ten thousand people are trying to kill each other," Jennifer said.

Mary hugged Jennifer to her. "How far away are they, Steve?"

"Less than two miles, I'd say."

Within fifteen minutes Paul, John, Douglas, two colonels, and a few captains had gathered not far from the lead wagon. After they had listened to the gunfire for a while, Steven said, "Any ideas, people?"

Colonel Jasper Potter spoke up, "It's too far away to tell what's going on, but it can't be good. I suggest we send scouts down there to check it out."

"I agree," Colonel Burnham said. The others nodded their approval.

"All right." Steven said. "John, choose a couple of men for the job. Tell them to stay together and be careful. How long do you think they'll need?"

"Two hours at the most," John said.

Steven checked his watch. "Okay, it's 2:00 p.m. now. That means we can expect them by 4:00. Tell them to hurry as fast as they can. In the meantime, we need to tell our people what's going on. They should remain as quiet as possible, but be ready to defend themselves."

The men sped away to alert the pioneers. An hour later they returned to await the report from the scouts. At 3:35 they saw the two young men running toward them. After the runners had climbed the embankment, they stopped and one, fighting for breath, blurted out, "A war... Looks like a war!"

Steven waited briefly for them to recover. "Who is fighting?"

The second runner said, "Bandits attacking families."

"And Indians!" the first runner added.

"Indians? Helping the bandits?"

"No, they're...they're attacking the bandits."

The leaders pumped the runners for all the information they had. Then they discussed what course of action they should take.

Seth Crowell contended, "We can't go down there. Such an action would be foolhardy. We have our families to think of. And the cause of Zion." Steven had considered relieving Seth of his leadership position because of his mutiny, but then decided to wait until they reached Independence. Even though Seth's disastrous experience should have taught him humility, he still had a tendency to use intimidation instead of love in his dealings with the people. Steven noticed, however, that most of the Saints in Crowell's charge no longer took him seriously.

"We can't just abandon those innocent people to a mob of devils," Colonel Burnham said.

"What do you say, John?" Steven asked.

"I say we help them. When the bandits see our Uzis and automatic rifles, they'll probably take off running."

"And you, Paul?"

"I agree with John. We have no choice."

"What about the rest of you?"

All of the leaders present, except Seth Crowell, indicated their desire to do their best to rescue the families, in spite of the danger.

Steven hesitated. "I think this is a decision the Saints must make. Their lives are at stake. Brethren, I want you to talk to each of them. Explain the problem, and ask for volunteers. Meet me back here in half an hour."

At 4:10 the leaders began to return. They grinned as they approached, with the exception of Seth. Jim Burnham remarked, "Most of my group say they know God wants them to come to the aid of their fellow man. The others ask for time to pray about it."

"I had the exact same reaction," Jasper Potter noted.

"All right," Steven shouted, "let's move them out. They've had plenty of time to pray."

Steven motioned to Mary and headed down the embankment, William tagging behind. Without hesitation, she released the brake, flicked the mules, and followed her husband. The two younger children were jammed in next to her, their eyes bright with excitement. Within twenty minutes every wagon and cart in the caravan turned off the freeway and followed their leader. Only one, the wagon of Seth Crowell, vacillated a minute near the edge of the road, but then rolled downward after the last wagon.

When the anarchists and militarists finally caught sight of 252 old wagons, 45 primitive handcarts, and 63 converted contraptions, rolling boldly into the war zone from the northeast, they lost heart. Especially when their scouts brought back frightening reports that every man, woman, and child in the caravan appeared to be armed with some type of high-caliber weapon, including submachine guns. First, two local colonies had to join forces. Then, the lousy Cherokees had to interfere. And now, a mob of strangers from heaven knows where! Within hours the anarchists and militarists had escaped to the safety of the wilderness fifteen miles to the west where they could decide in peace whether or not they wanted to tempt fate.

After making sure their enemies had truly left the area, the families of the Riff Community fell upon the Saints with tears of joy. The pioneers responded in the same way, and someone even claimed that he spied moisture in the eyes of Seth Crowell and his wife. After posting a heavy guard, the new friends sat around a multitude of fires in small groups to compare notes and share experiences.

"How long can you stay with us, Mr. Christopher?" Anthony Luce asked.

"Call me Steve."

"Okay—Steve!"

"We should move on right away to Independence."

Lee Bates said, "To build your New Jerusalem?"

"Yes."

"What a marvelous dream!" Anthony said with great feeling.

Mary affirmed, "An impossible dream that we will turn into a reality, with God's help!"

"So you're worried that the gangs will return?" John probed.

It was Jared Luce who responded. "There's no doubt. They'll never give up until they destroy us or we destroy them."

"Yes, that seems to be their nature," Anthony agreed.

"When do ya expect them?" Ruther Johnston asked.

"It's difficult to say," Anthony replied. "Probably in a few days. I have to admit that Lee and I hoped you might stay until the Cherokees come."

"I don't understand," Steven said.

Vernon Freeman, the Cherokee chief, explained, "We have five thousand braves traveling to this area from Oklahoma. They should arrive in less than two weeks."

"And we would be grateful if you could remain with us until that time," Anthony said.

Lee observed, "If you continue on alone, you'll be more vulnerable than if you stay here. The anarchists might decide to follow and attack you. But together we're much safer."

Steven said, "Yes, but..."

"And that's not all," Anthony said. "At this time Independence and the surrounding region for miles are no more than ruins and ashes. In fact, the area you're in now is one of the few places where you'll find trees, grass, herbs, wild animals, and decent water in the entire Midwest."

Steven was overwhelmed by the weight of that argument.

"And we might be able to sweeten our request even more," Anthony said slyly.

Steven smiled. "Meaning?"

Lee took over, "He means that we might be able to make you a good deal."

"What kind of deal?" Douglas Cartwright asked.

"Well," Lee continued, "some of our people have said that if you stay here until the braves come, they'd be interested in going with you to help build your great city. If you want them, of course. You may even find it in your hearts to find living space for them. Believe me, we are sick of living in tents and makeshift shelters."

"How can we refuse that, Steve?" Paul said.

"I say we accept," Jarrad Babcock added.

Steven replied, "The truth is, I feel the same way." He turned to the colony leaders. "I promise you that we'll stay in your camp a few days at least. In the meantime, I'll put it to the entire company to see if they want to stay until the Indian reinforcements arrive."

The pioneers chose to stay with the Riss Community. After learning that their leaders desired to accept the invitation of the community, they decided to follow their judgment. Both Saints and colonists were grateful for the time to make new friends, repair equipment, replenish supplies, make preparations for the defense of the colony, and restore their spirits. Four days later the gangs and militarists returned and surrounded the settlement. Since the enemy legions had increased to 2,500 soldiers, their camps pockmarked the entire region.

*****

At 4:00 a.m. on Tuesday, July 11, a coalition of Indian nations savagely attacked the eastern division of the Mexican Liberation Army near Soldier Summit, Utah on Highway 6. A great army of 109,000 braves surged out of the mountains near the highway and fell upon 100,000 sleeping Mexican renegades. As the Mexican army had traveled to Utah to conquer the Mormon Kingdom, they had murdered, raped, and pillaged both whites and native Americans. As a result, the Indians had followed them for months and had finally decided that this was the place to settle old scores.

When the Indians had first seen the evil army pushing through Mexico, then Arizona, they had fled for the safety of the wilderness. But after the renegades had passed, the tribal leaders had united their people with other tribes. In Mexico the descendants of the Aztecs, the Mayans, the Tarascans, and the Zapotecs had gathered as one. Then farther north the Navahos, the Hopis, and the Utes had joined their southern brothers. This confederation of tribes had accumulated supplies, arms, and numbers as they followed the outlaws north.

On Highway 6 in Utah the initial slaughter was terrible. However, because the Mexican renegades had good training and heavy weapons, thousands survived, regrouped, and held the Indians at bay. A half hour after the battle began, an express rider brought news of the struggle to the commander of a division of the Mormon Legion, stationed six miles to the northwest. Immediately, he ordered 40,000 soldiers to march to the bloody scene. As soon as the Mormon army arrived, they fell upon the enemy. As a result of this second assault, the renegade army disintegrated and fled in all directions. By the end of the day, most of the outlaws had been tortured and butchered by the braves tracking them.

On Wednesday, July 12, the two battles which occurred simultaneously farther west were even more terrible. The attack began with a sudden barrage of hundreds of mortar shells an hour before dawn, causing death and destruction in renegade ranks. At the end of the shelling, 167,000 Indian braves sprang from their hiding places, like shadows in the dark, and fell upon the outlaw troops on I-15. At the same time, 123,000 warriors assailed the bandits in Spanish Fork Canyon. As soon as the leaders of the Mormon Legion learned of the fighting, they ordered their armies to attack in force from several points in Utah County, as the Mormon commander at Soldier Summit had done. And the results were the same as they had been on Highway 6.

News of the astonishing victories spread rapidly through the communities of Utah, and the LDS people and their fellow citizens wept tears of relief and offered humble prayers of thanksgiving to the Lord.

*****

On Friday, July 14, the anarchists and militarists made a concerted attack against the Riss Community, but were repulsed by the defenders. The result was a stalemate which seemed to last forever. Because the main army of Cherokee braves did not arrive on the day expected, nor the day after, a great concern arose in the Riff camps that they were not coming at all. However, Chief Vernon Freeman insisted that his people would not let them down.

During the following days, from July 14 through July 22, fifty-six people in the settlement lost their lives, including twenty-two Saints. However, Steven was sure that Mormon casualties would have been greater if they had continued on immediately to Independence. The leaders of the colony estimated that the defenders had killed at least ninety-eight outlaws. They received many reports from their scouts, which at first puzzled them, but soon renewed their hope. The messages told of numerous fights and disagreements between the gang leaders and the heads of the militia. Also, bands of thugs actually raided other anarchist campsites and murdered those with whom they had some quarrel. Steven, Lee, and Anthony surmised that the power struggles within enemy ranks may have prevented them from overwhelming the community with their superior forces.

On Sunday, July 23, Steven awoke with a start at six in the morning. Several people stood outside his tent, calling him. Without dressing, he staggered past Mary and the children and stepped through the entrance of the tent. He shook his sleepy head, trying to straighten the uncertain images which resembled his brothers and colony leaders. "Yeah, what's up?" he mumbled.

"They're gone," Paul yelled.

"Gone?"

"Yes!" Lee Bates exclaimed. "Every last one!"

"The Gadianton robbers?"

John shook him vigorously. "Wake up, Steve! You must have been dreaming about the secret combinations in the Book of Mormon. We're saying that our enemies disappeared sometime during the night."

"But...why?"

Anthony replied, "We don't know yet. But our scouts report that nearly all of them are heading northwest on any road they can find. It looks like a herd of cattle in headlong flight instead of an organized retreat."

Vernon Freemen mysteriously appeared from nowhere. "They found out that our braves were coming and they took off."

A half hour later Steven watched through his binoculars as thousands of Cherokee warriors moved past the settlement on the south. Vernon had told him that his relief army had picked up five hundred extra men on their way north, but had been delayed by a few skirmishes with anarchists. Including Vernon's advance party, the total number of warriors now pursuing their foes was 6,500 men. During the day, several scouts returned to the community and reported that their adversaries had disappeared into the Kansas wilderness.

*****

On Monday, July 24, the pioneers anxiously insisted on setting out for their ultimate destination. At 7:00 a.m. they said good-bye to their non-Mormon friends and headed southeast on I-29. Two hundred and forty-one members of the Riff Community accompanied them. A strange sight it was to see thousands of people prancing through lands of utter desolation, laughing, joking, hugging one another, and singing continual songs of joy. By late after-noon they had covered the sixteen miles to the eastern border of Independence. They pulled their wagons into three separate circles near Independence Avenue and I-435 and walked in small groups into the eastern section of what used to be a city.

The Saints began to return at the approach of dusk. As Steven and Mary entered the camp with the three children, they noticed that many of the women were weeping, and some of the men struggled to hide their disillu-sionment. The young couple understood how the Saints felt because they also had been disheartened by the devastation they saw in their explorations.

Since there was a grove of trees not far away, which had partly survived the fires, the Saints gathered wood and began to build campfires. But not even this unforeseen blessing could lift their spirits. Leaving the children to prepare the evening meal, Steven and Mary left the camp again, climbed a low hill several hundred yards away, and watched the shadows gather in the east.

"Not much to see, is there?" Steven remarked, as he found a seat on a log burned at one end.

Mary sat next to him and put her right arm around his broad shoulders.

"That's an understatement. It's a terrible, ugly sight! I don't see how a small number of people with hand tools can transform this torn land into the greatest, most beautiful city on the earth! It's impossible!"

"I don't believe that. The Prophet told me that we would feel this way."

"He expected it?"

"Yes."

"And what did he say after that?"

"He said that with God's help we can do anything."

Mary began to cry. "I know, but it's so discouraging! How can we have a baby in these conditions?"

"Well, if we work together—" He stopped abruptly. He had focused on her tears, not her words. "What did you say?"

"How can we have a baby in such miserable conditions?"

"A baby! Are you serious? You're pregnant?"

"Yes. I have been for about five weeks."

Steven gazed at her in disbelief. "But how do you know? How can you be so sure?"

"A woman knows these things."

"Why didn't you tell me before?"

"I wasn't sure myself until a couple of days ago."

Steven jumped to his feet. He kissed Mary on the mouth and lifted her from the log. Pulling her close, he swung her in circles in the air. Then, suddenly, he lowered her to the ground. "Sorry. Did I hurt you?"

"Whew," she exclaimed, laughing. "Don't...worry. You can't...hurt me." She pushed her hair into place. "You took my breath away."

Steven was enchanted. Mary was going to have their first child! "I'd better tell everyone tonight."

"I'm not sure, but I think a few people already suspect."

"Oh? Who?"

"Andrea and Ruther."

"Ruther!"

Mary was embarrassed. "Yes, he saw how nauseated I was while preparing breakfast yesterday morning, and guessed the truth. I had only come to the same conclusion the day before that."

"Good old Ruther... Yes, he's very perceptive," Steven mused. He kissed her again. "Why didn't you tell me two days ago?"

"You've been so busy with all the problems, and I wasn't completely sure."

"I understand." As his eyes feasted on her beauty, another idea occurred to him. "There's something I don't understand, however."

"What?"

"I really don't see how you could be pregnant. You know, with the trials we've had, the kids around all the time, the cramped quarters."

"All I can say is, you're a very resourceful man."

They spent the next half hour discussing her pregnancy, the baby's sex, and all the names they might like. Finally, Mary said, "I'm sorry I was such a baby just now."

"No, I felt like crying too, but it's not something men do easily." There was another period of silence. "I was going to tell you what else the Prophet said."

"Yes?"

"He said we must do one small thing at a time. You know, set a goal, start the work, finish it, and rejoice in that accomplishment. Do one little thing at a time. Then we'll soon discover that we have performed a wonderful miracle, like building the New Jerusalem."

Mary kissed him on the mouth. "You make it sound so easy."

"Not easy, but possible."

Mary was smiling now. "Okay, young man, where do we start?"

"First we set up a semi-permanent camp, preferably not far from Independence. Next we plant late-growing crops, gather all the edible and medicinal plants we can, hunt for meat, and build solid houses."

"Is that all?"

"No. In our spare time we try to clear Independence of its debris."

"It seems to me as if that would take a lifetime."

"I think we'll all be surprised at what a thousand determined people can do."

Mary sighed and got to her feet. "Steve, I'd better check on supper. The kids have a tendency to burn everything. Are you coming?"

"I'll stay a few minutes longer."

Steven continued to watch the darkness spread gradually over the bleak scene before him, making it even more oppressive. He didn't really feel as courageous and enthusiastic as he had pretended for Mary's sake. She was right. It was an impossible task! How could a man with virtually no experience at construction or building achieve it? After all, he had spent most of his adult life training to be a translator in French and Japanese. With a heavy heart, he continued to stare into the gloom ahead.

A few minutes later he discovered scattered particles of light emerging in the dark vastness, as if a star-filled night was materializing magically before him. Soon both earth and sky glowed, and the brightness gradually intensified until it hurt his eyes. He continued to watch, fascinated, as the brilliance formed into shapes and patterns. At the same time, the mysterious light penetrated his mind and body, filling him with exquisite joy. Then, suddenly, he realized what he was seeing. It was a great city of dazzling splendor.

As the outline of the city slowly filled in, he perceived details of buildings, trees, animals, and people walking on golden streets! Before long, the radiance began to take on the hues of a dozen vivid colors. In the center of it all, he saw a spectacular building with many parts, and he knew it was the temple of the Most High. Finally, the resplendent scene faded until it disappeared, and nothing remained except blackness.

But the exhilaration of the marvelous panorama lingered in his soul. No longer did he feel so helpless and ignorant. Now he understood what could be, because the Lord in His kindness had given him a vision of the future City of God, which he would help to build!

After waiting in the darkness until the quickening subsided, Steven walked down the hill and headed for camp. From a distance he saw his family and friends sitting around a campfire close to his wagon. When he approached, they looked up and grinned. Steven guessed that Mary had already told them about the baby.

As he sat next to Mary, Douglas said, "Congratulations, Steve." Paul, John, and Ruther added their compliments. His wife stared at his face in the light of the fire.

"So Mary told you. Thanks. I'm very excited about it."

After they had discussed the baby for a while, Mary said, "What happened, Steve? You look so different."

Paul agreed, "Yeah, you've got this strange glow."

"He hasn't looked this happy and confident in a long time," Andrea said seriously.

"What's up, Steve?" John said.

"We will build the New Jerusalem. And it will be a city more glorious than you can possibly imagine. The Lord just showed me His holy city in a miraculous vision." As he described the vision in detail, Mary held his hand tightly, and his children sat at his feet, captivated. The Spirit of God filled every heart with a witness of the truth of his words.

Ruther acted as if he had been struck by lightning, and tears streamed from his eyes. "When ya were describin' your wunnerful city, I got touched with the same feelings I got while I was readin' your Mormon Bible on the plains of Nebraska... Listen, I ain't got no say here, but I suggest ya tell that thar vision ta your people tomorrow. They're mighty discouraged right now."

"I intend to, Ruther. I intend to."

Steven and his family got little sleep that night, because they passed the time talking about the gleaming city that Steven had seen, and how they might live there when it was built. Above all, they wondered what they would say and do and be when the Son of God Himself came to the city and filled it with his all-penetrating light.

The next morning at 9:00 a.m., Steven sent the caravan leaders to gather the pioneers for a short meeting. He had slept no more than four hours, but his joy exceeded his fatigue. As soon as the multitude stood around him, Steven stepped up on a charred stump and looked into their eyes. He saw many emotions. disappointment, pain, and fear, but also curiosity and hope.

He simply smiled and said in a loud voice, "Last night the Lord showed me a vision of the New Jerusalem, and so I desire at this time to describe exactly what I beheld." He spent the next ten minutes depicting the scene in minute detail. As he told his story, he saw a great change come over his listeners, and many of the sisters wept for joy. Their tears reminded him of those shed by the rough-and-ready old mountain man.

When Steven had finished, one of the brothers called out, "But what does it all mean, Brother Christopher?" Steven recognized him as the man named Clint, whom he had found repairing a wagon wheel after the great dust storm.

"It means many things," Steven said, his voice slightly lower now. The Saints strained anxiously to hear. He wasn't concerned, because he knew that those who did hear would spread the word quickly to the others as soon as he was finished "It means that the Lord is with us. He will strengthen and guide us in building a mighty city, the center place of Zion. From this spot, the land of Zion will grow and spread throughout the American continents. It may seem impossible to us now. But since God wills it, it shall be. No power in heaven or earth can prevent it. Let me reveal to you a truth: you are the only people on earth whom the Lord has prepared—made worthy—as a group, to begin the difficult task."

Steven paused a minute to let his words take effect. Then he said, "Now I wish to say that you can see the same vision as I beheld, if you desire it strongly enough. All you have to do is ask God, and He will reveal it to each of you individually. His Spirit has given me that promise. In this way, you can know as I do that, with God's help, you do have the power to establish the New Jerusalem."

As Steven delivered his message, a transformation came over the people. Instead of pain and disappointment, there was peace and confidence. Instead of sadness and doubt, joy and faith. And when he descended from the stump, the people of Pioneer One returned to their wagons with a new spirit. That same day, they began to do the great work of the Lord.